P9-BTL-911

PRAEGER WORLD OF ART SERIES

Readings in American Art Since 1900

A DOCUMENTARY SURVEY

Readings in American Art Since 1900

A DOCUMENTARY SURVEY

Edited by
BARBARA ROSE

FREDERICK A. PRAEGER, *Publishers*
New York • Washington

BOOKS THAT MATTER

Published in the United States of America in 1968
by Frederick A. Praeger, Inc., Publishers
111 Fourth Avenue, New York, N.Y. 10003

Library of Congress Catalog Card Number: 68-16421

Printed in the United States of America

Acknowledgments

Grateful acknowledgment is made for the use of the following material:

Excerpt from "The Illusion of Progress" by Kenyon Cox, *The Century Magazine,* Copyright, May 1913, and "The Painting of Today" by Edwin Blashfield, *The Century Magazine,* Copyright, April 1914. The Century Company. Reprinted by permission of Appleton-Century-Crofts, Division of Meredith Corporation.

Statement by David Smith, reprinted from "A symposium on Art and Religion," *Art Digest,* December 15, 1953, by permission of *Art Digest.*

Statements by Charles Burchfield and John Flannagan; excerpts from "Poverty, Politics, and Artists, 1930–45" by Burgoyne Diller and Reginald Marsh. All reprinted from the LIII, No. Four, 1965 issue of *Art in America* magazine, by permission of *Art in America.*

Excerpt from "Art-as-Art" by Ad Reinhardt, reprinted from *Art International,* December 20, 1962 (VI/10), by permission of *Art International* and the author.

Selected portions of an interview by G. Swenson with Roy Lichtenstein, reprinted from *Art News,* November 1963, and "Questions to Stella and Judd" by Bruce Glaser, reprinted from *Art News,* September 1966, both by permission of *Art News.*

Excerpts from "Epitaph for an Avant-garde" by John Ferren, reprinted from *Arts* Magazine, November 1958, and "Optical Art: Pending or Ending?" by Sidney Tillim, reprinted from *Arts* Magazine, January 1965, both by permission of *Arts* Magazine.

Statement by Jackson Pollock, reprinted from *Arts and Architecture,* February 1944, by permission of *Arts and Architecture.*

Excerpts from *An Artist in America* by Thomas Hart Benton (Rev. ed.,

Kansas City: University of Kansas City Press, Twayne Publishers, 1951). Reprinted by permission of the author.

"Thoughts on Sculpture" and "Second Thoughts on Sculpture" by David Smith, reprinted from *College Art Journal,* Winter and Spring 1954, by permission of *College Art Journal.*

Abridgment of chapters on Stuart Davis, Georgia O'Keeffe, Alexander Calder, and Josef Albers from *The Artist's Voice* by Katherine Kuh (New York: Harper & Row, 1960). Copyright © 1962 by Katherine Kuh. Reprinted by permission of Harper & Row, Publishers.

Excerpts from "The 'Modern' Spirit in Art" by Kenyon Cox, reprinted from *Harper's Weekly,* March 15, 1913 and "A Remarkable Art Show" by F. J. Gregg, reprinted from *Harper's Weekly,* February 15, 1913, both by permission of Harper's Magazine, Inc.

Excerpts from "The New Architecture: Principles" and "World Architecture" (quoted from *A Testament* by Frank Lloyd Wright), reprinted by permission of Horizon Press, from *Frank Lloyd Wright: Writings and Buildings.* Copyright 1960.

Statement by Mark Rothko, *Interiors,* May 1951, published through the courtesy of *Interiors.* Copyright 1951. Whitney Publications, Inc.

Excerpts from "An Address to the Students of the School of Design for Women, Philadelphia. Written in 1901" and "On Life Sketching" from *The Art Spirit* by Robert Henri, edited by Margery Ryerson (Philadelphia and New York: J.B. Lippincott Co., 1960). Copyright, 1951 by Violet Organ. Copyright 1930 by J.B. Lippincott Company. Published by J.B. Lippincott Company.

Selected portions of Clement Greenberg's introduction to *Post-Painterly Abstraction,* catalogue of the Los Angeles County Museum. First published in 1964 and reprinted by permission of the Los Angeles County Museum and the author.

Arshile Gorky on "Garden in Sochi," written in June 1942, at the request of Dorothy C. Miller, about the painting, "Garden in Sochi," which The Museum of Modern Art had just acquired. From the Collections Archives, The Museum of Modern Art, New York. Statement by Ivan Le Lorraine Albright from *American Realists and Magic Realists,* edited by Dorothy C. Miller and Alfred H. Barr, Jr., copyright 1943 by The Museum of Modern Art, New York. Statement by Willem de Kooning from "What Abstract Art Means to Me," *Bulletin of the Museum of Modern Art, New York,* Volume XVIII, No. 3, Spring 1951. Statements by Jasper Johns and

Robert Rauschenberg from *Sixteen Americans,* edited by Dorothy C. Miller, copyright 1959 by The Museum of Modern Art, New York. Excerpt from Josef Albers: *Homage to the Square* by Kynaston L. McShine, copyright 1964 by The International Council of The Museum of Modern Art, New York. All reprinted by permission of The Museum of Modern Art, New York.

Excerpt from *The Selected Writings of John Marin,* edited by Dorothy Norman (New York: Pellegrini & Cudahy, 1949). Reprinted by permission of Dorothy Norman and the author. Excerpt from "The Young Man in Architecture" by Louis Sullivan, reprinted from *Twice a Year,* Spring–Summer, 1939 and "Writings and Conversations of Alfred Stieglitz," edited by Dorothy Norman, reprinted from *Twice a Year,* Nos. 14–15, 1947, both by permission of Dorothy Norman.

"To Charles Demuth" and "To the American Abstract Artists" by George L. K. Morris, reprinted from *Partisan Review,* March 1938, by permission of *Partisan Review* and the author.

Excerpt from "Statement by Hans Hofmann," reprinted from *It Is,* Winter–Spring 1959, by permission of Philip Pavia.

Excerpt from *The Gist of Art* by John Sloan (New York: American Artists Group, 1939), reprinted by permission of Mrs. John Sloan.

Selected portions of "Interview with Franz Kline" by David Sylvester, reprinted by permission of David Sylvester from *Living Arts* magazine, edited by John Bodley and Theo Crosby; No. 1, 1963.

Excerpt from *Men of Art* by Thomas Craven (New York: Simon & Schuster, 1931). © 1931 by Thomas Craven. Reprinted by permission of Simon & Schuster, Inc.

Statement by Jules Olitski, reprinted from *Catalogue of the International Biennial Exhibition of Art,* Venice, 1966, by permission of The International Art Program, National Collection of Fine Arts, Smithsonian Institution.

Excerpt from "The Ides of Art" by Adolph Gottlieb, reprinted from *Tiger's Eye,* December 1947, and statement by Barnett Newman, reprinted from *Tiger's Eye,* December 1948, both by permission of Ruth Stephan.

Excerpt from *Arthur Dove* by Frederick S. Wight (Berkeley: University of California Press, 1958). Reprinted by permission of the University of California Press.

Excerpt from *Letters of John B. Flannagan* (New York: Curt Valentin, 1942). Reprinted by permission of the heirs of Curt Valentin.

"Aviation: Evolution of Forms under Aerodynamic Limitations," published in *Arshile Gorky* by Ethel Schwabacher (New York: Macmillan and Whitney Museum of American Art, 1957). Reprinted by permission of the Whitney Museum of American Art. "On Abstract Art," Stuart Davis' introduction to *Abstract Painting in America,* exhibition catalogue of the Whitney Museum of American Art. Published in 1935 and reprinted by permission of the Whitney Museum of American Art and Mrs. Stuart Davis.

Statement by Harold Rosenberg and Robert Motherwell, statement by William Baziotes, statement by Mark Rothko, and "My Painting" by Jackson Pollock, reprinted from *Possibilities,* No. 1, 1947–48. Excerpt from *Kindergarten Chats and Other Writings* by Louis Sullivan (New York: George Wittenborn, Inc., 1947). Excerpt from *Modern Artists on Art,* edited by Robert Motherwell and Ad Reinhardt (New York: Wittenborn Schultz, 1952). All reprinted by permission of George Wittenborn, Inc., New York, New York.

Contents

Index to Authors of Readings

(*References are to pages on which selections or statements appear.*)

List of Illustrations

(Plates follow page 224.)

Readings in American Art Since 1900

A DOCUMENTARY SURVEY

Editor's Note

These documents have been assembled for the purpose of providing a portrait of the artist in America through his own writings and those of contemporary critics. They are arranged to correspond with the chapter divisions of *American Art Since 1900: A Critical History,* so that they may be used as supplementary primary source readings. Original sources are cited at the beginning of each passage. Commentary has been supplied by the editor.

Introduction: The Practice, Theory, and Criticism of Art in America

PRACTICE

> Our drama, when it is anything but foolishness, is realistic; our engrossment, not with allegories and old-world myths, but with the actualities of the present; our life is a fast and strenuous race, heeding little of ceremonial formalities; the cast of our mind toward seriousness and subtleties; our capacity for pain and pleasure multiform and complex. For all the youth of the nation, we have been born into a late time.
>
> —Charles Caffin, in *Camera Work,* No. 17 (1907)

If the situation of the modern artist has always been precarious, then the practice of modern art in America has been particularly hazardous; this much, at least, emerges from the testimony offered in the following pages. The documents assembled record various ways in which American artists have responded to the fourfold task of founding and legitimizing a tradition of art in America; defining the American subject and extending its meaning to encompass an American style; imposing high art on a democratic, pluralistic society basically hostile to the concept; and creating a spiritual art in a materialistic environment.

Many factors have contributed to the difficulties of making art in America. To begin with, in Europe, the avant-garde, although divorced from the Academy and middle-class society, quickly established its own tradition and society, but, in America, Puritanism and provincialism for many years prevented the evolution of a Bohemian milieu capable of nourishing and sustaining an avant-garde. As a consequence, artists were isolated, not only from a hostile society but also from each other. Critic Sadakichi Hartmann complained:

> This lack of culture, this indifference to contemporary achievements is with us a natural condition . . . we are always twenty years behind the rest of the world in all artistic and literary matters. No wonder; the painters of New York do not even know their confreres in Boston and Philadelphia.
>
> For their excuse it may be said that the conditions to acquire such knowledge are exceedingly unfavorable. There is an utter lack of opportunities for the interchange of ideas. We have no *salons,* no art-centers of any pretension, and no *esprit de corps* among artists themselves. Everybody goes his own way, intellectually isolated, and depending largely on the observations of his student years.[1]

Isolation and alienation, characteristic of any avant-garde, came, in America, to be the defining conditions of the artist's life. Eventually, this lack of contact was seen as a positive virtue, even a necessity, not only by the artists themselves but by critics such as Harold Rosenberg and Clement Greenberg. Greenberg insisted, "The American artist has to embrace and content himself, almost, with isolation if he is to give the most of honesty, seriousness, and ambition to his work. Isolation is, so to speak, the natural condition of high art in America."

In addition to painful isolation, other problems vexed the American artist. Not only did he have to contend with the snide critical attacks and the lack of a market for his work that usually meet the avant-garde; he also had to face certain other, uniquely American, reactions. Take, for example, the popular suspicion that making art was not useful work, either because in a pioneer society it had been traditionally the province of women or because it was unremunerative and, therefore, of low status in a success-oriented culture. The result was that some artists, such as George Luks, compensated for feelings of inferiority with a swaggering braggadocio that emulated the respected "he-man" stereotype. More secure figures, such as Robert Henri, John Marin, Stuart Davis, and David Smith, held that the artist was first of all a worker, and that making art was the noblest kind of work. From such a position, it followed easily that the artist identified with the worker and that strong liberal, socialist, and sometimes anarchist leanings marked the political thinking of many American artists.

[1] Sadakichi Hartmann, "On the Lack of Culture," *Camera Work,* No. 6 (1904), pp. 19–20.

From the outset, the best artists in America have been among the most relentless critics not only of American politics but of American culture in general. In the early years of the twentieth century, this criticism often ended on an optimistic note; it was believed that, if the repressive and inhibiting pressures of the Puritan heritage could be discarded, the "art spirit," as Robert Henri called it, would naturally flourish and grow, defining and enlarging the intelligence and sensibilities of the people. This was essentially Whitman's view, and it is reflected in the optimistic, if not Utopian, hopes Henri and the architect Louis Sullivan, among others, had for American culture. Henri predicted:

> To have art in America will not be to sit like a pack rat on a pile of collected art of the past. It will be rather to build our own projection on the art of the past, whatever it may be, and for this constructiveness, the artist, the man of means and the man in the street should go hand in hand.[2]
>
> In America, or in any country, greatness in art will not be attained by the possession of canvases in palatial museums, by the purchase and bodily owning of art. The greatness can only come by the art spirit entering into the very life of the people, not as a thing apart, but as the greatest essential of life to each one.[3]

Similarly, Louis Sullivan attacked "our tentative and provisional culture," looking forward to a time "when a higher temperature shall infuse glowing vitality into root and stem, and exuberant foliation give more certain assurance of the coming flower of our soil." Criticizing "all that which Americans complacently call our art," Sullivan saw it as "too much a matter of heart and fingers and too little an offspring of brain and soul." Sullivan was critical of the dependence on sentiment and technique. He was also critical of the reliance on European models. Predicting that the struggle to introduce conceptual and spiritual power into the art of the nation would not be easy, Sullivan foresaw that "One must indeed have faith in the processes of nature to prophesy order eventuating upon so strange a chaos of luxuries." Nevertheless, Sullivan had such faith: "The presence of power, as a mental characteristic in one class of our people, augurs well for the belief that it may

[2] Robert Henri, *The Art Spirit,* compiled by Margery A. Ryerson (Philadelphia: J. B. Lippincott Co., 1960), p. 130.

[3] *Ibid.,* p. 190.

pervade our ranks. . . . We surely have in us the germ of artistic greatness—no people on earth possessing more of innate poetic feeling, more of ideality, greater capacity to adore the beautiful, than our own people."

Despite their Utopian optimism, Henri and Sullivan were not to see an aesthetic millennium. Others, like the caricaturist Marius de Zayas, grew pessimistic toward the prospects for art in the United States. In 1916, De Zayas gloomily assessed the situation:

> In all times art has been the synthesis of the beliefs of a people. In America this synthesis is an impossibility, because all beliefs exist here together. One lives here in a continuous change which makes impossible the perpetuation and the universality of an idea. History in the United States is impossible and meaningless. One lives here in the present in a continuous struggle to adapt oneself to the milieu. There are innumerable social groups which work to obtain general laws—moral regulations like police regulations. But no one observes them. Each individual remains isolated, struggling for his own physical and intellectual existence. In the United States there is no general sentiment in any sphere of thought.
>
> America has the same complex mentality as the true modern artist. The same eternal sequence of emotions and sensibility to surroundings. The same continual need of expressing itself in the present and for the present, with joy in action, and with indifference to "arriving." For it is in action that America, like the modern artist, finds its joy. The only difference is that America has not yet learned to amuse itself.
>
> The inhabitants of the artistic world in America are cold-blooded animals. They live in an imaginary and hybrid atmosphere. They have the mentality of homosexuals. They are flowers of artificial breeding.
>
> America does not feel for them even contempt.[4]

Soon, instead of fantasizing a Utopian community united through art, American artists would be happy receiving at least the measure of acceptance accorded to art in Europe. Of the artists forced to return to America by World War I, art dealer and critic Horace Holley wrote, "they have grown aware of the status enjoyed by the artists as a type essential to civilization," implying that artists were not yet acknowledged as a type essential to American civilization. Holley advised: "we should recognize the artist's status as it always has been recognized in civilized communities. In Europe successive generations of the same

[4] Marius de Zayas, in *Camera Work,* No. 47 (1916).

recurrent type have gradually impressed society with a tone favorable to the artist."

Holley's admonitions fell on deaf ears. Instead of raising the status of local artists, collectors continued to add to the prestige of the European masters by buying their works and neglecting the Americans.

Painter Marsden Hartley, too, agreed that art would have to reach a larger public before a native American art could take root. But, as Hartley foresaw, acceptance would go to popular and imitative art, not to the difficult and original art he and his friends were producing. In 1921, he wrote:

> Art in America is like a patent medicine, or a vacuum cleaner. It can hope for no success until ninety million people know what it is. The spread of art as culture in America is from all appearances having little or no success because stupidity in such matters is so national. There is a very vague consideration of modern art among the directors of museums and among art dealers, but the comprehension is as vague as the interest . . . the public finds no shock in the idea of art. It is not melodramatic enough and America must be appealed to through its essentially typical melodramatic instincts. . . . There is altogether too much of comfortable art, the art of the uplifted illustration. It is the reflex of the Anglo-Saxon passion for story-telling in pictures which should be relegated to the field of the magazines. Great art often tells a story but great art is always something plus the idea. Ordinary art does not rise above it.[5]

Gradually, the tone of these criticisms grew more hostile as it became clear that Whitman's vision of art rising from the people was not about to materialize. As Hartley ventured,

> I often wonder why it is that America, which is essentially a country of sports and gamblers, has not the European courage as well as capacity for fresh developments in cultural matters. Can it be because America is not really intelligent? I should be embarrassed in thinking so. There is nevertheless an obvious lethargy in the appreciation of creative taste and a still lingering yet old-fashioned faith in the continual necessity for importation. America has a great body of assimilators and out of this gift for uncreative assimilation has come the type of art we are supposed to accept as our own.[6]

[5] Marsden Hartley, *Adventures in the Arts: Informal Chapters on Painters, Vaudeville and Poets* (New York: Boni & Liveright, 1921), p. 60.

[6] Marsden Hartley, "Art—and the Personal Life," *Creative Art,* II (June, 1928).

Oscar Bleumner put it even more bluntly: "American art is, to my critical mind, and has been, absolutely European. . . . But the fundamental elements for an American art are here. . . . The art will come, of course."

Recognition did not come, however, for the American artist during the twenties, and Hartley became more discouraged. In 1928, he speculated, "I am not quite sure that the time isn't entirely out of joint for the so-called art of painting, and I am certain that very few persons comparatively speaking, have achieved the real experience of the eye either as spectator or performer."

But others saw brighter prospects. Stuart Davis, commenting on his trip to Europe, also made in 1928, claimed it enabled him "to spike the disheartening rumor that there were hundreds of talented young modern artists in Paris who completely outclassed their American equivalents." His trip proved to Davis "that work being done here was comparable in every way with the best of the work over there by contemporary artists." It proved to him as well "that one might go on working in New York without laboring under an impossible artistic handicap." Counting as positive factors in the American atmosphere its enormous vitality, "the hundreds of diverse scenes, sounds and ideas in a juxtaposition that has never before been possible," Davis came to the radical conclusion that one could "regard the necessity of working in New York as a positive advantage." This was, perhaps, to view the situation through rose-colored glasses; nevertheless, it marked a decided turning point in the self-esteem of the American artist. Although America would continue for years to import art, she would no longer export artists at the previous rate.

Davis' optimism, as well as his faith in the distinctiveness and vitality of American art, was shared by the critic Thomas Craven, whose preference for realistic art, however, was antithetical to Davis' abstract orientation. Two years after the 1929 Crash had destroyed the art market as well as the stock market, Craven, like Davis, saw salvation in acknowledging the cultural differences between America and Europe and in embracing and expressing those differences. In *Men of Art,* he wrote:

> Home again, after our long journey through European traditions, we enter a new environment for art. We are confronted not only with new

> physical conditions, but with what is more significant, a new mental attitude toward the world of the spirit. America possesses no revered or time-honored art culture, and our country as a whole, in word and deed, does not seem to regret it. If we do not look ahead, we surely do not look very far into the past for salvation, and the absence of an art tradition does not in the least interfere with our industrial development. America is the land of machines, and our new attitude toward the world—our indifference to cultural precedents and observances—is both the cause and the effect of our mechanized civilization. Our psychology is profoundly conditioned by our changing instruments and our control over them. Our machines wear out, and we construct newer and better models; we build and invent, destroy and replace, attaching no value to our handiwork beyond that of function and service. Thus we have come to have no use for things themselves, and no time to polish up memories of things when the moment of their usefulness is over.[7]

Even those who violently opposed Craven's critical position found themselves agreeing with his view that American art needed to free itself from its European ancestry. Beginning in the thirties, there was some justification for the feeling that a major art style might come out of the New World. Eminent European artists, like Fernand Léger, even began to visit the United States. Some, like George Grosz, refugees from the European catastrophe, remained in the United States, convinced, as was Clement Greenberg, that "the immediate future of Western art, if it is to have any immediate future, depends on what is done in this country." The development of Abstract Expressionism during the postwar period has proved the validity of Greenberg's prophecy. During this period, American painting at last emerged as an independent cultural force capable of evolving a major style and even of influencing European art.

But independence from the models of European art was won at a price. Victory was viewed with mixed feelings by those who had fought for it. Left to assess their situation, artists like Robert Motherwell began to ask how "our epoch meant to replace the wonderful things of the past—the late afternoon encounters, the leisurely repasts, the discriminations of taste, the graces of manners, and the gratuitous cultivation of minds." Now that American art was free to pursue its own course, there was the issue of the direction it would take. The question could not help but be raised as to whether the loss was not as

[7] Thomas Craven, *Men of Art* (New York: Simon & Schuster, 1931), p. 506.

great as the gain. In a 1960 journal entry, Jack Tworkov acknowledged, in a passage that echoes Henri's admonition:

> The old world, the world of aristocratic dreaming, has been shaken to bits; nothing but memories and pieces lie around like broken columns. It's a nuisance when we speak of culture to speak of the pieces we have inherited—however noble the pieces. The noblest libraries and museums and the noblest memories do not make us cultured. Only our own making gives being to our culture. Not the man who quotes—but the man who speaks out of himself for himself. Nothing archaic can help us or set us an example. Everything in the world is new—like ourselves. Not new like an invention for newness' sake—but new because it is out of our own nerves, our nerves vibrated by the world good or bad.[8]

Today, there is every reason to believe that the difference between the genuine and the spurious "new" is not widely understood. It is possible that the course of constant experimentation and restless invention that American artists have felt themselves impelled to take will be mistaken for a search for novelty. The danger is that the merely novel will usurp the position of the authentically inventive. The poverty of means that once afflicted American art having been overcome, there exists today the possibility that a high level of technical accomplishment will be confused with honest ambition.

Such confusions in the public mind leave the artist in many ways no better off than he was at the beginning of the century. For, although American artists were forced to accept the artificiality of an avant-garde situation, it was, to begin with, antagonistic to their basically egalitarian beliefs. So today, although the maturity of American art has brought acclaim, the nature of this acceptance has been so provisional and conditional that the artist continues to take for granted as a permanent condition—possibly still against his wishes—the breach between contemporary art and contemporary society. (Whether American society as it evolves will prove to be different from any other modern society remains to be seen.)

Among the first to doubt the authenticity of the popular response to art in America, Alfred Stieglitz observed, in 1916:

> There never has been more art talk and seeming art interest in this country than there is today. In my mind there is the constant question: Is the

[8] Jack Tworkov, as quoted in Edward Bryant, *Jack Tworkov* (New York: Whitney Museum of American Art, 1964), p. 48.

American really interested in painting as a life expression? Is he really interested in any form of art? . . . To me art as it is looked upon in America today is the equivalent in society to what the appendix is to the human body. Scientists are still differing as to whether the appendix is of value or not to the human organism. We do know the human being can enjoy life without it.[9]

Equal skepticism was shown recently by Harold Rosenberg in his description of the contemporary phenomenon of the "busy no-audience":

Considering the degree to which it is publicized and feted, vanguard painting is hardly bought at all. It is used in its totality as material for educational and profit-making enterprises: color reproductions, design adaptations, human-interest stories. Despite the fact that more people see and hear about works of art than ever before, the vanguard artist has an audience of nobody. An interested individual here and there, but no audience. He creates in an environment not of people but of functions.[10]

To Rosenberg's reservations, one can only add Stieglitz' caution: "No public may help the artist unless it has become conscious that it is only through the artist that it is helped to develop itself. When that is once actually understood, felt, art in this country may have taken root."

THEORY

In the seethe of things, in the interest of this, in the doing of that, terms, abstract, concrete, third or fourth dimension—bah. Don't bother me.

—John Marin, "John Marin by Himself," *Creative Art,* III (October, 1928)

Art theory in the United States, like art itself, has shown the same fluctuating dependence on, and independence of, European sources. Theoretical treatises, by means of which the ideologies of art movements are disseminated, are not popular in America. Neither are manifestoes. In fact, Synchromism, the only significant movement to issue a

[9] Alfred Stieglitz, Foreword to the *Catalogue of the Forum Exhibition,* Anderson Gallery (New York: Hugh Kennerly, 1916), p. 35.

[10] Harold Rosenberg, "The American Action Painters," *Tradition of the New* (New York: Horizon Press, 1959).

manifesto of aims and intentions, did so in Europe. On the contrary, the anarchistic spirit of the modern artist in America has kept him from banding together with others or issuing treatises or proclamations. His resistance to formulas and to art that is purely cerebral has made him wary of systems and theories. Marsden Hartley's view is representative of the American attitude: "Theoretical painting has little or no meaning for me, because it takes place above the eyebrows —I want the whole body, the whole flesh in painting." This does not mean, however, that twentieth-century American painting is without its theoretical foundations; it merely means that, for the most part, these premises are tacitly understood rather than explicitly stated. Daring and creative American artists did not, in general, concern themselves with abstract arguments; they preferred to derive their values from the general outlines of American culture, and to attack art with the pragmatic and empirical approach that characterizes American thought. Thus, Frank Lloyd Wright acknowledged as his sources not the philosophers or aestheticians of the past but "our own poets and philosophers, among them: Emerson, Thoreau, Melville, William James, Charles Beard, John Dewey, Mark Twain, our supreme humorist–story-teller; especially the giver of the new religion of democracy, Walt Whitman."

It is not surprising that, when an American artist has passed his ideas on, he has done so as teacher rather than as theoretician. In this way, many of the greatest teachers, suspicious of formulas and reluctant to freeze their beliefs into systems or ideologies, have communicated their advice as lessons to their students. Others have exchanged ideas with their peers over a drink.

The most challenging ideas in American art gained currency not in high-sounding publications but in the classroom or the barroom. (Only the patience of Henri's and Sloan's students in compiling their class notes has made it possible to reconstruct their lectures.) Despite such reluctance to formulate ideas into closed aesthetic systems, American artists have provided some theoretical literature that has had an influence on the practice of art in America and so deserves consideration. Arthur Wesley Dow, Denman Ross, Jay Hambidge, and Thomas Hart Benton are among the most important of these theoreticians who set out to systematize and codify the rules of composition and design. It is worth noting that they were all teachers.

Theories of Composition

As elsewhere in the Western world, awareness in the United States of the problems of two-dimensional design was first stimulated by contact with Oriental art. Returning from Asia sometime in the early nineties, the celebrated Orientalist Ernest Fenellosa drew attention to Chinese and Japanese art in his lectures at Harvard and the Boston Museum. These lectures on design and *notan* (light-dark contrasts) in Oriental art were early attempts to show that there were other possibilities than a naturalistic art. Tone, design, and pattern, rather than truth to nature, were stressed as compositional factors.

One of Fenellosa's eager listeners was Arthur Wesley Dow. Because he had come under Gauguin's influence in Pont-Aven, Dow was already prepared for such an approach to composition. Later, at Pratt Institute, where he instructed Max Weber, and subsequently at Teachers College, Columbia University, where Georgia O'Keeffe became his faithful disciple, Dow emphasized the importance of abstract design. In this, he was the most progressive art teacher in America of his time.

Pure design was also the concern of Denman Ross, another Harvard professor. In *A Theory of Pure Design,* published in 1907, Ross stressed pattern, abstract design, rhythm based on arithmetical measure, and movement. He advocated a vocabulary of form based on plant motifs that would suggest growth in a "gradual and regular change from one shape to another."

By isolating the purely plastic qualities of design from those of subject matter or representation, Ross found himself in the ranks of the most advanced aestheticians. His analysis of the formal elements, such as harmony, balance, rhythm, and movement, in pictorial composition influenced not only his own countrymen but the English critic Roger Fry as well. Singled out as particularly significant by Fry was Ross's observation that "a composition is of value in proportion to the number of the orderly connections it displays." Such an assumption was also to be at the root of most of the later theories of abstraction, such as Mondrian's manifesto on pure plastic art, which stresses the importance of formal relationships within a painting.

In the order of nature, Ross found "the order of a great number and variety of terms and of different principles in combination." From natural forms, he deduced a series of stylized plant motifs. These he cited as examples of harmony, balance, and rhythm—the three major compositional factors. The source of Ross's theory must be sought not in America but in the work of the nineteenth-century German and English theoreticians Alois Riegl, Gottfried Semper, and Owen Jones, who traced the transformation of natural forms into abstract motifs in the decorative arts. Shortly after it was published, Semper's work on ornament was translated into English by the architect John Wellborn Root, who apparently introduced Semper's ideas to Louis Sullivan. From this point of departure, it was but a short step to applying principles of abstraction to composition in general. But, despite the advanced concepts he explored, Ross stopped short of advocating that they become the basis for an abstract pictorial art. Typically, the analysis of art had outdistanced its practice in America.

Although Americans who worked in Europe naturally came into contact with Post-Impressionist assumptions about painting, art schools in the United States did not emphasize pattern, structure, and design. On the contrary, even progressive artists like Henri stressed realism based on observation, spontaneity, and personal expression. But the Armory Show helped make Americans more aware of the importance of form. George Bellows, Alfred Maurer, and even Henri himself, searching for the means to order and structure their compositions, found an answer in the system of dynamic symmetry proposed by Jay Hambidge. The most influential American art theoretician of the twenties, Hambidge had constructed a mechanical system, based on analysis of the structural principles of older art. In *Dynamic Symmetry,* published in 1919, Hambidge set forth a mathematical system of composition, purportedly of ancient origin, based on the relationship of the diagonal to the sides of the rectangle. As an added advantage, such structures supposedly conformed with certain types of plant growth, thus uniting the authority of history with that of nature. Hambidge, like Ross, lectured at Harvard. Later, he was an instructor at Yale, where he published the magazine *Diagonal* in 1919 and 1920.

According to Hambidge, "The difficulty is that while we have a more or less consummate science of draftsmanship, we have scarcely made an approach toward a science of design." This he sought to provide in a series of loose-leaf lessons illustrated with drawings and diagrams, which he began circulating in 1921. Like Henry R. Poore and Dr. Albert Barnes, who also analyzed works of art of the past for geometrical patterns and lines of construction, Hambidge was convinced that, once revealed, the underlying structure of the compositions of the masters could serve as models for contemporary artists.

This discovery he thought astonishingly modern, whereas he found Cubism an "academic union between an elementary geometry and those orthodox rules of composition that have been taught in art schools for many decades." In his article "The Ancestry of Cubism," Hambidge sought to find examples of "cubistic" reductions to simple geometric volumes in older art, from the Egyptians to Albrecht Dürer. His purpose was to prove that "Cubism is at bottom not radical, but blindly, haltingly conservative."

Hambidge's was a typically American confusion. He saw in Cubism only a superstructure, haphazardly applied as a stylistic effect, instead of a revolutionary new attitude toward art. His effort to reduce art to a scientific system of "foolproof" compositions paralleled Dr. Barnes's attempt to construct a verifiable scientific method of evaluating works of art. The search for some constant principle of authority, preferably scientific, occupied so many American artists, critics, and theoreticians that it must be taken as evidence of some very basic insecurity and discomfort that the practical American mind experienced when confronted with an art based not on science and observation but on the subjective qualities of feeling, imagination, and intuition.

Hambidge's investigations had some validity, however. Respected scholars defended his analysis of dynamic symmetry as a governing principle of ancient painting, and his diagrammatic analyses of paintings have been absorbed into art education and appreciation at all levels. It is likely that Dr. Barnes incorporated Hambidge's models in his own complex system of formal analysis.

Another formulator of mechanistic theories of composition was Thomas Hart Benton. Published as a series of articles in *The Arts,* in 1926–27, Benton's method, in opposition to flat, two-dimensional design, emphasized the deep space composition of Rubens and El Greco. Part of Benton's interest in movement in space, which stressed the interlocking of surface patterns with analogous patterns and rhythms in depth, must be attributed to his contact with the Synchromists, who were interested earlier in deep space composition.

Finding that "flat areas are inevitable," Benton counseled that they were also "mechanically necessary, affording a base for projection.

Their flat character emphasizes the cubic character of the forms with which they are associated." But, in general, Benton wished to eliminate flatness, considering deep space more meaningful because it was more complex and called forth greater empathy. Rejecting his Synchromist past on the question of color, he considered color a means, not an end—an excellent means, however, because of its ability to indicate space. According to Benton, "Color *is* a constructive factor in painting, but it is what it constructs that gives it its full sense and value."

Like the critic Willard Huntington Wright, Benton was interested in the *Einfühlung* (empathy) theory of the German philosopher Lipps. Although he rejected the ultimate physiological basis of the theory, he concluded, "In the practical field of actual construction, however, observation of the rich and intricate field of muscular action is responsible for much fine compositional work." Originally, it was his observation of Renaissance anatomy that led Benton consciously to apply the physiological principle in the building up of plastic structures. For Benton, this translation of muscular-action patterns into mechanical compositional forces had enormous value. Thus, he concluded:

> Forms in plastic construction are never strictly created. They are taken from common experience, re-combined and re-oriented. This re-orientation follows lines of preference also having a definite biological origin. Stability, equilibrium, connection, sequence, movement, rhythm, symbolizing the flux and flow of energy are the main factors in these lines. In the "feel" of our own bodies, in the sight of the bodies of others, in the bodies of animals, in the space of growing and moving things, in the forces of nature and in the engine of man the rhythmic principle of movement and counter-movement is made manifest. But in our own bodies it can be isolated, felt and understood. This mechanical principle which we share with all life can be abstracted and used in constructing and analyzing things which also in their way have life and reality.[11]

Theories of Expression

"It is an odd reversal of usual conditions," wrote Frank Jewett Mather, Jr., in 1914, "that the French writers on the new painting, MM. Apollinaire, Gleizes, and Metzinger, should be hopelessly unintelligible, whereas the most distinguished German practitioner and

[11] Thomas Hart Benton, "Mechanics of Form Organization in Painting," Part IV, *The Arts* (February, 1927).

critic of Post-Impressionism, Wassily Kandinsky, is entirely lucid." One can only speculate as to why the American mind found Cubist theory largely useless and Expressionist theory entirely compatible with local attitudes. It may have been the Neo-Platonic and abstract philosophical cast of Cubist thinking that alienated Americans, or perhaps its cold objectivity. In any event, although the core of Cubist thinking —that the painting represented an independent reality as concrete as actual experience—eventually came to be accepted by American artists, the idealistic bias and complex time-space metaphors of the French Cubists made virtually no inroads on American thinking. Instead, the single most important theoretical discussion in twentieth-century American art has centered around the issue of Expressionism.

The Expressionist controversy is linked directly with the argument that painting is related to music. Both find their roots in Kandinsky's essay *"Über das Geistige in der Kunst,"* excerpts from which appeared in English in 1912, the year of its German publication, in the pages of *Camera Work*. Translated completely into English, in 1914, as "The Art of Spiritual Harmony," Kandinsky's tract quickly found both disciples and enemies in America. Among the first to take a stand against Kandinsky's doctrine that art was the expression of an "inner need" was the conservative critic Mather. Writing in *The Nation,* in November, 1914, Mather dismissed Kandinsky's formulation that creation grows out of the artist's inner need as "at first blush . . . merely the familiar Romantic theory of the artist as self-sufficing titan." Antagonistic to abstract art to begin with, Mather dismissed Kandinsky's assertion that emotion provides the true content of art: "In bluntest words, the notion of a specialized emotion, creative or otherwise, wholly shut off from the residual feeling and thinking is merely bad psychology." As for Kandinsky's analogies between music and painting, Mather opposed assigning psychological and spiritual values to specific colors and forms. He observed, "Music itself does not play with fixed abstract terms, such as Kandinsky wishes the colors to be. An oboe, for instance, is neither a sad nor a glad instrument; it all depends on circumstances. . . . In short, any color may take on the most varied emotional values, just as the bow may draw from a single note of the violin the most various shades of feeling."

Numerous other critics agreed with Mather. In a much more scathing attack, Thomas Craven, in his 1931 discussion of modernism in

Men of Art, characterized Expressionism as the worst scourge of modern art:

> Like the other sects, *Expressionism* has flaunted a far-fetched aesthetic, but at bottom it professes a fairly simple creed: "Our contacts with nature—the facts of the visible world—for creative purposes are more important than any amount of learning or traditional knowledge. Given a genuine insight into the world of everyday experience, it is possible for the artist to dispense with all old forms and to create directly, trusting to the pull of such impulses as follow his sensations. So working, the artist inevitably produces new forms. The burden of dead learning which stultifies academic practice is overthrown by an earnest and truthful expression of experience." . . . This notion lends authority to that brand of self-satisfaction posing as genius; allows for every imaginable kind of stupidity, and lack of knowledge; and raises children, freaks and incompetents into the ranks of the masters.[12]

Stilled for a time in the thirties, when Cubist formalism and representational art held the field, the debate over Expressionism was renewed in the forties and fifties, with the rise of a painterly style that sought to add emotional content to the pure formalism of abstraction. From the first, Abstract Expressionism was primarily interested in emotional content, and its practitioners rejected any attempt to label them as formalists. The "subject" of the artist was uppermost, whether this subject was the myths of the collective unconscious or the personal autobiographical statement to be communicated through the charged stroke.

As a spokesman for Abstract Expressionism, Harold Rosenberg often reflected the artists' consensus in his writing. He explained:

> With regard to the tensions it is capable of setting up in our bodies the medium of any art is an extension of the physical world; a strike of pigment, for example, "works" within us in the same way as a bridge across the Hudson. . . . If the ultimate subject matter of all art is the artist's psychic state or tension (and this may be the case even in non-individualistic epochs), that state may be represented either through the image of a thing or through an abstract sign. The innovation of Action Painting was to dispense with the *representation* of the state in favor of *enacting* it in physical movement. The action on the canvas became its own representation.[13]

[12] Thomas Craven, "Cubes and Cones," in *Modern Art—the Men, the Movements, the Meaning* (New York: Simon & Schuster, 1934), pp. 225–26.

[13] Harold Rosenberg, "Hans Hoffman: Nature in Action," *Art News,* May, 1957.

Here we are not far from Kandinsky's system of equivalents, made less specific and modified by Existentialism's concern with "action" and a modernized version of the *"Einfühlung"* theory. In any event, whether or not the "ultimate subject matter of all art is the artist's psychic state or tension" was soon brought into question by a younger generation of American artists who rejected the subjectivity of Abstract Expressionism, exchanging it for the cool impersonality of pop art, the "new abstraction," and "primary structures." Weary of the rhetoric of Abstract Expressionism, and suspicious of the possibility of staging or simulating extreme psychic states, these young artists were, moreover, skeptical as to whether psychological states are, in fact, communicable in abstract art. Pop artist Claes Oldenburg, for example, assumed this detached position, characteristic of the present generation. He claimed, "It is possible for me to treat my subjectivity and that of others objectively and this is a unique thing in my art: the emotion in it is the observation of emotion."

Those who embraced the new abstraction, on the other hand, tended, tacitly at least, to maintain the art-for-art's sake view implicit in Symbolist theory, which has run as an aesthetic undercurrent in American art, though usually overshadowed by the more popular and more frequently discussed Expressionist point of view.

CRITICISM

> It is not entirely the fault of the American people that they lag far behind all other civilized nations in aesthetic appreciation. The aggressive ignorance and theopneustic cant fed them by the majority of native critics . . . are in themselves sufficient to bring about an indefinite deferment of intelligent artistic taste . . . and as long as their influence persists, America will retain its innocence of all those deeper problems of art which must be mastered before a true understanding be brought about."
>
> —Willard Huntington Wright, "The Aesthetic Struggle in America," *Forum,* LV (January–June, 1916)

Art criticism in America, denounced at every turn by its own practitioners, has, nonetheless, produced a substantial body of writing, some of it durable, and some of it distinguished. But, whether academic or progressive, American critics have tended to share a shortcoming:

they have taken too literally Baudelaire's advice that a critic ought to be passionate and partisan. The result has been that, no matter what the stature of the critic, he has aligned himself closely with one group or artist, and has been noticeably blind, antagonistic, or insensitive to other developments. Consequently, American criticism has at times had depth, but seldom breadth.

Critics in America have tended to fall into four major categories: moralist, social historian, formalist, or propagandist. As one would suspect, art criticism has seen equally varied interpretation. It has been interpreted as a branch of ethics, art history, sociology, aesthetics, or journalism. Seldom has art criticism been considered a profession. Many art critics earned their living as academics, and several of the most successful came to the field from literature, whereas lesser reviewers have been recruited from the ranks of artists and poets. Only recently have art historians entered the area of contemporary criticism.

Internecine warfare has characterized dealings among artists, at least since the Renaissance. But critics, too, have vehemently taken sides, and, in America, they have done so with particular venom. Outspokenness, brutal directness, and a general lack of delicacy are as characteristic of American art writing as of American art. In 1916, Willard Huntington Wright had this to say of his colleagues: "In America it is only too plainly evident that the majority of our critics choose, with fatalistic invariability, the inferior and decadent painters on which to spill their praise." To Wright's mind, his colleagues (with two exceptions, Leo Stein and Christian Brinton) were guilty of misleading the public. In order to expose their irresponsibility, he gave a devastating analysis of the competition, a favorite game of American literary critics as well.

In "The Aesthetic Struggle in America," Wright indicted his contemporaries on a number of counts. Royal Cortissoz, "the *doyen* of our art reviewers," he considered most guilty of all. Characterizing him as "an industrious, sincere, well-informed, commonplace, unillumined writer, who possesses a marked antipathy to all that is new," Wright chastised Cortissoz' timidity and fear of the present. "He belongs," Wright concluded, "to the aesthetic and intellectual vintage of the 'sixties: he is, in fact, almost pre-Raphaelitic in attitude."

For Charles H. Caffin, he had equally unkind words: "He is a compiler, a historian, a chronicler, a disher-up of information—a kind of head-master in the kindergarten of painting." Caffin's main fault, in Wright's opinion, was not his attitude toward modernism—Wright condescended to mention that "Mr. Alfred Stieglitz converted him to modern art, largely through hypnotism." It was to Caffin's lack of critical judgment and his willingness to tolerate all points of view that Wright objected.

Wright summed up Kenyon Cox's contribution as "his naïve assertion that all progress in painting is an illusion." He reprimanded Cox for his aggressive and loud tone. Cox, according to Wright, was "apparently unconscious that the world is moving forward. He belongs to the academy of antiquity. Even modern academicism is unknown to him. . . . He believes that painting stopped with the Renaissance and sculpture with Phidias."

Pointing out that Frank Jewett Mather, Jr., was a professor of painting at Princeton, Wright denounced him as a "typical scholastic pedant." Mather's mind he found conventional, and his prejudices, "of educational rather than emotional origin." As for what Mather chose to praise, Wright characterized it as "that which is inoffensive from the standpoint of puritan culture, provided it is thoroughly established and has the indelible imprint of traditional approval upon it."

Wright's judgments, though severe, were in many ways accurate. His basic criticism of art writing was the same as that leveled by Clement Greenberg nearly half a century later: that it lacked a firm grounding in aesthetics. As outspoken as Wright, Greenberg took his fellow critics to task in "How Art Writing Earns Its Bad Name." The interesting difference, however, is that, although the subject remained the criticism of American painting, many of the critics Greenberg named were European. Among the Americans, Harold Rosenberg was the major target. Of Rosenberg's interpretation of Abstract Expressionism, Greenberg wrote:

> The very sound itself of the words "Action Painting," had something racy and demotic about it—like the name of a new dance—that befitted an altogether new and very American way of making art: a way that was all the newer, all the more avant-garde, and all the more American because the art in question was not actually art, or at least not art as the stuffy past had known it. At the same time, Mr. Rosenberg's ideas them-

selves sounded very profound, and most art critics have a special weakness for the profound.[14]

In general, Greenberg found appalling "the fundamental repetitiousness of most criticism of contemporary art, as well as . . . its rhetoric and logical solecisms."

When American critics have not been throwing brickbats at each other, they have faced a number of common problems. For the critic as much as for the public, the question remained for much of this century whether America could produce a great artist. Forced to evangelize for American art, native critics had constantly to fight against an equation of European art with quality in art. They fought not only for the transcendence of their own personal point of view but also for the acceptance of American art in general, both at home and abroad. In 1917, Wright lamented that Henri, "like all significant Americans . . . has been victimized by the public's snobbery. His nationality weighs heavily against him; for I cannot help believing that, were he a foreigner (why did he not pronounce his name Ong-ree?), he would be hailed as a great painter." The situation had obviously not changed much when, in 1952, Greenberg complained that, had Pollock been a European instead of an American, he would already have been acknowledged as "maître."

In America, art criticism has been published in newspapers, general periodicals, and specialized art reviews, which tended to expire as new magazines, in touch with current developments, appeared on the scene. Usually, the art magazines were limited by an editorial policy that strongly favored one or another of the art-world factions. Thus, their scope was narrow, and their claim to objectivity, discredited. Criticism in newspapers, with a few important exceptions, such as the columns of Elizabeth McCausland in the *Springfield Union* and the recent reviews by Hilton Kramer in *The New York Times,* seldom transcended the journalistic level, and tended toward preserving the vested interests of conservative and academic viewpoints. From the first decade of the century, the *New York Sun* was one of the few exceptions; it printed the criticism of Gregg and Fitzgerald, which was favorable to the Eight, and later employed Henry McBride, a vocal partisan of modernism, as art critic.

[14] Clement Greenberg, "How Art Writing Earns Its Bad Name," *Second Coming,* March, 1962.

In the first two decades of the century, important criticism was published in such general magazines as *Century, Forum,* and *Harper's Weekly*. Several political journals, too, gave space to intelligent art writing. *The New Republic* employed Leo Stein from 1916 to 1926, and *The Nation,* beginning with Mather's tenure (1907–17) and continuing to the present, has enjoyed a distinguished line of critics, which included Clement Greenberg, Hilton Kramer, and Max Kozloff. Beginning in the late thirties, and continuing through the forties and fifties, *Partisan Review* published influential art criticism by, among others, George L. K. Morris and Clement Greenberg.

The art magazines, by and large, have passed in and out of vogue along with the artists they have supported. About the time of the Armory Show, the leading art magazines were *Arts and Decorations* and *The Craftsman*. Both were rather strongly oriented toward the Henri point of view, as was *The Touchstone,* edited by Henri's friend Mary Fanton Roberts. At the same time, the hyperreactionary *The Art World,* edited by F. Wellington Ruckstuhl, gave a fanatical interpretation of the academic position. Writing as Petronius Arbiter, Ruckstuhl denounced the "Bolsheviki" and "madmen" who were "foisting" modern art on an innocent public.

During the twenties, *The Arts,* intelligently edited by Forbes Watson, maintained a high level of discourse, printing the criticism of such informed critics as Virgil Barker, and alternating articles on contemporary European art with praise of the coteries of both Henri and Stieglitz. Since many avant-garde writers as well as artists gravitated toward Stieglitz, his protégés were particularly well received in the little magazines such as *Seven Arts, Broom,* and *The Little Review*. In their pages, writers like Paul Rosenfeld, Waldo Frank, and Lewis Mumford often defended Stieglitz' cause.

As art critic for *Dial* (1920–29) Henry McBride could be counted on to be sympathetic to the point of view of the moderns. Although his writing was enormously important in creating a climate of interest in modernism and as a bastion of defense for the American modernists, McBride's was not an incisive critical mind. He will be remembered for the excellence of his taste and eye, the balance of his judgment, and the courage of his convictions, rather than for the depth of his criticism. As a member of the Arensberg circle, he favored Dada—a fellow critic once characterized McBride's writing as "Da," because he was only partially Dada—but he did not neglect to praise a wide range of modern art.

Important art journals of the late twenties and thirties included *Creative Art,* edited by Lee Simonson, and *American Magazine of Art,* later *Magazine of Art.* During the late thirties, European magazines such as *Cahiers d'Art* and *Plastique* were often scanned by American artists eager for more sophisticated material. In the forties and fifties, *Magazine of Art,* which ceased publication in 1953, and *Art Digest,* which became *Arts* in 1955, published criticism by art historians such as Robert Goldwater, Robert Rosenblum, and Leo Steinberg. Magazines published briefly by the Surrealist artists in exile during the war, *Tiger's Eye* and *View,* printed statements by Americans as well. In the late forties and fifties, *Art News,* a relatively stodgy journal with a historical bias, which had been published since 1902, became, under the editorship of Thomas B. Hess, the champion of the new American painting. Although the mass of enthusiastic chauvinistic outpourings in its pages will be forgotten, essays by Hess, Rosenberg, Greenberg, and Meyer Schapiro in defense of Abstract Expressionism retain historical importance. In the late fifties, sculptor Philip Pavia published *It Is,* a magazine devoted exclusively to propagandizing for Abstract Expressionism, largely written by the artists themselves.

More recently, during the sixties, two new publications have gained importance. *Art International,* published in Switzerland by James Fitzsimmons, and *Artforum,* first in Los Angeles, later in New York, have emphasized post-Abstract Expressionist currents.

Besides artists, art historians, and assorted types of literati, collectors have also attempted art criticism. Since no credentials were needed, collectors often felt themselves to be—and in a few cases, indeed, were—as well equipped as any to enter the field. Beginning with two of the original buyers from the Armory Show, Arthur Jerome Eddy, who wrote the first book on Cubism to appear in English, and John Quinn, collectors have defended the points of view reflected in their collections. Duncan Phillips and Dr. Albert Barnes, the most sophisticated of the collector-critics, made substantial contributions to the literature on American art, and Katherine Dreier and A. E. Gallatin effectively evangelized for the recognition of modern art in America. In recent years, B. H. Friedman and Ben Heller, collectors of New York School painting, have defended their taste in writing.

The Issues

The history of American art criticism in this century may be reduced to a handful of controversial issues that have provided material for a series of lively, if vituperative, running battles, in which advocates and antagonists of a cause have lined up into viciously hostile enemy camps. Opening the century was the rather dusty matter of the battle of the ancients vs. the moderns, which had occupied the French art world some fifty years earlier. Supporters of academic art, the most articulate of whom were Royal Cortissoz, Kenyon Cox, and John Alexander, generally defended traditional art on the basis of its moral and technical superiority.

Besides the debate of academicism vs. modernism, there was the corollary issue of representation vs. abstraction. Whereas the first took fuel from the Armory Show and later declined as a serious issue, the second has occupied critics to the present. Sometimes, the discussion was carried out on a high philosophical plane, but, more often, abstraction was simply dismissed as socially useless because it carried no message, and undemocratic because it was unintelligible to the majority. The larger issue of art-for-art's sake vs. a socially useful art, which underlies a considerable amount of antimodernist opinion, was argued from the moment Henri took up the banner of life over art. It is still being debated, with the young abstractionists of the sixties avowing the autonomy and purity of art and its independence from life and with the pop artists and figure painters claiming that art separated from the concerns of life is sterile.

Another of the issues related to the art-vs.-life debate, that of form vs. content, continues to be one of the central concerns of critical discussion. On the other hand, some of the controversies of the thirties and forties, such as the ability of art to change society, and the relationship of American art to European art, seem to have died down.

Although the battle lines were drawn even before the Armory Show made the issue of academic vs. modernist art topical, the Armory Show attracted participants into the conflict. Some critics, mainly the defenders of Henri and the Realists, such as James FitzGerald, F. J. Gregg, and James Huneker, tended to steer a middle course, neither totally embracing nor categorically dismissing modernism. Others were to change their opinions during the debate, sometimes in an abrupt about-face. Duncan Phillips, for example, was a late convert to modernism, whereas Guy Pène du Bois and Leo Stein ended by abandoning its defense.

Among the most informed and least partisan early defenders of modernism were Christian Brinton and J. Nilson Laurvik, whose articles appeared regularly in *Century* and *International Studio.* Both posited the view that modernism was a continuation of traditional painting, although Laurvik felt that Fauvism and Cubism represented a decline from Post-Impressionism. Brinton, on the other hand, was one of the few critics familiar enough with developments in Europe to remark on the incompleteness of the Armory Show in its omission of the German and Austrian Expressionists and the Futurists.

But the real front-line fighters on the side of the modernists were Walter Pach, a painter, critic, and connoisseur, and Willard Huntington Wright, brother of the Synchromist Stanton Macdonald-Wright. The attacks against modernism they had to counter were largely based on the following grounds: (1) It was immoral and degenerate. (2) It was technically incompetent. (3) It was dehumanizing and unintelligible. (4) It was a hoax and a fraud. (5) It was insane. (6) It was a foreign conspiracy. These were the usual charges modernism had encountered when it appeared, except for the last, which seems a peculiarly American idea. A typical response to the paintings in the Armory Show was the editorial "Lawlessness in Art," which appeared in the 1913 *Century* magazine. It stated, "What drew crowds were certain widely talked of eccentricities, whimsicalities, distortions, crudities, puerilities, and madness, by which, while a few were nonplussed, most of the spectators were vastly amused. . . . The exploitation of a theory of discords, puzzles, ugliness, and clinical details, is to art what anarchy is to society, and the practitioners need not so much a critic as an alienist."

From the academic point of view, beauty of subject meant an elevated theme. Royal Cortissoz criticized the moderns because of the ugliness of their subjects: "I disbelieve in modernism because it seems to me to flout fundamental laws and to repudiate what I take to be the function of art, the creation of beauty." To Cortissoz, modernism was symptomatic of the moral decay found in "a world full of jazz." Like the isolationists who feared contamination by foreigners, he raised charges of conspiracy:

> The United States is invaded by aliens, thousands of whom constitute so many acute perils to the health of the body politic. Modernism is of precisely the same heterogeneous alien origin and is imperilling the republic of art in the same way. . . . The French post-Impressionists—Cézanne, Van Gogh, Gauguin—retained just enough contact with the normal conventions of art for their subversive tendencies to be overlooked to a certain extent. . . . By the time the cubists came along there was an extensive body of flabby mindedness ready for the reception here. . . . These movements have been promoted by types not yet fitted for the first papers in aesthetic naturalization—the makers of true Ellis Island art.[15]

Such a passage is illustrative of what may be termed, to paraphrase Professor Richard Hofstadter's expression the "paranoid style in American politics," the "paranoid style in American art criticism."

Charles Buchanan, quoting Royal Cortissoz, in a review of the Forum exhibition of 1916, also objected to the international character of modernism, as well as to its unintelligibility: "If a work of art does not explain itself you may depend upon it that there is something wrong there. . . . Now the paintings in the Forum exhibition were not only no more characteristically American than they were Chinese, they were absolutely lacking in any national characteristics whatsoever."

A novel argument against modernism was presented by Duncan Phillips, before he became converted to at least some of its manifestations. In the 1918 essay "Fallacies of the New Dogmatism in Art,"[16] Phillips echoed the opinion, held by a number of respectable critics, that modernism was not progressive but reactionary, because, from Cézanne onward, it preached the "cult of the archaic." This question—whether modern art was progressive or reactionary—was argued with great seriousness in the first quarter of the century; thereafter, it seems to have been found less interesting.

Frank J. Mather, Jr., found another unusual angle from which to attack the modernists. With a supercilious yawn, he condemned it as boring. Praising the National Academy show of 1916 over the Forum exhibition because of its greater variety, he concluded that "Monotony is the prerogative of the inwardly turned mind."

In all these debates, the most articulate advocate for the defense was

[15] Royal Cortissoz, *American Artists* (New York: Charles Scribner's Sons, 1923), p. 18.

[16] *American Magazine of Art,* IX (January, 1918).

Willard Huntington Wright. Against the charges of lunacy, he presented the evidence of a psychologist that there are no epidemics of pathological lunacy. "It is absurd," he said, "to accuse a large majority of the younger painters of the day and not a few among the elders of stark madness or perversity. One must, in all justice, recognize the sincerity of the new art and strive to comprehend its already considerable achievement." To the charge of unintelligibility, Wright countered in his Foreword to the Forum exhibition catalog: "Not one man represented in this exhibition is either a charlatan or a maniac; and there is not a picture here which, in the light of the ideal, is not intelligible and logically constructed in accordance with the subtler and more complex creative spirit which is now animating the world of art." For Wright, modern art was not only progressive, it was steadily evolving new forms, keeping pace with the progress of science. As thought and philosophy become more abstract, so, he concluded, must modern art, "the authentic expression of modern thought."

Wright's goal was to legitimize modernism. He chose to accomplish this by providing substantial evidence that "modern painting is not a fad" but a tradition that "has progressed and developed logically for a century." From Wright's point of view, modernism represented not a step backward into the primitive past but an advance into the future. In order for modernism to gain acceptance in this country, it was essential that this premise be understood. Unfortunately, Wright's was a minority opinion; not until a sufficient body of literature tracing the internal development and roots of modern art appeared in America could he hope to be taken seriously. In his own history *Modern Painting,* he made one of the earliest attempts to provide such a historical context for modernism. Another early attempt was Sheldon Cheney's *A Primer of Modern Art,* published in 1924.

As a critic, Wright had a record that was creditable but not flawless. He immediately recognized the quality of the work of Maurer, Walkowitz, Marin, and Dove, but he thought Hartley and Sheeler only promising and found Bruce, Weber, and Demuth imitators of Cubism and Futurism, although he later recanted on Demuth. He had, as well, a few personal enthusiasms such as his high opinion of the mediocre landscape painter George Of. And, like many of the best American critics, he had a blind spot—the work of his brother Macdonald-Wright and the other Synchromists. At first, this took the form of special pleading, but, ultimately, his need to establish a rationale for Synchromism as the culminating moment in the history of Western painting led Wright to assume untenable positions. It led him, for example, to reject categorically painting in which flatness, rather than three-dimensionality, was stressed. In his last critical writings, he concluded that, since the art of painting had reached its maturity in Synchromism, no further advances could be made in the medium. He predicted that the disembodied art of color, the art of the future implied in Synchromism, would free itself of the canvas to become an autonomous medium, as it had in the clavilux (color organ) of Thomas Wilfred. Given Wright's initial hypothesis, that the tones of painting were analogous to the tones of music, this was a logical if fallacious conclusion. In this state of error, Wright retired from the field of art criticism to become the successful detective-story writer S. S. Van Dine.

The nature of Wright's fallacies and errors in judgment are illuminating, because they are characteristic of the partial and mistaken understanding of modernism in the United States. He believed, first of all, that aesthetics was, or could be, a science and that criticism could be made scientific and exact. He believed as well that modern art could only be legitimized on the basis of its similarity to traditional art. Thus, like Dr. Barnes and innumerable others, Wright sought in older art consistent formal principles that would validate the new art. Searching for the authority of precedent, bewildered Americans for whom modernism, with its emphasis on the sensuous and the intuitive, was an alien experience cast about for sureness and solid ground. In criticism, such insecurity led to pseudo-scientific systems of analysis, and, in art, it led to abstract or semi-abstract paintings absurdly based on historical prototypes, which were merely academicism outside its usual context.

However, despite his limitations, Wright's contribution was impressive. He defended modernism with a sophistication equal to that of the academic critics; he insisted that the task of criticism was the separation of good from bad; and he refused to adopt a different set of standards for American art, constantly measuring it against advanced European art, thus forcing the realization that standards were still set in Europe and that American art would not come of age until it could conform to them. Berating the public, he claimed, "Modern art since Cézanne is the beginning of a new Renaissance; but the people in this country are unaware of its great significance." Wright took it upon himself to make them aware. If, in exasperation, he too became an eccentric, out of touch with the mainstream, his lot was not unlike that of many of the artists he championed.

The battle of abstract vs. representational art, hard fought throughout the second and third decades of this century, became, in the thirties, identified with the issue of European vs. American art. By this time, abstract art had come to be largely identified with European painting, whereas representational art was popularly considered the native mode of expression. Fostered by critics such as Thomas Craven, confusion between "modern" and "contemporary" helped to obstruct the development of modern American art, as it also protected Regionalists and American Scene painters from charges of academicism, to which they were certainly liable.

The leading apologist for abstraction in the thirties, George L. K. Morris, maintained that "during an epoch in history such as this, when everywhere the mind seeks some order for its broken cultural fragments, the abstract art-work takes on fresh significance. It has the 'look' of its time, the ability to hold its place among the mechanisms that characterize the new civilization we are just beginning to know." But Morris' position was compromised by the fact that he seldom if ever praised anything but abstract art. Critics of the forties, fifties, and sixties would be less exclusive, and less prone to attempt to objectify personal taste into prescriptive dogma.

The major issue currently occupying criticism, that of form vs. content, involves not only the position of the individual critic vis-à-vis the object under discussion or analysis but also the correct function, meaning, and role of art criticism as an autonomous discipline. Whether, as Royal Cortissoz insisted, "To say that a picture is bad in this or that respect is only incidentally to admonish the artist; the real purpose is to tell the lay reader what it is like" or whether, as John Dewey phrased it, "Criticism is judgment, ideally as well as etymologically" has yet to be resolved. Generally, serious critics side with Dewey. But, having decided that the evaluation of quality is the main task of the critic, they part company when it comes to determining on what basis this judgment is to be made.

The various attempts to make aesthetics or criticism scientific were undoubtedly naïve and mistaken; nevertheless, there arose from this concern with finding objective criteria of evaluation a type of criticism that endures as one of the strongest, perhaps *the* strongest, tradition of criticism in America. Although the roots of formalist criticism are usually traced to the English critics Clive Bell and Roger Fry, it is as much an American as an English tradition. Bell and Fry, as members of the Bloomsbury group, sought to put art criticism on an equal footing with literary criticism. Toward this end, they introduced some of the concepts of advanced literary criticism into art criticism, especially that which held form to be the expression of content. This was in contrast with the Americans who wished to eliminate the subjective factor entirely from criticism in order to provide systems of analysis that, transcending categories, personalities, and historical epochs, would prove their universality and general applicability.

Fry's attention was first focused on the problem of the analysis of form in art when, early in the century, he served as a young curator in the European-painting department of the Metropolitan Museum, where he might have remained to illuminate the course of American art, had his talents not gone entirely unrecognized. During these years, he became acquainted with Denman Ross's *Theory of Pure Design,* which must have influenced his thinking enormously, since it was the only work he acknowledged in his 1909 "Essay in Aesthetics."

Fry's definition of art as the expression of emotion, and his separation of aesthetic beauty from the beauty of "a woman, a sunset, or a horse," was immediately accepted by the American critics Walter Pach, Willard Huntington Wright, and Christian Brinton. Clive Bell, as Fry pointed out, supported this formulation in observing, "however much the emotions of life might appear to play a part in the work of art, the artist was really not concerned with them, but only with the expression of a special and unique kind of emotion, the aesthetic emotion." The aesthetic emotion, for Bell, was communicated through "significant form."

Convinced of the rightness of Bell's and Fry's positions, Dr. Albert Barnes spent many years and devoted several books to the definition of "significant form." His search not only provided the basis for an extensive method of formal analysis, it influenced the thinking of some of our most important historians, critics, and aestheticians, including John Dewey, whose *Art as Experience* is dedicated to Dr. Barnes.

Published in 1934, *Art as Experience* touched the thinking of a generation of American critics, and continues to be an important step in the development of American criticism.

During the thirties, under the rising tide of realism and illustrational painting, formalist criticism underwent a relative setback. It came under direct attack from critics who felt, as Virgil Barker did, that "the very conception of a 'pure' art, the very demand for a 'pure' aesthetic response could have arisen only in an unhealthy state of civilization." In a review of Fry's book on Cézanne, Barker summed up the humanists' arguments:

> It is a mark of malease and incomplete living for the painter to want to escape from ordinary life and to attain in his art an unconditioned state of being. . . . art is reduced to an excrescence on life, something on the margin, a mere means of escaping from conditions there which have proved too much for the subduing and harmonizing power of the personality. Its separation from life is fatal—to art and to life both.[17]

The most telling case against formalist criticism, however, was made by Meyer Schapiro, in a review of Alfred Barr's *Cubism and Abstract Art* ("Nature of Abstract Art," *Marxist Quarterly,* January–March, 1937). Schapiro criticized Barr's book, which still stands as the most lucid and thorough study of Cubism, on the grounds that it was unhistorical and separated art from its historical context. Objecting to Barr's presentation of art history as a cyclical process of exhaustion of forms and styles and reaction to this exhaustion, Schapiro stated that "The theory of immanent exhaustion and reaction is inadequate not only because it reduces human activity to a simple mechanical movement, like a bouncing ball, but because in neglecting the sources of energy and the condition of the field, it does not even do justice to its own limited mechanical conception."

This conception, that art history undergoes periodic cyclical reversals, was the view of the German art historian Heinrich Wölfflin, and it is one of the understood givens of a formalist interpretation of art history. Such an interpretation traces the evolution of forms in art independent of the personalities and conditions that generated them. To Schapiro, and other historians and critics opposed to this point of

[17] Virgil Barker, "The Limitations of 'Pure' Art," *The Arts,* XIII, No. 1 (January, 1928).

view, stylistic change is directly tied to social, cultural, and political change. In Schapiro's words: "The broad reaction against an existing art is possible only on the ground of its inadequacy to artists with new values and new ways of seeing . . . the banal divisions of the great historical styles in literature and art correspond to the momentous divisions in the history of society."

Attacked for being unhistorical, the formalist position has also been characterized as overly dependent on the judgments of history. Reviewing Clement Greenberg's collection of essays *Art and Culture,* published in 1961, Hilton Kramer accused Greenberg of taking the stand that "critical judgments if they are to carry the authority and force of something more than a merely personal taste, must be made in the name of history." Kramer interpreted Greenberg's attempt to construct an infra-logic of the relations among abstract forms as the presentation of "the impersonal process of history . . . in the guise of an inner logic."

A more serious criticism of the formalist position than that it is unhistorical or unduly historical—to the degree that it attaches positive value to "advanced" art—is the argument that it ignores the question of content in art by concentrating exclusively on formal relationships. Many critics, ranging from partisans of representational art to moralists and social philosophers, have maintained that content—ethical, emotional, social, or political—takes precedence over form as the primary criterion of value in art. Harold Rosenberg has recently taken such a stand, insisting that the validity of Abstract Expressionism resides in its "crisis content," rather than in its sense of pictorial form.

As a rule, formalist critics have stopped short of a discussion of content. Roger Fry, fearful such a discussion would plunge him into the "depths of mysticism," stopped "on the edge of that gulf." Greenberg is apparently equally wary of plumbing the ineffable. In neither case, at any rate, can the accusation of illogicality or muddled metaphysics be made as it can be of many critics of modern art. The issue becomes, instead, if the aesthetic emotion and significant form are ineffable, how much can the critic tell us about art? This is one of the questions younger American critics find themselves discussing today.

If the contribution of Americans to twentieth-century art criticism has been undervalued, it has been so because often it was buried in an eccentric frame of reference. Thus, even so excellent a study as Milton Brown's *From the Armory Show to the Depression,* the basic source for any discussion such as the foregoing, dismisses the work of Denman Ross, W. H. Wright, and Dr. Barnes as "pseudo-scientific." Given the extent to which their findings have been incorporated, without acknowledgment, into current thinking, such an evaluation seems unjust. Like the advanced artists whose work was misunderstood, these thinkers worked in a situation where a lack of tradition or context for their work put them constantly on the defensive. As a result, Wright and Barnes, at any rate, became eccentric and offensive, and those whom they offended attributed to their work the shortcomings of their persons. At this point, it seems fitting to restore to them the credit due to pioneers.

Chapter One

Apostles of Ugliness

ROBERT HENRI: THE STUFF AND PRACTICE OF ART

• Robert Henri's advice to his students and friends, mainly consisting of lecture notes compiled by students during his forty years as a teacher, provides a guide to his philosophy as teacher and liberal humanist. These aphorisms and observations document Henri's courageous and successful attempt to replace nineteenth-century academic conventions with practical attitudes more suitable to the conditions of the new century and to the conditions of American life.

[FROM *The Art Spirit,* compiled by Margery A. Ryerson (Philadelphia: J. B. Lippincott Co., 1960).]

The sketch hunter has delightful days of drifting among people, in and out of the city, going anywhere, everywhere, stopping as long as he likes—no need to reach any point, moving in any direction following the call of interests. He moves through life as he finds it, not passing negligently the things he loves, but stopping to know them, and to note them down in the shorthand of his sketchbook, a box of oils with a few small panels, the fit of his pocket, or on his drawing pad. Like any hunter he hits or misses. He is looking for what he loves, he tries to capture it. It's found anywhere, everywhere. Those who are not hunters do not see these things. The hunter is learning to see and to understand—to enjoy.

There are memories of days of this sort, of wonderful driftings in and out of the crowd, of seeing and thinking. Where are the sketches that were made? Some of them are in dusty piles, some turned out to be so good they got frames, some became motives for big pictures, which were either better or worse than the sketches, but they, or rather the states of being and understandings we had at the time of doing them all, are sifting through and leaving their impress on our whole work and life.

• From an address to the students of the School of Design for Women, Philadelphia, 1901.

The real study of an art student is generally missed in the pursuit of a copying technique.

I knew men who were students at the Académie Julian in Paris, where I studied this year and found some of the same students still there, repeating the same exercises, and doing work *nearly* as good as they did thirteen years ago.

At almost any time in these thirteen years they have had technical ability enough to produce masterpieces. Many of them are more facile in their trade of copying the model, and they make fewer mistakes and imperfections of literal drawing and proportion than do some of the greatest masters of art.

These students have become masters of the trade of drawing, as some others have become masters of their grammars. And like so many of the latter, brilliant jugglers of words, having nothing worth while to say, they remain little else than clever jugglers of the brush.

The real study of an art student is more a development of that sensitive nature and appreciative imagination with which he was so fully endowed when a child, and which, unfortunately in almost all cases, the contact with the grown-ups shames out of him before he has passed into what is understood as real life.

Persons and things are whatever we imagine them to be.

We have little interest in the material person or the material thing. All our valuation of them is based on the sensations their presence and existence arouse in us.

And when we study the subject of our pleasure it is to select and seize the salient characteristics which have been the cause of our emotion.

Thus two individuals looking at the same objects may both exclaim "Beautiful!"—both be right, and yet each have a different sensation—each seeing different characteristics as the salient ones, according to the prejudice of their sensations.

Beauty is no material thing.

Beauty cannot be copied.

Beauty is the sensation of pleasure on the mind of the seer.

No *thing* is beautiful. But all things await the sensitive and imaginative mind that may be aroused to pleasurable emotion at sight of them. This is beauty.

The art student that should be, and is so rare, is the one whose life is spent in the love and the culture of his personal sensations, the cherishing of his emotions, never undervaluing them, the pleasure of exclaiming them to others, and an eager search for their clearest expression. He never studies drawing because it will come in useful later when he is an artist. He has not time for that. He is an artist in the beginning and is busy finding the lines and forms to express the pleasures and emotions with which nature has already charged him. . . .

What you must express in your drawing is not "what model you had," but "what were your sensations," and you select from what is visual of the model the traits that best express you.

I do not want to see how skillful you are—I am not interested in your skill. What do you get out of nature? Why do you paint this subject? What is life to you? What reasons and what principles have you found? What are your deductions? What projections have you made? What excitement, what pleasure do you get out of it? Your skill is the thing of least interest to me.

The tramp sits on the edge of the curb. He is all huddled up. His body is thick. His underlip hangs. His eyes look fierce. I feel the coarseness of his clothes against his bare legs. He is not beautiful, but he could well be the motive for a great and beautiful work of art. The subject can be as it may, beautiful or ugly. The beauty of a work of art is in the work itself.

I love the tools made for mechanics. I stop at the windows of hardware stores. If I could only find an excuse to buy many more of them than I have already bought on the mere pretense that I might have use for them! They are so beautiful, so simple and plain and straight to their meaning. There is no "Art" about them, they have not been *made* beautiful, they *are* beautiful.

Some one has defined a work of art as a "thing beautifully done." I like it better if we cut away the adverb and preserve the word "done," and let it stand alone in its fullest meaning. Things are not done beautifully. The beauty is an integral part of their being done.

Low art is just telling things; as, There is the night. High art gives the feel of the night. The latter is nearer reality although the former is a copy. A painter should be interested not in the incident but in the essence of his subject.

Here is an emotional landscape. It is like something thought, something remembered.

Reveal the spirit you have about the thing, not the materials you are going to paint. Reality does not exist in material things. Rather paint the flying spirit of the bird than its feathers.

Don't worry about the rejections. Everybody that's good has gone through it. Don't let it matter if your works are not "accepted" at once. The better or more personal you are the less likely they are of acceptance. Just remember that the object of painting pictures is not simply to get them in exhibitions. It is all very fine to have your pictures hung, but you are painting for yourself, not the jury. I had many years of rejections.

ROBERT HENRI: THE ARTIST IN AMERICA

• In a review of the Exhibition of Independent Artists, organized in 1910 by Rockwell Kent and other former Henri pupils, Henri set forth the dominant ideas of his democratic philosophy of art in which echoes of Walt Whitman's *Democratic Vistas,* James Jackson Jarves' *Art Thoughts,* and Tolstoi's *What Is Art?* may be found. Henri's insistence on the connection between art and life announces one of the two main lines of thought in American art—that which holds that art is a reflection of life, a current traceable from the Ash Can School through the American Scene painters of the thirties to the present-day pop artists. His notion that art is a vital process constantly in a state of organic growth reflects the extent to which the Vitalist philosophy of Henri Bergson had penetrated American art theory early in the century.

[FROM "The New York Exhibition of Independent Artists," *Craftsman,* XVIII, No. 2 (1910).]

Freedom to think and to show what you are thinking about, that is what the exhibition stands for. Freedom to study and experiment and to present the results of such essay, not in any way being retarded by the standards which are the fashion of the time, and not to be exempted from public view because of such individuality or strangeness in the manner of expression. What such an exhibition desires is all the new evidence, all the new opinions that the artists have, and then their work must either succeed by its integrity or fail from the lack of it. We want to know the ideas of young men. We do not want to coerce them into accepting ours. Every art exhibit should hear from the young as well as the old, and in this one we want to present the independent personal evidence which each artist has to make and which must become a record of their time and a proof of the advancement of human understanding. . . .

As I see it, there is only one reason for the development of art in America, and that is that the people of America learn the means of expressing themselves in their own time and in their own land. In this country we have no need of art as a culture; no need of art as a refined and elegant performance; no need of art for poetry's sake, or any of these things for their own sake. What we do need is art that expresses the *spirit* of the people of today. What we want is to meet young people who are expressing this spirit and listen to what they have to tell us. Those of us who are old should be anxious to be told the things by those who are to advance beyond us, and we should not hate to see them in their progress. We should rejoice that a building is rising on the foundation that we have helped and are still helping to erect. I personally want to see things advance. I want to see work done better by others than I have found possible in my life. I want to see progress. It should be impossible to have any feeling of jealousy toward those who are young and who are to accomplish the future.

It is necessary for the people in this country to understand that it is the expression of the temperament of our people, that it is the development of the imagination which in the end must affect not only the production of painting, of sculpture, of poems, music, architecture, but every phase of our daily existence. If art is real it must come to affect every action in our lives, every product, every necessary thing. It is, in fact, the understanding of what is needed in life, and then the pursuit of the best means to produce it. It is not learning how to do something which people will call art, but rather inventing something that is absolutely necessary for the progress of our existence. Our artists must be philosophers; they must be creators; they must be experimenters; they must acquire a knowledge of fundamental law in order that those who seek them and listen to them may learn that there are great laws controlling all existence, that through the understanding of these laws they may live in greater simplicity, greater happiness and greater beauty. Art cannot be separated from life. It is the expression of the greatest need of which life is capable, and we value art not because of the skilled product, but because of its revelation of a life's experience. The artists who produce the most satisfactory art are in my mind those who are absorbed in the civilization in which they are living. Take, for instance, Rockwell Kent. He is interested in everything, in political economy, in farming, in every phase of industrial prosperity. He cannot do without this interest in his art. The very things that he portrays on his canvas are the things that he sees written in the great organization of life and his painting is a proclamation of the rights of man, of the dignity of man, of the dignity of creation. It is his belief in God. It is what art should mean.

Another is John Sloan, with his demand for the rights of man, and his love of the people; his keen observation of the people's folly, his knowledge of their virtues and his surpassing interest in all things. I have never met Sloan but what he had something new to tell me of some vital thing in life that interested him, and which probably was eventually typified in his work.

William Glackens is in this exhibition as usual, unique in mind, unique in his appreciation of human character, with an element of humor, an element of criticism, always without fear. He shows a wonderful painting of a nude that has many of the qualities that you notice in the neo-impressionist movement. But Glackens seems to me to have attained a greater beauty and a more fundamental truth. There is something rare, something new in the thing that he has to say. At first it may shock you a little, perhaps a great deal; you question, but you keep looking; you grow friendly toward his art; you come back and you get to feel towards the things that you have criticized as you do toward the defects in the face of a person whom you have grown to like very much. They become essential to you in the whole, and the whole with Glackens is always so much alive, so much the manifestation of a temperament intensely sincere and intensely brave. . . .

What a mistake we have made in life in seeking for the finished product. A thing that is finished is dead. That is why the student interests me so. He is in the process of growth. He is experimenting; he is testing all his powers; he has no thought of any finished product in his expression. A thing that has the greatest expression of life itself, however roughly it may be expressed, is in reality the most finished work of art. A finished technique without relation to life is a piece of mechanics, it is not a work of art. Some of the things that may hold one's attention in this present exhibition are possibly the very slight sketches. . . .

I have been asked if this Independent Exhibition will become a permanent organization. I have not the slightest doubt but what the *idea* will go on, but I personally have no interest whatever in forming it into a society, and if an institution were formed and I were to become a member of it, I would probably be the first man to secede from it, because I can see no advantage to art in the existence of art societies. The thing that interests me in this is the idea of it, the idea of independence, the idea of encouragement of independence and individuality in study and the giving of an opportunity for greater freedom in exhibitions.

JOHN SLOAN

• Along with Robert Henri, William Merrit Chase, Arthur Wesley Dow, and Hans Hofmann, John Sloan was one of the great teachers who shaped the art of America through their classes and lectures. In *The Gist of Art,* compiled mainly from notes taken by his students at the Art Students League, Sloan's tart, outspoken style is vividly preserved. Sloan's emphasis on "realization," a term Cézanne used to describe the artist's transformation of reality into something more durable and permanent, testifies to his consciousness of the importance of form and organization in art. In insisting that the function of art was to transform rather than to record the stuff of life, he was more clearly a twentieth-century artist than Henri. He counseled independence from formulas; and, like his former mentor, he was optimistic about the future of American art.

[FROM *The Gist of Art* (New York: American Artists Group, 1939).]

Art is the result of the creative consciousness of the order of existence. How can there by any ultimate solution of that? Art is the evidence of man's understanding, the evidence of civilization. Humanness is what counts. Man doesn't change much over the centuries, but there is some evidence that he is growing more human, very slowly, although it is his one great reason for being.

The artist has a song to sing. His creative mind is irritated by something he has to say graphically. You don't need to paint masterpieces or monumental subjects. Look out the window. Use your imagination. Get a kick out of that spatial adventure, the textures of things, the reality of the world. Find the design in things.

Seeing frogs and faces in clouds is not imagination. Imagination is the courage to say what you think and not what you see. Max Eastman has said: "The scientist describes water as H_2O; the poet goes further and says 'it is wet.'" We want to describe things that way. An ideograph is better than the thing itself. A better work of art tries to say the thing rather than to be the thing. The image has greater realization than the thing itself. That is the great beauty of poetry—realization brought about by the use of images.

An artist is a product of life, a social creature. Of necessity he cannot mingle with people as much as he would like, but he reaches through his work. The artist is a spectator of life. He understands it without needing to have physical experiences. He doesn't need to participate in adventures. The artist is interested in life the way God is interested in the universe.

The artist has his own life to live; he has to pause and select and find something to say about it. The man of integrity works for himself alone, spurning all temptations to sell out his ability for commercial success. Any artist who paints to suit buyers and critics is what Walter Pach calls an Ananias, and unworthy of the name artist.

We live in a complex world in which we are mutually interdependent. But the artist must be independent. I think he always had to fight for his life, for freedom of expression, for the right to say what he believes. . . .

The great artist is the bloom on a plant, which is the art of the period. There may be more than one bloom. All the rest of us are the roots, shoots and branches of that plant or falling petals from the flower. The work we are doing today is a preparation for the great artists who are to come.

GUY PÈNE DU BOIS

• Although critics who were partisans of academic art reacted unfavorably to the realism of The Eight, The Eight also had their defenders in the press. James FitzGerald, James Huneker, and Frederick James Gregg supported their work from the outset, as did Guy Pène du Bois, a former Henri pupil who also wrote criticism. Later, Henri's friend Mary Fanton Roberts would devote considerable space to them in her magazine *The*

Touchstone. During the twenties, Forbes Watson, as editor of *The Arts,* often featured their work. And, as Davies had his special champions among critics who could not tolerate realism, Glackens and Prendergast found a friend in that redoubtable champion of modernism, Dr. Barnes, who not only bought their work, but subjected it to the same rigorous formal analysis with which he scrutinized Cézanne and Matisse.

[FROM "George B. Luks and Flamboyance," *The Arts,* III (February, 1923).]

The tonic thing that Luks says is only newly said in this country. Europe has heard it at intervals: Germany in music, France and England in literature, Italy, Flanders and, especially, Holland, in paint. The best word to describe it, I should think, is flamboyance, which has a root in flame and suggests the gesture of fire. Luks' art makes that gesture along with the man. In pointing to Holland in preference to Italy the point made lies in that while the Italian manifestation has had an aristocratic turn, the one in Holland as in the instance of Hals and the Little Masters, on the contrary, has been republican. Very little of art is practical or, if this is plainer, very little of it may successfully be tried on the facts of life. Perhaps the facts which are the truths of small people (most of us are that) are too near them. The artist assembles great masses of facts and uses only those which appeal to him. It is out of his selection that he builds his truth. It may be conceptional or perceptional, come before or after the fact. This though in the former case it is questionable whether he can swallow another man's philosophy whole and retain enough of his precious personality to make a definite imprint with it. The artist is a sensitized plate gathering impressions from an environment, from the voice of a people and a place and giving them out again intellectually ordered and marshalled, giving them out in a more direct or evident or comprehensive form.

Art is too generally confused with artisanship by the conception that it is made in three parts at least of good taste. In America good taste resides in the Eastern States—by the confession of these states—and is composed almost entirely of fear. In any case it is inconceivable that any flamboyance could exist within the confines of its precedential conservatism. Architects, as I have said perhaps too many times before, are the high priests of it. It may be that they have influenced American canvases. If they have, however, their way has been roundabout, their influence insidiously injected, for every artist will deny it. The fact is, anyway, that there is an enormous amount of willfulness, of intellectual direction, in the consistent good taste of most American canvases. This is true to a nearly intolerable extent in the prize-winning examples, and in their case is an evidence which cannot be taken lightly, for prizes are usually awarded by a consensus of opinion. Indeed, even when they are awarded through political machinations or favoritism of one kind or another there must still be some attention paid to the impression created upon those outside the ring and care taken to waylay or avoid their suspicion.

Good taste or the thought of it, as we know it in this country, is very largely a middle-class concern which begins at the manner of holding a fork, as an example, and ends at the pronunciation of a word or the decoration of a drawing room. It is considered so much a factor in the computation of social status that those persons who are uneasy upon the question of their position in the social scale, fortify it by the employment of instructors in fork holding and drawing room decoration. Indeed, taste is one of the most fearsome bugaboos in ordinarily comfortable lives.

George Luks, the flamboyant, has nothing to do with good taste of one kind or another. I do not know whether this makes him seem an especially honest or an especially ingenuous man, and do not think that it matters in the least. Nor does the fact that he is a Pennsylvanian and an Easterner make much difference. The fact that he was born under a republican form of government in the nineteenth century accounts for the nature of the flamboyance, but it does not account for the flamboyance. This is essentially his own, a natural gift of vitality just as in the instances of Rabelais and of Rubens. This vitality is the sort of power that will tear through fences and quite gaily pull at the pillars of established temples. It is not necessarily iconoclastic.

George Luks begins by having the bad taste of the braggard and goes on with a mad extravagance in untempered garrulousness and the impertinence, quite unconsidered on his part, to exhibit canvases fat in form and luscious in color to a people accustomed to the cramped works of painters with whom good taste is a dominating idol. . . . Luks will go to those whose strength almost carries an odor with it. The choice is quite often one of need and not of politeness or chance with Luks. He wants to make a record of the fullness of life, to render its rich flavor and warmth. This he does with a quality akin to mellowness and a sensuousness that is its counterpart. There are no static moments in a single one of his successful canvases. They do not flow with the swift urbanity of the lines of Rubens.

[FROM "William Glackens," *Arts and Decoration,* September, 1914.]

Had Glackens been a cerebralist he would have covered up his tracks. He would have formed a Renoiresque style such as we see in so many German pictures of the day. But Glackens took Renoir just as he took the bathers playing pranks on the beach, or the flowers in the fields. Renoir for him is part of the beauty of the world. He gladly acknowledges his obligations to Renoir. For Glackens doesn't have to try to be original.

Look for example at the reproduction of the young nude girl that was in the New Society exhibition this year. The form is pure Glackens. The Glackens' point of view remains an entity that can easily be traced throughout his extensive production of drawings, pastels and paintings. That point of view is uncomplicated by the problems of the chess player. Men like Marcel Duchamp, for example, get their artistic pleasure from setting up intellectual problems for themselves and working them out. Instinct plays a very small part in such work. It is almost purely intellectual and has a strong appeal to the intellectuals.

Glackens plays at painting. There is no tormented, morbid struggle with profound life facts disturbing him. He doesn't delve deeply into psychology. The color of the world makes him thoroughly happy, and to express that happiness in color has become his first and most natural impulse. He lives in a kind of dream of painting, absorbed, distrait, unaware of the problems that bother more unhappy natures. . . .

If we were not so timid about our own painters, or if Glackens had any of the publicity sense that nearly all European artists have found necessary for salvation, there would not be a museum in America which did not have some of his works. He is one of the gayest . . . most delightful and accomplished painters in the world today. If he were more heavyhanded and ponderous there would be much more made of our good fortune in having such a painter in our midst.

Chapter Two

291: The Largest Small Room in the World

ALFRED STIEGLITZ

• Although poles apart in many ways, Robert Henri and Alfred Stieglitz shared certain basic assumptions: that art must be alive, not dead (i.e., academic); that "it is the spirit of the thing that is important"; that art cannot be labeled or compartmentalized. Stieglitz' statement, recorded by his friend Dorothy Norman, is characteristic of the salty, if not arrogant, tone that offended many, but earned the life-long devotion of others.

[FROM "Writings and Conversations of Alfred Stieglitz," edited by Dorothy Norman, *Twice a Year,* Nos. 14–15 (1947).]

I do not see why photography, water colors, oils, sculptures, drawings, prints . . . are not of equal potential value. I cannot see why one should differentiate between so-called "major" and "minor" media. I have refused so to differentiate in all the exhibitions that I have ever held.

People are constantly trying to compare, when the important thing is to see what is before one, in its own right. I refuse to label. . . . People are constantly asking if one likes this picture better than that; this medium better than that; the full-blown blossom better than the bud; Beethoven's Ninth Symphony better than the First. Had it not been for the First Symphony, Beethoven never would have developed to the point of being able to write the Ninth. It is the spirit of the thing that is important. If the spirit is alive, that is enough for me.

It is as if there were a great Noah's ark in which every species must be separated from the other species, so that finally, as they are all placed in their separate cells, they grow so self-conscious that finally, if one were to take them out and put them together they would all fall upon one another and kill each other.

CAMERA WORK: BENJAMIN DE CASSARES

• In the photography review, *Camera Notes,* which soon expanded into *Camera Work,* a collection of criticism of photography and the visual arts published from 1903 to 1917, Stieglitz presented dissonant views of American culture and defenses of modernism in art and literature. The first American magazine to publish Gertrude Stein, *Camera Work* regularly published the criticism of Marius de Zayas, Benjamin de Cassares, Sadakichi Hartmann, and Charles Caffin, whose scathing attacks on the Academy made lively reading. De Zayas, a Mexican caricaturist, ultimately branched out on his own to open the Modern Gallery in 1915, with the financial aid of Marcel Duchamp's friend, Walter Arensberg. Here he continued Stieglitz' tradition of showing the best European works, as well as examples of primitive art.

Cassares' pieces often had a *fin-de-siècle* air about them, and his sympathy was clearly with the nineteenth-century "decadents."

Insisting on the lack of true culture in the United States, the *Camera Work* critics set the stage for the more trenchant and systematic criticism of American culture that took place in the twenties. Other themes sounded were prophetic, too. Cassares' article on irony, excerpted below, was typical in that it discussed a radical subject that would crop up again and again in twentieth-century criticism of American culture.

[FROM "The Ironical in Art," *Camera Work,* No. 37 (1912).]

Irony in art is the expression of a lifelong vendetta of a penned-up, often impotent Ego against the commonplace and the limited; the cry for perfection *a rebours*. . . . The root of nihilism in art is spite. *Les Fleurs du Mal* is spite. *The World as Will and Idea* is spite. All Futurism, Post-Impressionism is spite. Great men are known by their contempts. There have been geniuses who have never given their spite to the world; it was because they lacked the time, not the will.

All great movements begin with the gesture of hate, of irony, of revenge. This is as true of art as in social history. Irony is the perpetual heaven of escape. Nothing can follow the mind into that sanctuary. . . . Why should the dreamers and painters of the Other Plane despise this age we live in?—this age of sheds and pasteboard, of superficialities and stupidities, of inanities and material prosperity? Has it not given to us the divine ironists, the supreme haters, the mockers, the merry-andrews of art?

SADAKICHI HARTMANN

• Sadakichi Hartmann and Charles Caffin were two of the earliest apologists for modernism in America. Both published in *Camera Work,* as well as in more widely-read periodicals, such as *Forum* and *Century.* Hartmann's denunciation of Puritanism, excerpted below, presents an example of his writing for *Camera Work.* Caffin gained importance as an art critic for *Harper's Weekly, International Studio,* and later the *New York Sun,* and Hartmann was the author of an early history of modern art.

One of the regular contributors to *Camera Work,* Hartmann, like Henri, deplored the notion of art as a luxury commodity, outside the understanding or pocketbook of ordinary citizens. Reacting against the monopolization of art by the new rich and the "robber barons," who sought by buying art to buy themselves a pedigree, Hartmann analyzed the structure of the art world in order to expose its shams. Unfortunately, later critics of the American art audience would continue to find the same faults Hartmann uncovered in 1910.

[FROM "Puritanism, Its Grandeur and Shame," *Camera Work,* No. 32 (1910).]

[Puritanism is the] skeleton in the family closet, which saps the best life blood of our nation and makes it impossible for literature and art to expand in a free and wholesome manner. In the life of the Puritan all worship of the beautiful was wanting. . . . All we possess in the domain of higher esthetics is the art of delicate transitions, of refinement, freshness of immediate observation and mechanical skill. And there can be no vital art of any sort until there has grown up an appreciation of the Rubens-Goya spirit; until we dare face our passions, until we are unashamed to be what we are, until we are frank enough to let wholesome egotism have its sway.

[FROM "The American Picture World, Its Shows and Shams," *Forum* (July–December, 1910).]

Foreigners of discernment, visiting this country, are astonished at the scarcity of American paintings on public exhibition. They wonder if the United States, so advanced in other things important to civilization, has as yet produced an art as distinctively American as the painters of the Barbizon School are distinctively French. America has no Luxembourg, no representative collection of pictures by American painters, and the chance of acquiring such a national treasure seems remote for years to come.

There is no doubt that we have done some big things in art, that we have produced some big men in painting, sculpture, illustration and other aesthetic pursuits, that the era of 1875–1900 has produced a group of men (as Inness, Homer Martin, Winslow Homer, A. P. Ryder, Abbott Thayer, St. Gaudens) of which any country could well be proud. But we Americans do not seem to value its significance or to be able to impress it on the European mind. We lack the graces of self-assertion in appreciation and enthusiasm. We consider aesthetic accomplishments inferior to attainments that directly benefit vital needs.

Americans have the reputation of being the most generous picture buyers in the world. Donations are readily made, and art museums crop up everywhere. This very year three huge buildings, involving an investment of millions of dollars, are under construction in Kansas City, Toledo, Ohio, and Worcester, Massachusetts. But the American collector has not yet learned to buy art for art's sake. He patronizes art for self-aggrandizement, for the sake of direct advertisement, of notoriety, of speculation, of crude and selfish reasons. It is with him not a healthy demand for needed things, but just a gambling device. He treats art as a mere sport and delights in the reports of phenomenal prices that he paid for a single painting. And so the average citizen gets the erroneous idea that art is not for such as he, that the only pictures worthy [*sic*] the name are the few famous ones in the galleries of the rich, and that, like diamonds, automobiles, and race horses, they represent a luxury, a superfluity beyond the reach of an ordinary income. . . .

Picture buying depends almost entirely on individual trust and personal magnetism. The average collector, who has little knowledge of art and is often even doubtful as to what is best for him to buy, can do nothing but accept the word and blindly abide in the judgment of the salesman. The latter is all powerful. If he has once succeeded in securing the confidence of a customer, he has but himself to blame should he forfeit it.

The salesman of the large metropolitan establishments is shrewdness personified. Suave and self-possessed, he applies the kid-glove treatment to all prospective buyers. He is very dignified in deportment. He knows how to arouse the hush of expectancy. A vocabulary as picturesque as that of a poet accompanies the manners of a Chesterfield.

It is the credulity of the *nouveau riche* which has proved such a faithful source of revenue to the art dealer that, from small beginnings dating back to the civil war, he has risen to absolute control of the picture market. His methods show at times a striking similarity to the stock jobbing of Wall Street. Picture dealers work up an artificial demand for the productions of those artists they control. They "bear" prices on all pictures that lack the popular, salable quality, and "bull" those of which they control the supply. By misrepresentation and a nimble juggling of facts they unload worthless canvases upon confiding "lambs" after the fashion set by Wall Street with watered stocks. The ludicrous height to which the prices of Inness landscapes soared after the artist's death can only be compared to the shrewd operations in Spring wheat. . . .

In Europe, municipalities accumulate a collection before acquiring a suitable structure to shelter it. We, however, first erect a most expensive and elaborate building, and then try to fill it with donations. To walk through the empty exhibition halls of a museum in the Middle West is, indeed, a sad and melancholy pastime.

Art museums seem to have become necessary adjuncts to civilization. If people of ordinary means could afford to patronize art, there would be little use for museums. A certain educational value cannot be denied to them, although an actual influence like that of the Parthenon Frieze on modern English art is seldom noticeable. The only museum picture in America I know that can claim this distinction is Whistler's *Sarasate* at the Pittsburg Carnegie Institute. The tendency for dark tonality and the triumphs of pictorial photography have received a considerable impetus from this canvas. The majority of these accumulations are so tentative, so incomplete, badly arranged and meaningless, that one might come to the conclusion that museums serve no purpose but that of a morgue—for dead pictures which nobody wants.

THE MEANING OF 291

• In 1914, Stieglitz requested statements about the meaning of 291. The following are among the responses he received.

[FROM *Camera Work*, No. 47 (1917).]

Djuna Barnes

291 is the Attic near the Roof. It is nearer the roof than any other attic in the world.

The insomnia is not a malady—it is an ideal.

Abraham Walkowitz

Two-Ninety-One and Rockefeller Institute are doing research work.

291—Art is a living thing in relation to life.

291—Where one can live and feel one's own life.

Arthur B. Carles

All who come there [291] forget, in a sense, who they are. If they don't get this feeling of being part of a comradeship which is above prejudice, they drift off to where they are of more importance. . . . The things shown are like the frequenters—they test and prove each other —to think of one is to think of all.

Adolf Wolff*

Here in prison everything is institutional, uniform, routinal, dogmatic, academic, counted, fastened, barred and hopeless; there at "291" everything is free, informal, enthusiasm, struggle, attainment, realization, expansion, elation, joy, life. I have always felt it, but now I feel it more than ever that next to my own little studio, "291" is for me the freest and purest breathing place for what is commonly called the soul.

Arthur Dove

The question "What is 291?" leaves one in the same position in explaining it as the modern painter is in explaining his painting. The modern painting does not represent any definite object. Neither does "291" represent any definite movement in one direction, such as Socialism, suffrage, etc. Perhaps it is these movements having but one direction that make life at present so stuffy and full of discontent.

There could be no "291ism." "291" takes a step further and stands for orderly movement in all directions. In other words it is what the observer sees in it—an idea to the nth power.

One *means* used at "291" has been a process of elimination of the nonessential. This happens to be one of the important principles in modern art; there "291" is interested in modern art.

It was not created to promote modern art, photography, nor modern literature. That would be a business and "291" is not a shop.

It is not an organization that one may join. One either belongs or does not.

It has grown and outgrown in order to grow. It grew because there was a need for such a place, yet it is not a place.

Not being a movement, it moves. So do "race horses," and some people, and "there are all sorts of sports," but no betting. It is more interesting to find than to win.

* A political prisoner in jail on Blackwell's Island.

MARCEL DUCHAMP

• Founded by emigré artists in New York at the same time as several short-lived publications associated with Dadaism, the magazine *291* joined *Camera Work* in printing the iconoclastic opinions of the avant-garde. Although the first *291*, published in 1915, bore as title the address of Stieglitz' gallery, its editors were Francis Picabia and Stieglitz' former associate, Marius de Zayas, who had recently opened his own gallery. Later, in 1917, Walter Arensberg, one of *291*'s backers, along with H. P. Roche, financed the publication of *Rongwrong* and *The Blind Man.* The following article was contributed to *The Blind Man* shortly after Marcel Duchamp resigned as an officer of the Society of Independent Artists over the issue of the society's refusal to exhibit the urinal titled "Fountain" by "Mr. R. Mutt." Testing the Americans' capacity to tolerate extremism, Duchamp quickly exposed the fallacy of the open exhibition; for, although all entries submitted were to be shown, Duchamp's found object was rejected, revealing that tacit considerations of taste and decorum still colored judgments.

[FROM "The Richard Mutt Case," *The Blind Man,* 1917.]

They say any artist paying six dollars may exhibit.

Mr. Richard Mutt sent in a fountain. Without discussion this article disappeared and never was exhibited.

What were the grounds for refusing Mr. Mutt's fountain:—

1. Some contended it was immoral, vulgar.

Others, it was plagiarism, a plain piece of plumbing.

Now Mr. Mutt's fountain is not immoral, that is absurd, no more than a bath tub is immoral. It is a fixture that you see every day in plumbers' show windows.

Whether Mr. Mutt with his own hands made the fountain or not has no importance. He chose it. He took an ordinary article of life, placed it so that its useful significance disappeared under the new title and point of view—created a new thought for that object.

As for plumbing, that is absurd. The only works of art America has given are her plumbing and her bridges.

THE FORUM EXHIBITION

• The catalogue of the Forum Exhibition, organized in 1916 with the help of Stieglitz, Henri, and a group of critics, contains statements by a number of 291 artists. Below are those made by Dove, Oscar Bluemner, Abraham Walkowitz, and Alfred Maurer. Taking a consistently modernist stand, Stieglitz' protégés stressed that art was the expression of the unique, personal vision that allowed no compromise.

[FROM *Catalogue of the Forum Exhibition,* Anderson Gallery (New York: Hugh Kennerly, 1916).]

Arthur Dove

I should like to enjoy life by choosing all its highest instances, to give back in my means of expression all that it gives to me: to give in form and color the reaction that plastic objects and sensations of light from within and without have reflected from my inner consciousness. Theories have been outgrown, the means is disappearing, the reality of the sensation alone remains. It is that in its essence which I wish to set down. It should be a delightful adventure. My wish is to work so unassailably that one could let one's worst instincts go unanalyzed, not to revolutionize nor to reform, but to enjoy life out loud. That is what I need and indicates my direction.

Oscar Bluemner

Any new work of art explains and reveals itself only to that degree that the spectator is unprejudiced and receptive. Indeed, a picture ought not to be and cannot be fully explained. Rather must explanation needs be obscure, so that the spectator may try to explain to himself the explanation by the aid of the pictures. Then these will the sooner become lucid to him.

The painter to-day as formerly in an ethical sense aims at a liberation of feelings. Only the ideas of the present age create emotions wanting liberation through expression in form and beauty that are different from those of the past and are more varied; because man's intellect progresses, widens, deepens. Hence the arts become more manifold and freer, less bound by traditional and antiquating points of view.

Why then should American painting be limited by either old canons or any single new "ism"? We have a climate and a mind of our own—greater intellectual freedom demands for its pictorial expression a corresponding freer use of line, form, tone and color. The only law a picture must conform to is that which it carries within itself, instead of submitting to rules from without; just as true art springs from within, while that which is caused from without is imitation.

The intensity and purity of this character of modern painting is greater than it was in by-gone art, so that we have even come to speak of abstract painting. Whatever inner impulse we address towards nature is abstract. Thus a landscape, as a motive for expression, undergoes a free transformation from objective reality to a subjective realization of personal vision. Thus the forms, tones, colors we call natural are so changed that the painting harmoniously corresponds to the idea by which it is inspired. Any pictorial idea imposes upon the process of transformation only one law—that of harmony. Hence painting may be as varied and novel, as characterized and personal, as music is: free, bound only to its own inner laws.

Abraham Walkowitz

What one picks up in the course of years by contact with the world must in time incrust itself on one's personality. It stamps a man with the mark of his time. Yet it is, after all, only a dress put on a man's own nature. But if there be a personality at the core then it will mould the dress to its own forms and show its humanity beneath it.

In speaking of my art, I am referring to something that is beneath its dress, beneath objectivity, beneath abstraction, beneath organization. I am conscious of a personal relation to the things which I make the objects of my art. Out of this comes the feeling which I am trying to express graphically. I do not avoid objectivity nor seek subjectivity, but try to find an equivalent for whatever is the effect of my relation to such a thing, or to a part of a thing, or to an afterthought of it. I am seeking to attune my art to what I feel to be the keynote of an experience. If it brings to me a harmonious sensation, I then try to find the concrete elements that are likely to record the sensation in visual forms, in the medium of lines, of color shapes, of space division. When the line and color are sensitized, they seem to be alive with the rhythm which I felt in the thing that stimulated my imagination and my expression. If my art is true to its purpose, then it should convey to me in graphic terms the feeling which I received in imaginative terms. That is as far as the form of my expression is involved.

As to its content, it should satisfy my need of creating a record of an experience.

Alfred Maurer

My main concern in painting is the beautiful arrangement of color values—that is, harmonized masses of pigment, more or less pure.

For this reason, it is impossible to present an exact transcription of nature, for the color masses in nature are broken up by many minute color notes which tend to eliminate the mass effect. Consequently, I often use the dominating color in a natural object, and ignore the minor notes. By this process the natural *effect* is retained, and at the same time the picture becomes a color entity divorced from mere representation: and I have acquired a volume of color which will take its place in the conception of the picture. This, of course, would be lost if all the details were truthfully set down: the many inconsequent aspects of an object would detract the eye from the final and pure effect of the work.

In order that I may express myself through the medium of color alone, I have eliminated, as far as possible, the sombre effect of black masses, and have keyed my pictures in a high articulation, so that the reaction to them will be immediate and at the same time joyous and understandable. Black, I believe, has a deadening effect in a pure color gamut, and I am trying to express the emotional significance of a scene without it, for pure colors are more moving than black, which is a negation of color.

It is necessary for art to differ from nature, or we would at once lose the *raison d'être* of painting. Perhaps art should be the intensification of nature; at least, it should express an inherent feeling which cannot be obtained from nature except through a process of association. Nature, as we all know, is not consciously composed; and therefore it cannot give us a pure aesthetic emotion. I believe that the artist who paints before nature should order his canvases; and in doing this he is unable to adhere exactly to the scene before him. The principles of organization and form, which animated the older painters, must not be ignored. They form the true basis for artistic appreciation. But the modern men can make use of these principles through a different medium. He can find a new method of presentation.

The artist must be free to paint his effects. Nature must not bind him, or he would have to become more interested in the subject-matter before him than in the thing he feels need expression. In my case, where I am interested in the harmonic relation of color volumes, I consider the tonal values first. This is why my pictures differ from the scene which they might seem to represent.

GEORGIA O'KEEFFE

• Although Georgia O'Keeffe has denied that photography provided the example for her enlarged close-ups of flowers, there is an undeniable similarity between certain of her compositions, both floral and abstract, and the photographs of her husband, Stieglitz, and his colleagues Strand and Haviland. The uniformity of texture and suave, simplified modeling, not only in O'Keeffe's flowers but in the paintings of Charles Demuth and Joseph Stella, suggest undeniable affinities to the transformations effected by the camera. The frequency with which the composition based on the cropped photograph, the rectangle selected out of a larger scene, appears in American art makes it clear that in many ways representational art in America is as closely tied to photography as it is to illustration. Given an already established taste for the factual and the concrete, it is not surprising that the documentary objectivity of the camera became something artists wished to emulate. Paradoxically, however, what they wished to borrow from the photograph was not its precise realism, but it ability to reduce a variety of objects and textures to a common denominator so as to treat them as equal elements in an abstract composition.

[FROM Katherine Kuh, *The Artist's Voice* (New York: Harper & Row, 1960).]

QUESTION: Why have you always been so interested in simplifying and eliminating detail?

O'KEEFFE: I can't live my life any other way. My house in Abiquiu is pretty empty; only what I need is in it. I like walls empty. I've only left up two Arthur Doves, some African sculpture and a little of my own stuff. I bought the place because it had that door in the patio, the one I've painted so often. . . . Those little squares in the door paintings are tiles in front of the door; they're really there, so you see the painting is not abstract. It's quite realistic. The patio is quite wonderful in itself. You're in a square box; you see the sky over you, the ground beneath. In the patio is a well with a large round top. It's wonderful at night—with the stars framed by the walls.

QUESTION: Do you always paint what you see? What about changing light?

O'KEEFFE: You paint *from* your subject, not what you see, so you can't be bothered with changes in light. I rarely paint anything I don't know very well.

JOSEPH STELLA

• Besides *Camera Work,* the little magazines, such as *Broom* and *Seven Arts,* would sometimes publish the statements of modern artists. The heights of fantasy reached in his late paintings are hinted at in this macabre indictment of academic art by the avant-garde modernist Joseph Stella.

[FROM *Broom,* December, 1921.]

But then a little worm, born of envious sterility, began to crawl: it became gigantic and pestiferous: The graces, horrified, flew from his evil eye and he got hold of Art left alone and destitute of means. He chained her, closed her in a dungeon called "Academy," debarred the sun from her view (since then the north light for the studios) and for amusement during her slavery, as toys, gave her colored ribbons and tinkling medals. Besides he builded a kind of martial court house. A crowd of parasites got employed and self appointed judges enthroned themselves at the entrance of many bridges of sighs through which the artist had to go to give a daily account of his doings.

You could call this worm with various names: chaperon, censor, or better, aesthete, critic, teacher—I don't know why but when I look at the face of an aesthete, critic, teacher, I provoke the same feeling of immense sadness as when I see wax-tears sliding gentle upon a coffin. I was eight years old and my hatred for the school was assuming alarming proportions. By the way I have always considered the school as the punishment for our original sin—in a glorious day of May the window was open and I was looking at the blossoms of a cherry tree in full bloom. A bird came. I thought he was saying "Come and have fun outside." As [if] pushed by the imperative force of fate I rushed straight to the teacher.

"I have to go out."

"Why?"

"He is calling me."

"Who?"

"The bird."

He struck me, but I got hold of his spongy fingers. I chewed half of it and runned [*sic*] away. That's exactly what has happened with modern art. The dungeon still exists and some day we hope that it will be declared [a] national monument. Cowards are still satisfied with ribbons and medals, but the living ones are all outside and the judges have the sad appearance of kings in exile.

The motto of the modern artist is freedom—real freedom. We cannot have enuf [*sic*] of it because in art license doesn't exist. The modern painter knowing that his language deals with form and colour proclaims above all the purity of his own language and repudiates the assistance of all those red-cross societies which camouflage themselves: literature, philosophy, politics, religion, ethics. Although many prejudices still cling to him—and generations have to pass before he will reach the absolute freedom, he has lost that idiotic religious feeling which urges fanatics to nominate a leader, a pope. He recognizes personalities and not their derivations, the schools. But while he recognizes merit and he has respect for it, no matter what period and what race it belongs to (it is to modern art the credit of having enriched the knowledge of beauty to be found in the most glorious forgotten periods) he is far from fetishism because his chief interest lies in the venture through the untrodden path knowing that he belongs to his own time, he does not only accept it but he loves it—and therefore he can't go back to any past to borrow material. He does not feel obliged to follow any tradition; only tradition lies in him. The only guide to follow is his own temperament and that's the reason why abstractions and representations in the strict sense of the word don't mean anything. Rules don't exist. If they did exist everybody would be [an] artist. Therefore he can't recognize as modern artists those who having left an old slavery are chained by a new one. In other words chinasism [*sic*], indianism, persianism, negro sculpture with Cézannism and Renoirism—which most prevail nowadays—cannot but disgust him. If Cubism has declared the independence of Painting, by suppressing representation and in order to purify the vision is gone back, with abstractions, to geometry, the source of the graphic Arts, he feels that every declaration of Independence carries somewhat a declaration of a new slavery. And according to his credo he will always prefer the emotions as expressed by a child to the lucubrations of those warbling theorists who throw harlequin mantles on insipid soapy academic nudes or to those anatomical forms in wax chopped a sang froid by necrophiles. When we think that our epoch, like every other epoch, is nothing else but a point in the immensity of time, we have to laugh to those standards that people considered eternal. The masterpiece—a phrase of the infinite speech running through the centuries can't be the final word it is supposed to be. You cannot consider a phrase no matter how perfect it is, complete and final when the whole sentence is not finished.

Innumerable are the roads leading to heaven and innumerable are the treasures in the illimitable ocean of Art to be unsealed to light by the master hand.

Master is the rolling mountainous wave which darts in challenge to the Gods, against the blue of the heaven, the suspected fantastic floor wrested from the abyss, and fame is the shell which preserves the thunder of the vehemence of this wave in dashing against the dead dunes of oblivion the monuments of the continuous wrecks of idiocy in grotesque opposition to its full sweep.

MARSDEN HARTLEY

• Both Hartley and John Marin expressed themselves poetically, and both wrote poetry whose subject was often the same as the lyric nature studies they chose to paint. Acerbic New Englanders, they condensed language as they condensed imagery in their paintings, in order to make the strongest statement in the fewest words. Hartley's faith in individualism and the importance of the subject is expressed below.

[FROM *Catalogue of the Forum Exhibition,* Anderson Gallery (New York: Hugh Kennerly, 1916).]

Personal quality, separate, related to nothing so much as to itself, is a something coming to us with real freshness, not traversing a variety of fashionable formulas, but relying only upon itself. The artist adds something minor or major more by understanding his own medium of expression, than by his understanding of the medium or methods of those utterly divergent from him. Characteristics are readily imitable; substances never; likeness cannot be actuality. Pictural notions have been supplanted by problem, expression by research. Artistry is valued only by intellectualism with which it has not much in common. A fixed loathing of the imaginative has taken place; a continual searching for, or hatred of, subject matter is habitual, as if presence or absence of subject were a criterion, or, from the technical point of view, as if the Cézannesque touch, for instance, were the key to the aesthetic of our time, or the method of Picasso the clew to modernity.

I am wondering why the autographic is so negligible, why the individual has ceased to register himself—what relates to him, what the problematic for itself counts. I wonder if the individual psychology of El Greco, Giotto and the bushmen had nothing to do with their idea of life, of nature, of that which is essential—whether the struggle in El Greco and Cézanne, for example, had not more to do in creating their peculiar individual aesthetic than any ideas they may have had as to the pictural problem. It is this specialized personal signature which certainly attracts us to a picture—the autographic aspect or the dictographic. That which is expressed in a drawing or a painting is certain to tell who is its creator. Who will not, or cannot, find that quality in those extraordinary and unexcelled watercolors of Cézanne, will find nothing whatsoever anywhere. There is not a trace anywhere in them of struggle to problem: they are expression itself. He has expressed, as he himself has said, what was his one ambition—that which exists between him and his subject. Every painter must traverse for himself that distance from Paris to Aix or from Venice to Toledo. Expression is for one knowing his own pivot. Every expressor relates solely to himself—that is the concern of the individualist.

It will be seen that my personal wishes lie in the strictly pictural notion, having observed much to this idea in the kinetic and the kaleidoscopic principles. Objects are incidents: an apple does not for long remain an apple if one has the concept. Anything is therefore pictural; it remains only to be observed and considered. All expression is illustration—of something.

JOHN MARIN

• In his frequent letters to Stieglitz, Marin insisted, like Hartley, on individuality, intensity, freedom of expression, and quality. Like Stieglitz, Marin was against simplification; he held that the attempt to explicate the unexplainable poetic core of the work of art was doomed to failure. Typical of the attitude of American artists, who tended to identify with the proletariat, rather than with a Bohemia, was Marin's contention that art is, above all, work.

[FROM *Selected Writings of John Marin,* edited with an introduction by Dorothy Norman (New York: Pellegrini & Cudahy, 1949).]

To Stieglitz, July 21, 1921/Taos, N.M.

Freedom, what is it? Let's disobey the law. To first find out, to recognize, the elemental, the big laws then, one must perforce disobey the fool law, to keep the big law. But so many seek to break the big law. Well, nature has something to say about this.

Stonington, Me., Sept. 12, 1923

Yesterday I heard a bird singing. Well, I might go down in Africa and hear a lion roar down the street, the honk of an automobile down to the city, a jazz band. There was quality to the bird's singing, wonderful quality. So in the lion's roar, could be in the honk of the auto, could be in the jazz band. *Quality.* That's what the few of the world will always cry out for, till doomsday. I know it. That's one of my convictions if I have any.

To Hell with Walt Whitman's hymn to death, say I. He was already beginning to croak. No man is old until he begins those croakings. Some are born with it, they love to call the work of others *light, airy.* There is plenty of light if you can see it, away down deep in the uttermost depths. Go down and haul it up—no need to parade where you have been with the damned literature of romance. If you really have *been,* those who see will know, without smearing tatooing, skull, crossbones all over the body.

Out of doors painting as such is just a *Job*—to get down what's ahead of you—water you paint the way water moves—Rocks and soil you paint the way they were worked for their formation—Trees you paint the way trees grow.

If you are more or less successful these paintings will look pretty well indoors for they have a certain rugged strength which will carry them off in a room—though they seemingly bear no relationship to the room

In *indoors* painting—as such—things should bear a close relationship to the room

And I find that now I am hovering close to a statement that in using the term *indoors* I am approaching a supposition of *inward travelling* which throws us back on our haunches again

But—I would like to sound myself to those—would like to roar at those

Those critics
Those feeble painters
Those who gasp out "Interpret myself"
Those—Art creatures
Those—Art exponents

That painting after all—*is painting*—just that—and that if you'll paint and paint—and when you get through your paint builds itself up—moulds itself—piles itself up—as does that rock—this very set of things—why then you might call yourself a painter—you might have one or two of the *old boys*—could they come back—give you a deserved pat on the back

So I stand firm—I refused to be budged by the Spiritual crowd—the maybe so and maybe not—crowd

Yes I'll have it that painting is a *Job*—a *Job* in paint—and I am afraid that in the crazed desire to be modern—to have ideas—to be original—to belong to the tribe *intelligencia* [*sic*]—we have gotten away from the paint job which is a *lusty thing* . . . and I almost feel like saying "what you have to say don't amount to so much"—but the *lusty* desire to splash about—submerge oneself in a medium—you might come up to surface with something worth while—Oh there be phases and phases and still more—but at the present I sing to the LUSTY

Your
MARIN

To Stieglitz from Addison, Me., July 1933

Also I know that when I quit this Expression in *Water Colors*—the which I am now playing with—and get to the dignified—the high micka muck medium Oils—I know that my clothes 'l' a'gin to have paint spots on em and that my wife 'l' a'gin to say things

I find that I begin to think about oil [paints] when the Wells begin to get low—which bears out Demuth's vision of Marin and his slopping water buckets

Once in a while, after a fellow has laid or is laying down some

Solid Red Brick thoughts, or thinks or others think he has laid down these things of Grit and Color, building up, tearing down, often more tearing down than building up—thus bearing out the old saw, "What goes up must come down"—there happens along some one or ones: the curious, too the really interested, and they want to know what it's all about, this brick laying, or what calls for brick in the specifications. And there are those aplenty to tell them. Mostly loiterers. A few try hard and a fewer still with something to tell. But it has been in the past rather hard for those few to find place or space to tell.

It's getting better now. You can see the signs.

Quite a few people are getting nauseated with platitudes, the platitudes of those who write upon things about which they sense mighty little.

So that it's become the thing now to ask the worker himself about his carrying on.

There will be this, though. The worker is one rather given to observing, thinking and doing. It's not easy for him to talk about and explain his work, but as he and his work have been placed in false positions many times, I suppose that he owes it to himself and his world to say something.

To lay off for a while, which is not too difficult, to ponder over, to think on, to vision, what I have done, am doing, am to do, what I have seen, am seeing, am to see, in, of and on this world about me on which I am living, that impels the doing of my do—that's more difficult.

And too what others are doing. For the trend of the doing, from the seeing, must certainly bear out a sort of collective of today.

For the worker to carry on, to express his today, with the old instruments, the old tools, is inexcusable, unless he is thoroughly alive to the relationships of things and works in relationships. Then he can express his today in any material, preserving that material's relationship; as the relationship of two electric bulbs of different strength can be the same as the relationship of two pieces of lead of different weights.

Considering the material sides of today with its insistence: glass, metals, lights, building of all kinds of all kinds of purposes with all kinds of material. Lights brilliant, noises startling and hard, pace setting in all directions, through wires, people movements, much hard matter.

The life of today so keyed up, so seen, so seeming unreal yet so real and the eye with so much to see and the ear to hear. Things happening most weirdly upside down, that it's all—what is it? But the seeing eye and the hearing ear become attuned. Then comes the expression:

taut, taut
loose and taut
electric
staccato.

The worker in parts, to create a whole, must have his parts, arrange his parts, his parts separate, his parts so placed that they are mobile (and though they don't interchange you must be made to feel that they can); have his lines of connection, his life arteries of connection. And there will be focussing points, focussing on, well, spots of eye arrest. And those spots sort of framed within themselves. Yes, there will be big parts and small parts and they will all work together, they will all have the feel, that of possible motion.

There will be the big quiet forms. There will be all sorts of movement and rhythm beats, one-two-three, two-two-three, three-one-one, all sorts, all seen and expressed in color weights. For color is life, the life Sun shining on our World revealing in color light all things.

In the seethe of things, in the interest of this, in the doing of this, terms, abstract, concrete, third or fourth dimension—bah. Don't bother us.

For the worker, the seer, is apt to damn all terms applied by the discussionists. But the glorious thing is that we cannot do, elementally do, other than our ancestors did. That is, that a round conveys to all who see it a similar definite, a triangle a similar definite, solids of certain forms similar definites, that a line—what I am driving at is that a round remains, a triangle remains, a line remains and always was.

To get to my picture, or to come back, I must for myself insist that when finished, that is when all the parts are in place and are working, that now it has become an object and will therefore have its boundaries as definite as that the prow, the stern, the sides and bottom round a boat.

Though as I said before, all things of today are keyed up to the pitch of today.

So that the worker of today, as of old picks up each of these things with recognition. And as to color, we pick out red today as the old Chinamen did. And as for race language of color, all races of all times, I am sure, have had color language otherwise, they are as dead people. And it's all similar elementally.

And that it is my picture must not make one feel that it bursts its boundaries. The framing cannot remedy. That would be a delusion and I would have it that nothing must cut my picture off from its finalities. And too, I am not to be destructive within. I can have things that clash. I can have a jolly good fight going on. There is always a fight going on where there are living things. But I must be able to control this fight at will with a Blessed Equilibrium.

Speaking of destruction, again, I feel that I am not to destroy this flat working surface (that focus plan of expression) that exists for all workers in all mediums. That on my flat plane I can superimpose, build up onto, can poke holes into—By George, I am not to convey the feel that it's bent out of its own individual flatness.

Too, it here comes to me with emphasis that all things within the picture must have a chance. A chance to play in their playground, as the dancer should have a suitable playground as a setting for the dance.

Too it comes to me a something in which I am curiously interested. I refer to Weight balances. As my body exerts a downward pressure on the floor, the floor in turn exerts an upward pressure on my body.

Too the pressure of the air against my body, my body against the air, all this I have to recognize when building the picture.

Seems to me the true artist must perforce go from time to time to the elemental big forms—Sky, Sea, Plain—and those things pertaining thereto, to sort of re-true himself up, to recharge the battery. For these big forms have everything. But to express these, you have to love these, to be a part of these in sympathy. One doesn't get very far without this love, this love to enfold too the relatively little things that grow on the mountain's back. Which if you don't recognize, you don't recognize the mountain.

And now, after looking over my scribblings on various pieces of paper, I think that what I have put down is about what I have wanted to say, the gist of it anyway. My present day creed, which may show different facets on the morrow.

ARTHUR DOVE

• In a letter to Chicago collector Arthur Jerome Eddy, Dove attempts to answer Eddy's question as to what he was driving at in the painting *Based on Leaf Forms and Spaces,* which Eddy had bought in 1912 from Dove's Chicago show. Explaining that he will not make propaganda on modern art, Dove offers instead an "explanation of my own means."

[FROM Frederick S. Wight, *Arthur G. Dove* (Berkeley: University of California Press, 1958).]

Inasmuch as the means continually changes as one learns, perhaps the best way to make it understood would be to state the different steps which have been taken up to the present time. After having come to the conclusion that there were a few principles existent in all good art from the earliest examples we have, through the masters to the present, I set about it to analyze these principles as they occurred in works of art and in nature.

One of these principles which seemed the most evident was the choice of the simple motif. This same law held in nature, a few forms and a few colors sufficed for the creation of an object. Consequently I gave up my more disorderly methods [Impressionism]. In other words I gave up trying to express an idea by stating innumerable little facts, the statement of facts having no more to do with the art of painting than statistics with literature. . . .

The first step was to choose from nature a motif in color and with that motif to paint from nature, the forms still being objective.

The second step was to apply this same principle to form, the actual dependence upon the object (representation) disappearing, and the means of expression becoming purely subjective. After working for some time in this way, I no longer observed in the old way, and, not only began to think subjectively but also to remember certain sensations purely through their form and color, that is, by certain shapes, planes of light, or character lines determined by the meeting of such planes.

With the introduction of the line motif the expression grew more plastic and the struggle with the means became less evident.

Chapter Three

The Armory Show: Success by Scandal

WILLIAM GLACKENS

• Publicity for the Armory Show was solicited and well planned. Although some of the criticism published by sympathetic writers like Gregg and Huneker was closer to propaganda, their support was helpful in stemming the tide of negative reaction. The Armory Show touched off a prolonged series of critical debates on the validity of modernism, which lasted several years. To help gain an audience for the exhibition, Guy Pène du Bois devoted the entire March, 1913, issue of *Arts and Decorations* to the Armory Show. The following is an interview with William Glackens, chairman of the domestic committee, on the American Section of the Armory Show, which was ghostwritten by du Bois in that issue.

[FROM "Interview with William Glackens," *Arts and Decoration,* March, 1913.]

American art is above everything else skillful. American painters and sculptors are technical marvels. I mean the majority. They work with great fluency, manipulate the medium with an astonishing and almost sensational ease. Their painting is the kind of painting that wins prizes. But it is not the kind of painting in which one feels that the artist is actually enjoying himself. Indeed this skill in America is limited, limited by a lack of bravery—a fear of freedom or of honesty. It is skill enslaved by academies, skill answering to the dictates of a rigidly defined prescription—a prescription made general in order that it may fit everything, and, therefore, fitting nothing exactly.

We have had no innovators here. But I do know surely what is meant by innovators in art. American art is like every other art—a matter of influence. Art, like humanity, every time has an ancestry. You have but to trace this ancestry with persistence and wisdom to be able to build the family tree. The cubes of the cubists that must inevitably give us a sense of weight and seem to be a marked departure from the much trodden paths of art are derived directly from Cézanne, who, in turn, is indebted to the impressionists and to the classicists—to the order-loving Ingres, for example.

Everything worth while in our art is due to the influence of French art. We have not yet arrived at a national art. The old idea that American art, that a national art, is to become a fact by the reproduction of local subjects, though a few still cling to it, has long since been put into the discard. This quite naturally and for very obvious reasons.

The early Americans were illustrative. They followed in the tracks of the writers, and that is out of the way that art should follow. It was France that showed them the error of their project. Even Winslow Homer so much lauded as a purely native product, was never good, never the power that he became, until he got under the influence of France. It was through France that Homer, with America, began to get a knowledge or, in fact, a first sight of actual values. That is true, too, in the instance of George Inness, who worked his way out of the rut of the Hudson River School only after he had secured the assistance of the art of France.

But the national art, the truly national art, must be the result of growth; it has never come as a meteor, it never will come as a meteor. Our own art is arid and bloodless. It is like nothing so much as dry bones. It shows that we are afraid to be impulsive, afraid to forget restraint, afraid above everything to appear ridiculous.

Perhaps it is a reflection of the racial characteristic come down to us from Anglo-Saxon forefathers—the same thing that inspires the sobriety of our clothes, the reserve in our manners. For while we have learned to throw off a lot of the formalism that is a veil between every Englishman that has remained a long time in England and life, it is being drawn again tighter and tighter over us as we grow older. Perhaps it is inevitable that the Gauls, who put no masques over their emotions, should become the leaders, pointing the way to us, infusing a little of their fire into our dead wood.

As to the trend of our art, whether it is realistic, classic or romantic, I cannot correctly define. These are, after all, but terms made up for cataloguers who hug index systems to their breasts, as though these might become or were the only coherent histories of the devious ways in which the efforts of mankind travel. They may be in a sense; index systems may casually place men in their proper relations to one another. But the best of them is very general and must inevitably be very superficial. Heaven knows what an impressionist may be. The cataloguers here assuredly fuddled the original meaning.

The man with something to say is the important man in art—in fact, the only man who may claim the title of artist. The manner of his expression matters very little. That will take care of itself. The man with something to say generally says it pretty well.

I am afraid that the American section of this exhibition will seem very tame beside the foreign section. But there is promise of a renaissance in American art. The signs of it are everywhere. This show coming at the psychological moment is going to do us an enormous amount of good. It will go a long way. Up to the present time, of course, there are exceptions, the much-lauded American energy has been displayed everywhere but in our art. It may be that the country, going through the process of building, has not had time for art. It may be that the money god has been a prepondering influence, a gaudy lure for our eyes, a too-strong appeal to our senses. I am not so sure of this, however. It may be that our most energetic men have not had time for art. But inoculate the energy shown elsewhere into our art and I should not be surprised if we led the world.

F. J. GREGG

• The apologetic tone of the critic F. J. Gregg, who examines the attitude of the Americans, is symptomatic of the second thoughts of the Armory Show's organizers.

F. J. Gregg

[FROM "The Attitude of the Americans," *Arts and Decoration,* March, 1913.]

This is not by way of an apology but only in strict justice.

The American painters and sculptors who have arranged for the International Exhibition of Modern Art, and those of them who are co-operating as exhibitors, have reason to claim for themselves the credit of true disinterestedness. It may be that they will benefit as much, or more, than the general public, but, on the other hand, it must be remembered that they are running a risk with their eyes open, the risk of the deadly comparison which is sure to be made by the newly awakened and even by the casual spectator.

The Americans who have done this thing with their eyes open are of all sorts and conditions. Some of them are academicians, others are occasional exhibitors at the Academy; others, again, exhibit anywhere and don't care what side of the street they are found on; others are members of various groups in New York who have nothing whatever in common; others have given up exhibiting altogether, having become convinced of the futility of reaching the public in that way, and others believe only in "one man shows" under ordinary circumstances. It is something that individuals varying so on the subject of the display of art should have worked together harmoniously for what they regard as a great public purpose.

In the practice of their art the members of the Association and their fellow exhibitors present just as decisive contrasts as in the other matter. There is no doubt that in the case of a number of them it will be found that through their individual vitality they have been developing along their own lines, with the result that their works will hold their own even in the neighborhood of the innovators from aboard. This is no more than saying that a number of the Americans have been growing because they were alive and couldn't help it. But undoubtedly one thing the exhibition will show, as anybody might have imagined without it, these are the men who have had no or next to no influence on their fellow countrymen.

It is possible that, when the affair is over, the verdict will be that the vast mass of the American works exhibited represented simply arrested development, and had nothing in them to suggest anything like the hope of posterity while, in the work brought here from Europe, and in that of the few Americans who have been dissatisfied and are struggling after something better was to be found all that was worth any serious attention. But if there was a great contrast and a discouraging one, that in itself will be but the clinching argument that the enterprise was necessary if the lethargy into which our painters and sculptors had fallen was to be put an end to.

We have had various exhibitions of so-called "Independents" and "Insurgents" and so on, but even in the case of the smallest of these it was hard for any man of sense to see what logical relation there was between the artists who showed their work together. There were always several of the associates who, you felt, ought not to have been there. Taking this fact into consideration it is not so surprising that there should be a great variety of importance, or lack of importance, in so large an exhibition as the present one.

What is undoubtedly to be found in the Frenchmen is a quality in their work which, however it may irritate, or puzzle, or disturb, never produces dullness. If it indicates nothing but what is embryonic, that very fact stands for growth into fulness of existence. On the other hand, American art, or that part of it with which the ordinary man is perfectly satisfied, is deadly dull and suggests decay instead of growth.

The manner in which Americans have regarded their own painters and sculptors has affected their purchases of foreign works. Of course there were some daring collectors who bought Post-Impressionists' paintings before they were accepted abroad, but the tendency here was to wait until the drift of fashion had made itself felt. . . .

Some persons who view the great exhibition in the 69th Regiment Armory, and even some artists, will have no idea of the amount of work performed by the members of the Association, at home and abroad, in getting the great show together. It is easy enough to collect pictures for an International Exposition. In such a case the result is a hodgepodge, each nation being represented by what is good, bad, or indifferent, but in the main by what is known as "official art." In this case a body of painters and sculptors set out to do a definite thing, to obtain a certain definite unity which was never lost sight of. The result is that as far as they were able to accomplish it, the exhibition has a positive unity.

Even if the American work in these rooms represents no such vigor as the European work, nothing was accepted or asked for which did not at any rate show a susceptibility on the part of the artist to the vital influences of his period.

Not only was it a difficult task to get the works together, but the exhibition and the preparation for it involved so many details, and such a mixture of details, that the members of the Association had to give up a great deal of their time in committees and otherwise to hard and continuous office work. It is true that they expect to benefit from the exhibition, but this is not the thing that they have kept in mind. The main thing was to get the foreign paintings and sculptures here, and each man made the question of how his own work would look under such trying circumstances quite a secondary consideration.

As one distinguished American painter put it: "I am just as anxious as you fellows are to see how bad my pictures look."

[FROM "A Remarkable Art Show," *Harper's Weekly,* February 15, 1913.]

The exhibition of International Art (February 17th to March 15th), at present the main business of the Association of American Painters and Sculptors, a body incorporated under the laws of the State of New York, was planned to introduce to the public the works of a number of foreign artists, who, though they are well known in Europe, are for the most part but names to New York and America. The method adopted, however, was not to throw our "extreme" contemporaries at the heads of the public, but to show, by a process of selection, from what they had developed. So Ingres was taken as the starting-point, the line continuing with Delacroix, Courbet, Corot, Daumier, Puvis de Chavennes, Degas, Renoir, Monet, Sisley, Pissarro, and so down to Cézanne, Gauguin, Van Gogh, Matisse, Picasso, and the "Futurists."

Until the present occasion the most that Americans knew, in America, of the "movement" abroad, outside some few examples shown at certain small exhibitions here, were the works of certain young men who had gone to France and become immediately and deliberately, perhaps, sensitive to their new environment. Many of them were but weak imitators. It seemed that it was the extravagance of the new foreign painters and sculptors that affected them, and of that extravagance they were the feeble reflectors, all the strength of the originals having evaporated in the process.

The result was the natural one, the public looked on the productions of these disciples as a joke, and could not be convinced that it had any real or valid reason for its existence. The Association, in bringing over the work of the men so eagerly imitated wished to allow Americans to see among other things the difference between the substance and the shadow, between what has set a fashion unwittingly and what was merely fashionable. In the case of those who are now really influential there can be no difficulty about comparing a man's early with his later work. It will be found, on comparison, that the change is the result of a certain logical development. Each step has been in a definite direction and follows the one before. It was not a case of "going somebody one better," or intended to cause surprise or even astonishment. If there was an explanation offered, though it might not explain, at any rate it gave people something to think about.

It was found by Mr. Davies and Mr. Kuhn, the committee of the Association of American Painters and Sculptors which was sent abroad to select works for the New York exhibition, that most of the German Post-Impressionists were adapters, the result being that very little of what they had done had any real significance. A German of Cologne, speaking of the tendency of his fellow-countrymen, said that they were becoming "ultra-intellectual" as distinguished from "ultra-intelligent"; that they went so far, deliberately, as to make their work "sickly." As for the English advanced men, or so-called advanced men, with certain notable exceptions, their work did not exhibit much force or show real development, which is the reason why they are not more widely represented. At the same time there are British painters and sculptors not shown here who ought to be here. But, owing to the shortness of time, all committees, foreign as well as American, found it impossible to cover the field. This is why, for instance, the Russian Modernists, who are affected by the naïve folkart of the empire, are not shown.

As for the "system" followed in selecting the work, it is to be kept in mind that the entire exhibition is the result of a plan of the committee. It decided to go out and find American and foreign art that it considered suitable to its purpose. This it did. But it also had to consider American work that it had not invited, in cases where artists asked to have their paintings and sculptures inspected. It is to be observed that this is a very different matter from sending out a general invitation for works which would have to be dealt with by a regular jury. In fact, the association might put it this way: "This is our show—we have had a special purpose in view in arranging it. We did not try to put so many pictures on view, or wish to give an opportunity to exhibit to this, that or the other person. We desired to give our public the chance to see what has been going on abroad, as it is important for us to know to what extent we have not come under the influences of our period, whatever they may be."

THEODORE ROOSEVELT

• Expressing the honest bewilderment of the man in the street, Theodore Roosevelt lashed out against the array of radical painting and sculpture on view at the Armory Show. His equation of modernism with the lunatic fringe has endured as a popular stereotype; so has his allegation that modern art is a hoax and a fake. Acknowledging the importance of the show, he nonetheless denied the value of the works exhibited.

[FROM "A Layman's Views of an Art Exhibition," *The Outlook*, XXIX (March 9, 1913).]

The exhibitors are quite right as to the need of showing to our people in this manner the art forces which of late have been at work in Europe, forces which cannot be ignored.

This does not mean that I in the least accept the view that these men take of the European extremists whose pictures are here exhibited. It is true, as the champions of these extremists say, that there can be no life without change, no development without change, and that to be afraid of what is different or unfamiliar is to be afraid of life. It is no less true, however, that change may mean death and not life, and retrogression instead of development. Probably we err in treating most of these pictures seriously. It is likely that many of them represent in painters the astute appreciation of the power to make folly lucrative which the late P. T. Barnum showed with his faked mermaid. There are thousands of people who will pay small sums to look at a faked mermaid; and now and then one of this kind with enough money will buy a Cubist picture, or a picture of a misshapen nude woman, repellent from every standpoint.

KENYON COX

• The most intelligent rejection of modernism in the name of academic art came from Kenyon Cox, the articulate painter, critic, and member of the National Academy. Cox saw the breakdown of academic conventions in painting as an indication of the general breakdown of the moral structure. In many ways he was right: the Armory Show did signify the end of an age of cultural innocence in America, as World War I closed the Belle Époque in Europe. Both art and social moral structure were changing, if not crumbling, as Cox feared. But unlike his colleague Royal Cortissoz, Cox was not an hysterical reactionary condemning foreign art as "Ellis Island art"; rather, he was a highly rational conservative. Nevertheless, he could not refrain from charging the modern movement with charlatanism, decadence, and lunacy, the most popular of the indictments against the new art.

While Kuhn and Davies laid plans for the forthcoming Armory Show, Cox delivered a lecture on "The Illusion of Progress" before the American Academy of Arts and Letters on December 13, 1912. The argument declares the supremacy of Renaissance and Baroque art. Progress has meant that "the balance has turned against us; our loss has been greater than our gain; and our art, even in its scientific aspect, is inferior to that of the sixteenth and seventeenth centuries." Moreover, according to Cox, "Being no longer intimidated by the fetish of progress, when a thing calling itself a work of art seems to us hideous and degraded, indecent and insane, we shall have the courage to say so and shall not care to investigate it further." His advocacy of the maintenance of the *status quo* and his conception of the Renaissance as a golden age, lost to corrupt modern man, find many echoes today in academic writings.

Kenyon Cox

[FROM "The 'Modern' Spirit in Art," *Harper's Weekly,* March 15, 1913.]

It is proper to begin an account of the extraordinary exhibition of modern art recently held in New York with an acknowledgment that it is well such an exhibition should be held and that, therefore, the thanks of the public are due to the gentlemen who got it together. We have heard a great deal about the Post-Impressionists and the Cubists; we have read expositions of their ideas and methods which have had a plausible sound in the absence of the works to be explained; we have had some denunciation and ridicule, some enthusiastic praise, and a great deal of half-frightened and wholly puzzled effort to understand what, it was taken for granted, must have some real significance; but we have not heretofore had an opportunity of seeing the things themselves—the paintings and sculpture actually produced by these men. Now the things are quite indescribable and unbelievable. Neither the praises of their admirers, the ridicule of their opponents, nor the soberest attempt at impartial description can give any idea of them. No reproduction can approach them. They must be seen to be believed possible, and therefore it is well that they should have been seen. From this point of view my only regret is that the Association of American Painters and Sculptors did not see fit to include some representation of the Futurists in their exhibition, that the whole thing might be done once for all. In a case of necessity one may be willing to take a drastic emetic and may even humbly thank the medical man for the efficacy of the dose. The more thorough it is the less chance is there that it may have to be repeated.

Of course I cannot pretend to have approached the exhibition entirely without prejudice. One cannot have studied and practised an art for forty years without the formation of some opinions—even of some convictions. But I remembered the condemnation of Corot and Millet by Gérome and Cabanel; I remembered the natural conservatism of middle age; I took to heart the admonition of the preface to the catalogue, that "to be afraid of what is different or unfamiliar is to be afraid of life." I meant to make a genuine effort to sort out these people, to distinguish their different aims and doctrines, to take notes and to analyze, to treat them seriously if disapprovingly. I cannot do it. Nor can I laugh. This thing is not amusing; it is heartrending and sickening. I was quoted the other day as having said that the human race is rapidly approaching insanity. I never said it, but if I were convinced that this is really "modern art" and that these men are representative of our time, I should be constrained to believe it.

In recollecting the appalling morning I spent in this place certain personalities do, however, define themselves and certain tendencies make themselves clear. It is no time for squeamishness or for standing upon "professional courtesy," and such persons as I may mention I shall treat quite frankly—in that respect, at least, I may follow their own example. Fortunately there is little necessity of dwelling upon the American part of the show. It contains some good work by artists who must wonder at the galley aboard which they find themselves, some work with real merit by men who have aided in the launching of the galley, and a great deal of bad work which, however, seldom reaches the depths of badness attainable by Frenchmen and Germans. But this work, good, bad, and indifferent, is either perfectly well known or is so paled by comparison that it needs no mention. Some of it is silly, but little of it is dangerous. There is one American, however, who must be spoken of because he has pushed the new doctrines to a conclusion in some respects more logical and complete than have any of the foreigners. In the wildest of productions of Picabia or Picasso there is usually discernible, upon sufficiently painstaking investigation, some faint trace of the natural objects which are supposed to have inspired them; and even when this disappears the title remains to show that such objects have existed. It has remained for Mr. Marsden Hartley to take the final step and to arrange his lines and spots purely for their own sake, abandoning all pretense of representation or even of suggestion. He exhibits certain rectangles of paper covered with a maze of charcoal lines which are catalogued simply as Drawing No. 1, Drawing No. 2, and so forth.

This, I say, is the logical end, for the real meaning of this Cubist movement is nothing else than the total destruction of the art of painting—that art of which the dictionary definition is "the art of representing, by means of figures and colors applied on a surface, objects presented to the eye or to the imagination." Two years ago I wrote: "We have reached the edge of the cliff and must turn back or fall into the abyss." Deliberately and determinedly these men have stepped over the edge. Now the total destruction of painting as a representative art is a thing which a lover of painting could hardly envisage with entire equanimity, yet one may admit that such a thing might take place and yet an art remain that should have its own value. A Turkish rug or a tile from the Alhambra is nearly without representative purpose, but it has intrinsic beauty and some conceivable human use. The important question is what it is proposed to substitute for this art of painting which the world has cherished since there were men definitely differentiated from beasts. They have abolished the representation of nature and all forms of recognized and traditional decoration; what will they give us instead? And here is the difference between Mr. Hartley and his Parisian brothers. His "drawings" are purely nugatory. If one finds it impossible to imagine the kind of human being that could take any pleasure in them one is free to admit that there is nothing especially disgusting about them. But one cannot say as much for the works of the Frenchmen. In some strange way they have made their work revolting and defiling. To have looked at it is to have passed through a pathological museum where the layman has no right to go. One feels that one has seen not an exhibition, but an exposure.

Of course the work of these artistic anarchists formed only a part of the exhibition. A serious attempt was made to get together a representative showing of the artists whom they consider their forerunners, and a number of the smaller galleries contained what might be considered a series of illustrations of Meier-Graefe. A good many critics who find the latest manifestations of the "modern" spirit quite intolerable are yet able to maintain a complacent satisfaction in these earlier exemplifications of it and even, by contrast, to increase their pleasure in work which seems relatively sane and wholesome. I wish I could feel, as they do, that there is a sudden dislocation with the appearance of Matisse and that everything before him falls naturally into its place as a continuation of the great tradition. I wish I were not forced to see that the easy slope to Avernus began as far back as the sixties of the last century. The lack of discipline and the exaltation of the individual have been the destructive forces of modern art, and they began their work long ago. For a time the persistence of earlier ideals and the possession by the revolutionaries of the very training which they attacked as unnecessary saved the art from entire dissolution. Now all discipline has disappeared, all training is proclaimed useless, and individualism has reached the pitch of sheer insanity or triumphant charlatanism.

The decadence did not begin with Ingres and Delacroix and Corot, though the ultras would fain utilize the glory of these masters as a covering for their own nakedness. It seems to me clear that it did begin with Manet and Whistler. It is impossible not to sympathize with the revolt against an unintelligent literalism which these men began. It is equally impossible not to see that they suffered from the lack of training and from the lack of a normal relation to their public, and that, in spite of great beauties, their work is ineffectual and fragmentary. There was little of it here, and that not of the best, but there was enough of it, as there was of the more purely Impressionist work of Monet and Renoir and the rest, to show its relation to the *dégringolade* which followed. The Impressionists denied the necessity of any knowledge of form or structure and decried the acquisition of such knowledge. They preached "the innocence of the eye." It was not the business of an artist to know what anything is like or how it is made—his affair was only how it looks. Neither had he any right to compose or select, though, as a matter of fact, they could not help composing and selecting. The colored spot and the vibration of light—these were the sole objects of study. . . .

Cézanne is by far the most interesting as he is the most extravagantly praised of the modernists. I believe him to have been a perfectly sincere searcher, and I admit in him some of the elements of genius. He seems to have had a sense of essential character in portraiture, just as he had a sense of the essential squareness of houses and the essential roundness of apples. He seems always to have aimed at the great things. But he seems to me absolutely without talent and absolutely cut off from tradition. He could not learn to paints as others did, and he spent his life in the hopeless attempt to create a new art of painting for himself. Fumblingly and partially he can express himself to the few—he will never have anything for the many. If Cézanne is a builder, Gauguin is a decorator, but a decorator tainted with insanity. His arrangements of line are sometimes noble and graceful, but the things he represents are often hideous. His color is sometimes beautiful, but it is always unnecessarily false and often unpleasantly morbid. "The Spirit of Evil" haunts more of his pictures than the one so named. In the work of Van Gogh which was shown at the armory

I can find little either of the great qualities he is said to have possessed or of the madness that finally overcame him. All I can be sure of is an experiment in impressionistic technique by a painter too unskilled to give quality to an evenly laid coat of pigment.

All these men were, I think, honest enough; unbalanced, undisciplined, and self-absorbed, but not self-glorifiers. I cannot think the same of the two I have next to name. How far mental disease mingles with inordinate self-esteem and immoderate self-exploitation in the later work of Rodin it is difficult to say. Some of his later sculpture and almost all of his drawings are the more lamentable in that they mark the ruin of a great talent. As to Matisse I am no longer in doubt; it is not madness that stares at you from his canvases, but leering effrontery.

Believing, as I do, that there are still commandments in art as in morals, and still laws in art as in physics, I have no fear that this kind of art will prevail, or even that it can long endure. But it may do a good deal of harm while it lasts. It may dazzle the young students of art with the prospect of an easily attained notoriety which they cannot distinguish from fame, and prevent their acquiring any serious training during the years when, if ever, such training must be acquired; it may so debauch criticism that it shall lose what little authority or usefulness it still retains; it may corrupt public taste and stimulate an appetite for excitement that is as dangerous as the appetite for any other poisonous drug; finally, it may juggle out of the pockets of the gullible a few dollars that will be far more wasted than if they were thrown into the sea. To the critics it is useless to speak. How shall we instruct our self-appointed instructors? The students and the public may possibly listen, and for them I have a few words of earnest advice.

To the student I would say: Distrust all short cuts to art or to glory. No work worth doing was ever done without long preparation and continuous endeavor. The success that is attained in a month will be forgotten in a year. To the public I would say: Do not allow yourselves to be blinded by the sophistries of the foolish dupes or the self-interested exploiters of all this charlatanry. Remember that it is for you that art is created, and judge honestly for yourselves whether this which calls itself art is useful to you or to the world. You are not infallible, but your instincts are right in the main, and you are, after all, the final judges. If your stomach revolts against this rubbish it is because it is not fit for human food. Let no man persuade you to stuff yourselves with it.

[FROM "The Illusion of Progress," *Century,* LXXXV (May, 1913).]

In these days all of us, even Academicians, are to some extent believers in progress. Our golden age is no longer in the past, but in the future. We know that our early ancestors were a race of wretched cave-dwellers, and we believe that our still earlier ancestors were possessed of tails and pointed ears. Having come so far, we are sometimes inclined to forget that not every step has been an advance, and to entertain an illogical confidence that each future step must carry us still further forward; having indubitably progressed in many things, we think of ourselves as progressing in all. And as the pace of progress in science and in material things has become more and more rapid, we have come to expect a similar pace in art and letters, to imagine that the art of the future must be far finer than the art of the present or than that of the past, and that the art of one decade, or even of one year, must supersede that of the preceding decade or the preceding year, as the 1913 model in automobiles supersedes the model of 1912. More than ever before "To have done, is to hang quite out of fashion," and the only title to consideration is to do something quite obviously new or to proclaim one's intention of doing something newer. The race grows madder and madder. It is hardly two years since we first heard of "Cubism" and already the "Futurists" are calling the "Cubists" reactionary. Even the gasping critics, pounding manfully in the rear, have thrown away all impedimenta of traditional standards in the desperate effort to keep up with what seems less a march than a stampede.

But while we talk so loudly of progress in the arts we have an uneasy feeling that we are not really progressing. If our belief in our own art were as full-blooded as was that of the great creative epochs, we should scarce be so reverent of the art of the past. It is, perhaps, a sign of anemia that we have become founders of museums and conservers of old buildings. If we are so careful of our heritage, it is surely from some doubt of our ability to replace it. When art has been vigorously alive, it has been ruthless in its treatment of what has gone before. No cathedral builder thought of reconciling his own work to that of the builder who preceded him; he built in his own way, confident of its superiority. And when the Renaissance builder came, in his turn, he contemptuously dismissed all medieval art as "Gothic" and barbarous, and was as ready to tear down an old façade as to build a new one. Even the most cock-sure of our moderns might hesitate to emulate Michelangelo in his calm destruction of three frescos by Perugino to make room for his own "Last Judgment." He at least had the full courage of his convictions, and his opinion of Perugino is of record.

For this seems, finally, to be the law of all the arts: the one essential prerequisite to the production of a great work of art is a great man. You cannot have the art without the man, and when you have the man you have the art. His time and his surroundings will color him, his art will not be at one time or place precisely what it might be at another; but at bottom the art is the man, and at all times and in all countries is just as great as the man.

Let us clear our minds, then, of the illusion that there is in any important sense such a thing as progress in the fine arts. We may with a clear conscience judge every new work for what it appears in itself to be, asking of it that it be noble and beautiful and reasonable, not that it be novel or progressive. If it be great art, it will always be novel enough; for there will be a great mind behind it, and no two great minds are alike. And if it be novel without being great, how shall we be the better off? There are enough forms of mediocre or evil art in the world already. Being no longer intimidated by the fetish of progress, when a thing calling itself a work of art seems to us hideous and degraded, indecent and insane, we shall not care to investigate it further. Detestable things have been produced in the past, and they are none the less detestable because we are able to see how they came to be produced. Detestable things are produced now, and they will be no more admirable if we learn to understand the minds that create them. Even should such things prove to be not the mere freaks of a diseased intellect that they seem, but a necessary outgrowth of the conditions of the age and a true prophecy of "the art of the future," they are necessarily the better for that. It is only that the future will be very unlucky in its art.

Chapter Four

Cubism in America

EDWIN BLASHFIELD

• Although Walter Pach, the leading spokesman for French modernism in the United States, and other champions of the new art, inveighed against the sterility of academic art, many came to its defense. To Abraham Walkowitz' statement that dead art like dead meat could have its buyers and its use, Edwin Blashfield countered that there is no dead art. In "The Painting of Today" (*Century,* April, 1914), Blashfield, an academic painter, warned against the excesses of an unbridled modernism. And the compromise between academic art and modernism that he counseled was a solution accepted by many American artists who produced innumerable tepid, Cubist-tinged still lifes and landscapes from the moment of the Armory Show on through the twenties and thirties. That this marriage of the old and the new would result, not in an ideal synthesis, but in a pastiche of the academic and the modern, ought to have been evident; but, on the contrary, where the imported modernist style was insufficiently understood, the unlikely partnership Blashfield advocated had a great appeal.

[FROM "The Painting of Today," *Century,* LXXXVII (April, 1914).]

I believe that the new movement is potential for great good in its development, through experiment, of effects produced by broken color and the novel manipulation of material. But there is in this no excuse whatever for other tendencies, which occasionally seem to accompany the new movement, that are dangerous, and that may be even mortal, if pushed to their ultimate conclusion. Once the experiments made, the best effects of color and light found, there is no reason why the vigor and freshness acquired should not be applied to correct proportion, correct forms, and correct values. There are in the new movement two tendencies that cannot be too persistently combated: the tendency to consider labor bestowed on a work as a hindrance to excellence, and the tendency to a fatuous contempt for the lesson of the past.

Certain phrases have been referred rightly or wrongly to those who stand for "advance." For instance: "Anything in a work of art which shows evidence of training in the author is bad," or "Freedom and feeling are all that should be required from an artist," or "All that has been done in the past is useful only to show us what to avoid." This seems to me puerile nonsense, negligible, were it not dangerous. What freedom is greater than that of the man who has mastered methods? What slavery is more complete than that of him who can control no method? Since a flat surface is all a painter has on which to exhibit feeling, how can he exhibit it freely unless he can *govern* that surface?

"Labored" is also an expression which has become a bogy to many a student, frightening him away from his work before his dough is half baked. What work is good if accomplished without thought? Indeed thought is labor in its most strenuous form. And to decry laboriousness is to play with a two-edged tool. Not only does the intimidated pupil leave his work before he has accomplished it, but he is also fascinated by a promise of facile accomplishment; he is befooled and frightened at once.

Indeed, it is hard to conceive of any one idea more dangerous to a beginner than the idea that work is superfluous and even hurtful. Most dangerous of all, perhaps, is the fact that a truth is mixed up with this —the truth that work which does not look labored is better than work which does.

It is difficult to compress into a short article what I should like to try to state, but surely the unprejudiced art lover will admit this at least: A, B, and C, men who possess a brilliant technic, may safely throw aside much of it for a time as hampering while they concentrate themselves on new effort and solve fresh problems; but X, Y, Z, beginners in art, who start with the idea that truth, freedom, and strength lie in forswearing a technic which they have never acquired, and disdaining the discipline to which they have never submitted, will wreck themselves, and become dangerous and deplorable examples to others who wish to "arrive" easily and quickly. It is quite possible to adopt some of the methods of the new movement with advantage; it is *mortal,* in my opinion, to adopt some of its principles, as they are stated by votaries. Variation of technic is helpful, eschewal of technic is deadly, and technic without training is nonexistent.

ANDREW DASBURG

• Among the most successful of those who attempted to reconcile Cubism with older styles of representational art, Andrew Dasburg analyzed the impact of this school on American art. His criticism of the American understanding of Cubism was a remarkably incisive, contemporary account of its limitations, but his distaste for extremism reveals that he shared many of the prejudices that inhibited the development of American modernism and, incidentally, of his own art.

[FROM "Cubism—Its Rise and Influence," *The Arts,* IV (November, 1923).]

The influence of Cubism on American Art is apparent; yet in writing of Cubism in America one must hesitate to call themselves so. *Isms* and classifications are "taboo." The illusion of individuality has cast its spell upon the artist. He resents being associated with any particular group. To him classification impiles a loss of identity. This attitude is so general among our painters that one cannot write of "actual Cubism" in America, but only of the effort.

This ambition to achieve the distinctly personal would be admirable were it not accompanied by a self-deception which, admitting nothing, takes from many sources the formal material for our art. We fail to recognize that form arises in personality and bears the impress of its origin. An idea can belong to all and become the way to individuality, whereas merely to adopt the results of another's use of the idea is essentially a negation of self. We lack the intellectual integrity to work logically within the limitations inherent in an idea. We want instead to gather what is best from many sources, forgetting that art is not compounded from extracts of different significant qualities found in great art. We have yet to learn that each development has a character of its own which remains forever intact. One cannot, for example, present simultaneously the quivering aspirational movement of El Greco and the gravitational weight of Cézanne; the absolute loss of both would result.

This idea of combining a variety of forms of perfection into one complete ideal realization prevents any creative work being done which possesses the contagious force of Cubism. Usually we weave into the fabric of a new conception enough of current traditions to destroy its integral character, a process of peaceful penetration wherein little is risked and much may be gained. Not until it is realized that originality never follows from this attitude of assimilation and refinement can we become innovators. Though we fail in this rôle there are, among American artists, men of unusual talent whose work compares favorably with the best being done in Europe, excepting that of a few great figures. Almost everyone that can be called "modern" has at some time or other shown an influence of Cubism in his work. Among these are Sheeler, Man Ray, Hartley, McFee, Wheelock, Demuth, Marin, Cramer, Burlin, Sterne, Wright, Haweis, H. F. Taylor, Dasburg, the Zorachs, A. Lohr, Baylinson, Judson Smith and lastly, Max Weber, who has worked more consistently within the discipline of Cubism and developed it further than any of these. . . .

Before attempting to trace the modifications of Cubism by American painters, it seems necessary to define Cubism more completely. Cubism can be separated into three developments—movement, spatiality and pure form.

Cubism is a geometry of rhythm and an architecture of matter. Two considerations are fundamental to the understanding of rhythm. One is the force of gravity, the other, the upward impulse in living things. All matter shows the effect of one or both of these conditions, and they are two important factors in the invisible moulding of all forms. The so-called static nature of inanimate things is controlled by one; the organic materializes under the influence of both. Movement as opposed to the static effect of gravity on inanimate things—as, for example, the formation and action of the human figure—implies a displacement from the center of gravity and a sequence of adjustments against resistance to a state of equilibrium. This adaptation is a constant sensory experience of man. He, in all his movements, instinctively seeks an attitude of poise and ease. Rhythm is the effect of the harmonious accomplishment of this action. And when the essence of this is achieved in a work of art, without expenditure of energy on our part, we receive a sense of freedom from the physical difficulties of a resisting world. These forces in the mechanism of growth are the underlying principles upon which a feeling for rhythm and rhythmic composition is founded.

The instinctive experience of our natures is then the truest guide for the proportioning and directing of form into significant symbols of rhythm. In this principle Picasso found a plan that served to coordinate the form element of planes. Not content with the bilateral displacements resulting through movement, he added yet greater and more vivid interest through asymetrical surprises in the breaking up of his objects. This gave a complex and astonishing combination of dynamic and static elements. Here began the dissolution of the objective image until it ultimately became incorporated into the space surrounding it. A transformation obtained through the extension of planes through planes, forming an architectonic unit in which the remaining fragments of the dissolved objects were held together only by the law of association. Even though the sculptural aspect of things was destroyed and transformed into purely spatial sensations, the technique for bringing about illusional depth was still employed.

Painting has a two-dimensional objective reality, a plane on which depth and modeling are illusional occurrences supplied through the process of association. In the non-illusional elements of painting, such as color, line, tone, and in the unlikeness of images, exists a separation which for the painter should be the key to plastic space. Qualities that are dissimilar, like contrasts of color, differences of tone and line, exist on the same plane only in a tactile sense, i.e., on the surface of the canvas; the difference of their appearance is a spatial interval.

Picasso with a fecundity of invention finally achieved the method in which the means he employs becomes the motive for his composition. In this last phase of Cubism, so remote from the original conception, the emphasis is upon the material reality of the means involved, color existing for color, and all the other elements used accentuating their own reality through the fundamental aesthetic law of contrast. As aesthetic achievement which in its finest examples penetrates into a high region, having a quality akin to great Buddhistic art—one of ultimate poise wherein the conflict of elemental forces is transcended.

As in Europe, so in America; with a few distinguished exceptions, the idiosyncrasies of Cubism rather have permeated our art in varying degrees with a severity of line and acute angles just as Impressionism did before it with blue and orange. These, the essential symbols which remain intact always, will have to serve as an index for identifying those who come under its influence.

Among these, H. L. McFee combines a theme of planes, objects and cubical depth, which receive, through his sensitiveness, an appearance of poised solidity. Marin, in certain water colors, crystallizes exquisitely the spatial relation of things. Demuth, another artist of distinction, through a division of planes extending from his objects into their environment achieves an effect of displacement like the reflection of an image in a crystal. Haweis, Stella and Wheelock arrive at similar surprises in a distinctly personal manner. In contrast to the effect in the work of these men, that of Bluemner, Dickinson and the sculpture of Wolf and Nakian have a static simplicity, which in Hartley, Sheeler, and in recent improvisations of Paul Burlin, is especially fine.

Man Ray, in his Invention Dance, can be called a one-dimensional Cubist, carrying simplification to a point where his figures appear like paper patterns. The "Cubist-Futurist" settings designed by Robert Edmund Jones for the production of Macbeth were the most extraordinary of their kind by an American seen in America.

It is singular that "Synchromism," which Willard Huntington Wright calls "the last step in the evolution of present-day art materials," which "embraces every aesthetic aspiration from Delacroix and Turner to Cézanne and the Cubists," should have at one stage of its kaleidoscopic career borrowed from Cubism a scaffolding on which to support its color theories while at the same time denying its aesthetic validity.

Instead of finding Synchromism, as Appolinaire did in 1913, "*vaguement Orphist,*" New York in 1915 only recognized in it the influence of Cubism. I refer to the figure composition of MacDonald-Wright based on the attitude of Michael Angelo's Slave, where the form is reduced to planes, distributed co-ordinately with the movement of the figure, dividing the color contrast and making an appearance like that of a gay Harlequin suit. I refer also to Morgan Russell's radiations of angular planes circulating spirally throughout his canvas.

Aside from the influence of 291, which stands unique, the work of these two Americans, with that of Max Weber, who undoubtedly was our first "extremist," together with the phenomenal success of the International Exhibition, tended more than any other influence to bring to notice the new formal element entering into French art. But the single novelty that broadcasted Cubism throughout America was Duchamp's Nude Descending the Stairs—the sensation of the hour, making the term "Cubism" become in the mind of the layman synonymous with "Modern Art."

Among all the crafts—architectural decoration, textile designing—the flotsam of Cubism is scattered. For the gentle temperament, Cubism serves as a geometric web to support his lyrical theme. To the more energetic talent, it becomes a way into the wonder of creation. But for all, after the shock of its angularity and asymetrical deformities, the influence of Cubism, with that of Matisse, resulted in a greater liberation from tradition than even Impressionism achieved.

STANTON MACDONALD-WRIGHT

• The two groups of American artists to have the firmest grasp of the principles of Cubism were the European-based Synchromists and the Precisionists, or Immaculates. As leader of the former, Stanton Macdonald-Wright formulated the color-oriented aesthetic of the Synchromists.

[FROM *Catalogue of the Forum Exhibition,* Anderson Gallery (New York: Hugh Kennerly, 1916).]

I strive to divest my art of all anecdote and illustration, and to purify it to the point where the emotions of the spectator will be wholly aesthetic, as when listening to good music.

Since plastic form is the basis of all enduring art, and since the creation of intense form is impossible without color, I first determined, by years of color experimentation, the relative spatial relation of the entire color gamut. By placing pure colors on recognizable forms (that is, by placing advancing colors on advancing objects, and retreating colors on retreating objects), I found that such colors destroyed the sense of reality, and were in turn destroyed by the illustrative contour. Thus, I came to the conclusion that color, in order to function significantly, must be used as an abstract medium. Otherwise the picture appeared to me merely as a slight, lyrical decoration.

Having always been more profoundly moved by pure rhythmic form (as in music) than by associative process (such as poetry calls up), I cast aside as nugatory all natural representation in my art. However, I still adhered to the fundamental laws of composition (placements and displacements of mass as in the human body in movement), and created my pictures by means of color-form which, by its organization in three dimensions, resulted in rhythm.

Later, recognizing that painting may extend itself into time, as well as being a simultaneous presentation, I saw the necessity for a formal climax which, though being ever in mind as the final point of consummation, would serve as a *point d'appui* from which the eye would make its excursions into the ordered complexities of the picture's rhythms. Simultaneously my inspiration to create came from a visualization of abstract forces interpreted, through color juxtapositions, into terms of the visual. In them was always a goal of finality which perfectly accorded with my felt need in picture construction.

By the above one can see that I strive to make my art bear the same relation to painting that polyphony bears to music. Illustrative music is a thing of the past: it has become abstract and purely aesthetic, dependent for its effect upon rhythm and form. Painting, certainly, need not lay behind music.

CHARLES SHEELER

• In contrast to the Synchromist color-oriented aesthetic set forth by Stanton Macdonald-Wright, Charles Sheeler, as spokesman for the Precisionists, formulated more down-to-earth views of the "business of the artist." His statement, as Macdonald-Wright's, comes from the Forum Exhibition catalogue.

Cubism in America

[FROM *Catalogue of the Forum Exhibition,* Anderson Gallery (New York: Hugh Kennerly, 1916).]

I venture to define art as the perception through our sensibilities, more or less guided by intellect, of universal order and its expression in terms more directly appealing to some particular phase of our sensibilities.

The highest phase of spiritual life has always in one form or another implied a consciousness of, and, in its greatest moments, a contact with what we feel to be the profound scheme, system or order underlying the universe; call it harmonic rhythm, law, fact, God, or what you will.

In my definition I used the expression "through our sensibilities more or less guided by our intellects," and I here add "less rather than more," for I believe that human intellect is far less profound than human sensibility; that every thought is the mere shadow of some emotion which casts it.

Plastic art I feel to be the perception of order in the *visual* world (this point I do not insist upon) and its expression in purely plastic terms (this point I absolutely insist upon). So that whatever problem may be at any time any particular artist's point of departure for creative aesthetic endeavor, or whatever may be his means of solving his particular problem, there remains but one test of the aesthetic value of a work of plastic art, but one approach to its understanding and appreciation, but one way in which it can communicate its most profound significance. Once this has been established the observer will no longer be disturbed that at one time the artist may be interested in the relation of straight lines to curved, at another in the relation of yellow to blue or at another in the surface of brass to that of wood. One, two or three dimensional space, color, light and dark, dynamic power, gravitation or magnetic forces, the frictional resistance of surfaces and their absorptive qualities capable of visual communication, are material for the plastic artist; and he is free to use as many or as few as at the moment concern him. To oppose or relate these so as to communicate his sensations of some particular manifestation of cosmic order—this I believe to be the business of the artist.

FORBES WATSON

• The Synchromists had an apologist in the critic Willard Huntington Wright, brother of Macdonald-Wright, and, unfortunately, when Wright stopped writing art criticism, writing about their work virtually ceased. Others who wrote sympathetically of the American Cubists in the twenties were Henry McBride and Forbes Watson, editor of *The Arts,* whose essays on Sheeler and Demuth are exceptionally perceptive.

[FROM "Charles Sheeler," *The Arts,* III (May, 1923).]

The past decade in American art has been a spectacle to watch, and those whose eyes were not too much distracted by the mere spectacle, have seen developments of a more permanent kind than healthy noise alone can make. The tremendous whoop, with which the decade began, was necessary, else the rock-bound would have continued to retain the fort of public opinion. Yet, though whooping may shake existing foundations, or at least rattle the windows above them, a calmer faith is needed to produce something that will outlive the waves of sound.

Since the business of being modern, as a business, soon attained its final capacity to shock, it followed that with every successive beat of the big drum the noise grew fainter and many a promising noise-maker, with paint, is now a salesman of automobiles—or horns. The band-wagon of "modernism," after a period of immense usefulness, is pretty well deserted and the word "modern," after fifteen years—or is it fifteen centuries—of perpetual strain, is an invalid requiring long rest and comparative seclusion. Many fell asleep on the band-wagon and have rolled off into oblivion. Others are still jumping up and down on it trying to make themselves believe that it is going somewhere, while the more intelligent stepped down quietly when it had served its inspiring purpose, the only purpose of a band-wagon, and took their way along a path of their own choice. And to these, real things have happened. They are the only important younger artists, the rock-bound having brought forward none of any importance whatsoever.

In days of hasty thought transference it did not take people long to find out that the bright idea of imitating this French "modern" or that French "modern," would not necessarily end in producing an American "modern," however much it might give, for the moment, to the American imitator's painting, a certain fancy dress of "modernism." One couldn't go on forever painting by theory unless one had the particular racial characteristics of those who enjoy muddling their paint with philosophy, even as the English enjoy muddling their paint with literature. One couldn't go on forever asking the world to judge a work of art, not as something created for itself to serve the artist's purpose or idea, but, on the contrary, as a logical exposition of a theory outside of itself.

Sooner or later the American was sure to demand that the art which he produced should bear up without support from threatening jargon or heavy bombast. Having himself a simple nature, the American, like the Frenchman, takes his painting simply. He likes to select, eliminate, arrange, unless he happens to belong to that dying school of American landscape wherein much is said about following nature and very little done about it, and wherein, instead of selection, there is on the one hand a submerging of nature in a pot of brown sauce, or on the other hand, the unselective makeshift of pretty color-photography.

Dismissing these last two phases as being outside the field of art the American artist, by and large, still has his being in the dark ages of good taste, and I hope he will stay there. Good taste is his native inheritance. Witness, for example, American architecture, so choice in its early stages, and in its latest developments so superior to any other contemporary architecture, and witness also American furniture, American glass, Whistler, Davies, Demuth, Marin, and, finally, Charles Sheeler, the subject of this review, whose work is now on exhibition at the Denver Art Association, Denver, Colorado. It is easy to trace, through more than a century of American art, an inherent refinement, a definite quality of good taste which are part of a tradition to which the art of Charles Sheeler belongs. . . .

[FROM "Charles Demuth," *The Arts,* III (January, 1923).]

Charles Demuth came in with the rush of "modernism" that made its tardy arrival in America after the famous Armory exhibition;

which means that as an artist before the public, Mr. Demuth belongs to the past or passing decade. He is one of that group of aesthetic young Americans who specialized in the new movement imported from France, and decided that the opportunity to be saved from the obvious, which the new movement offered, together with its other advantages and disadvantages, was too good to be missed.

The disadvantages of the new movement were, that it called many who have turned out not to be chosen—heavy-minded young men (Demuth is the opposite of heavy-minded) who tramped into "modernism" to the accompaniment of a kind of fog-horn chorus of blah. Demuth has been tagged with the nickname modern, and he carries this nickname as airily as Grace Christie balances the bubble in her bubble dance. For Demuth is mentally agile; he's the Whistler of his little circle, but he doesn't talk as much about it as Whistler did. I suspect that he often smiles at the demi-intellectual sentiments of the earnest members of the little circle, all that stuff about this being the age of machinery and the artist, in order to realize the dynamic forces, etc., etc. . . .

His art is light and floating. It moves through the air. It is agile, poised in a space above the world, but not out of reach of theatrical lights. And that certain skill of the acrobat, that sense of freedom and complete escape from rubber heels and office chairs . . . that all belongs to Demuth.

It is part of that excessive *finesse,* his most cherished attribute, which he protects behind a mask of disdain.

Fantasy, the light touch, the art quality (aesthetic), the whimsical, the ironic, the delicate (never the sweet), the biting—Charles Demuth.

Between himself and his spectators he likes to maintain a barrier of aloofness. He is *fin* in the French sense. He enjoys Duchamp's *blagues,* but he has more creative energy than Duchamp. Yet Duchamp has been his strongest influence of late years as Demuth himself says. From Duchamp he has gained an increased interest in good workmanship; but Demuth naturally has the sense of medium. Water color fits him like a glove. It belongs to and is a part of his expression. And in this medium he has done his finest work.

Oil is a medium for an exuberant nature. And Demuth despises exuberance. He is far too selective for that. His inventions are utterly intentional. He is not interested in fact for its own sake, and the display of much emotion would seem a little ridiculous to him, not to say vulgar. In this he makes me think of Jane Austen.

Many of his illustrations of vaudeville are among the American prizes in the Barnes collection.

His later art is Post-Cubist. It couldn't have been done before Cubism. It is only one of the manifestations that go to prove that Cubism as an art is far less important than Cubism as an influence. Every day makes this fact clearer.

But Demuth has not gone to work with Hebraic intensity and made a problem play of Cubism. Like a dainty canary he has picked seeds neatly here and there.

GEORGE L. K. MORRIS

• Fifteen years later, George L. K. Morris lamented Demuth's premature death (at the age of 52 in 1935) on the occasion of his retrospective at the Whitney Museum. He cast his appreciation of the largely unappreciated Demuth in the form of an open letter.

[FROM "To Charles Demuth," *Partisan Review,* March, 1938.]

To Charles Demuth.

There are many who regret that you are not here to see this exhibition. You would be surprised yourself, perhaps, at the poise and monumentality that your work retains, even from as far back as 1913. To many who had previously known your pictures through isolated examples, the present complete display comes as a revelation. There are inherent native qualities here, and a structural fabric that can support them. Your stature increased, while much that was more ambitious has been forgotten in the meantime.

It may have been for the best that, like Juan Gris, you did not live through the disturbing cycle. For you are free to go down among recent American painters as the only one who knew to the end what you were doing. There is no strain, your accent was never forced;

everything in this exhibition holds within its limits to the wall. Perhaps you knew that it would be the only one. It may have been the disease of your body—the fact that you always knew when your work must cease—which creates the sense of completeness.

During your lifetime your work was referred to as cold. You were indeed always aloof. The passion for realism inherent in America never touched you. Your pictures are not lively, but they live with an internal vitality that will endure. You were fortunate in your contact with the European structural renaissance at an early date. By 1912 your aesthetic accent was already established. The electric line, the very personal manipulation of shape and contour, your peculiar secret of letting the picture breathe through its unpainted areas, were there before the War. Of course there were pitfalls. You ran into difficulties when you tried to fuse abstraction with landscape and house-forms, the only time when there is a disturbing divergence of spirit. And you did not imbibe the later teachings of abstraction, your color does not completely absorb the form. But, on the other hand, you were never impeded by Marin's Impressionist hangover. You were always an architect within the canvas boundary, with a passion for exhausting every means whereby the parts might be welded together. Your gifts are most congenial to still life; there, where the shapes are more readily and simply defined the full emotional gamut lies securely at rest.

Influences are difficult to trace throughout your work; only occasionally will the echo of an early American flower-painting protrude or (as in "Mme. Delaunois") of Constantin Guys. Neither has your own influence been wide, but in depth it can be incalculable. To enter these exhibition rooms is to discover a world where everything is digested and understood. There are no "cocktails," no quickly-shaken mixtures of alien styles—a trend that has become the bane of American art. And the coldness that was once attributed to you seems to have vanished now. Few of the enduring monuments from any period have been ingratiating at the start. The supreme achievements often "refuse" the spectator and he is forced to try again. So it is that when your world is finally broken into, there is no trace of vulgarity, for there had never been disturbing inducements to attract the casual eye. You present the quality we need most today if we can withstand the shocks with which the artist is being continually bombarded.

Chapter Five

The Thirties: Reaction and Rebellion

THOMAS CRAVEN

• The quarrel that rent the art world in the thirties began with a criticism of superficial imitations of European art and ended in a violent rejection of internationalism in art. That chauvinistic strain, which sought to make America safe for American art, was publicly announced when Royal Cortissoz dismissed the foreign sections of the Armory Show as "Ellis Island art." Henri's espousal of American subjects and the American scene was distorted in a manner he and his friends ultimately repudiated.

In the interest of creating a distinctively American art, Thomas Hart Benton and his friend the critic Thomas Craven launched diatribes against internationalists like Stieglitz ("a Hoboken Jew"), calling for an art based on regional themes, which would be intelligible to the common man. In the name of a democratic art, they proposed to abandon the genuinely democratic pleas of Henri and Sloan for a plurality of styles in favor of a prescription for the single style they considered suitable to express their nationalistic message.

Like earlier moralistic critics, Craven saw modernism as a degenerate style. He praised, instead, the American Regionalists who had rejected modernism and exalted "life" over art. Urging others to emulate Benton's abandonment of abstraction and return to realism, Craven attacked what were, to his mind, the inadequacies and weaknesses of abstract art and railed at the formalist approach to art.

[FROM *Men of Art* (New York: Simon & Schuster, 1931).]

Among the younger painters there is plenty of talent worth mentioning, but more important than talent is the growing desire to throw off the European yoke, to rebel against the little groups of merchants and esoteric idealists who control the fashions and markets in American art, and who maintain little stables of thoroughbred artists just as the sporting millionaires deal in thoroughbred horses. These little groups, comprising collectors, connoisseurs whose fathers got rich in pork, oil, or iron, lady art students, and students of philosophy mired in aesthetics, feed on transplanted European cultures—or American imitations of the same—support museums, cliques, and various uplifting societies, but they have only the mildest of contacts with the swift and brutal realism of American energy. The consciousness of slavery among the younger men has bred unrest and dissatisfaction with foreign cults, and this unrest, together with the immense possibilities in architectural decoration, augurs well for a revival of painting in America. For it is in North America, or Russia, or perhaps in a combination of the two, that we must plant our hopes for the significant expression of the new age. Certainly we have profited little by the culture of Western Europe. . . .

This, translated into terms of aesthetics, means that art for its own sake, or beauty's sake, or for the sake of any abstraction whatever, will not thrive in America. It means that the kind of painting exploited by our international dealers is a hothouse product nurtured in little pots of imported soil, and that it will never exert an iota of influence on American life or thought. It means that if we are ever to have an indigenous expression, it will be an art proceeding from strong native impulses, simple ideas, and popular tastes, an art reflecting the color and character of a machine age. We had some years ago in the United States a popular expression of a minor sort in prints and illustrations, the form of which, intimately related to the social scheme, is not to be sneered at; and we have today all the talent and energy requisite to great painting, as well as an environment of immeasurable artistic richness.

But, the idealists object, the machine is strangling the creative impulse. This terrible ogre, by destroying handicrafts, has destroyed the background of the fine arts, leaving the sensitive soul no foundation for a spiritual edifice. Furthermore, the machine is supposed, in some mysterious fashion, to have affected our responses to "formal relationships. . . ."

The Modernists were men of the strongest antisocial propensities.

They took pride in their aloofness and gloried in their refusal to traffic in bourgeois sentiments and vulgar emotions. "To hell with the public!" they cried. "There is no such thing as popular art! The public has always demanded trash and we will leave that to the academicians!" But these aristocrats of art, these aesthetic thoroughbreds, were not wholly above commerce with the rabble: they employed the most extraordinary tactics in order to persuade, cajole, and bully the public into buying their pictures. In such an atmosphere art turns inward, feeds upon itself, takes refuge in abstractions. It was only natural that men living in a little world of metaphysical disputations should have produced an art divorced from its human context; it was to be expected that the defence of this art should be the hopeless effort to separate social, moral, and sentimental activities from what was snobbishly labelled "pure aesthetics." This critical attitude, propped up by the tenets of an unstable psychology, sprang from two bases, the scientific and the emotional, but the machinery involved was identical.

It consisted in restricting the significant factors in the production and appreciation of art to those whose understanding rested upon special training or unusual experience. Thus technique, essentially a matter for painters and a few specialists, became the whole of art, a field completely isolated from vulgar understanding. Into this exclusive field the thoroughbreds dragged the values belonging to the profoundest art and annexed them to minor technical issues. Furthermore, by describing technical problems in the terms of physiological mechanics and psychology, painters made the simplest processes enormously impressive. The "purification of painting" was the fine name given to this dehumanizing tendency, and to be looked upon as in the know, one was forced to subscribe to the high-sounding chatter about abstraction, empathy, significant form, dynamic relationships, and so forth.

The purification of painting! An enchanting fallacy indeed! "Pure beauty," as Winckelmann said long ago, "is like pure water—it has no taste." Yet this tasteless art multiplied by leaps and bounds. The various purity cults founded on the technique of line and color organization raised mediocrity to a glorious eminence and provided the initiate with the regalia for personal distinction. Poor old Cézanne's little sensation was father to a thousand perversions. To be "highly sensitive" in the esoteric fashion was the supreme honor, and any painter ingenious enough to erect a precious mythology round a few lines, or daubs of color, was assured of enviable notoriety. A tangle of lines, a swirl of tones, and he had produced a subjective cryptogram entitled *Psychic Portrait, Symphony in Blue-Green,* or *Centripetal Force.* Every little technical operation, every shade and detail, was magnified to epochal proportions. He was willing to die to make a table cloth pictorially interesting, willing to sacrifice his life to a pattern of spots and curves, the sole value of which lay in its "abstract beauty" —a theme for the humorist. He was so self-contained that he esteemed man as less valuable than a bowl of fruit or a congestion of cubes. The growth of humanity did not concern him—he was painting the growth of abstractions or the soul of pots and pans. Eventually he talked more about himself and his strange soul-states than about his art, and consulted the Freudian doctors to ascertain the full import of the psychic orgasms aroused within him by a piece of still life.

Increasing in purity, painting shrank proportionately in human values until, at last, it appealed to a few souls divinely endowed with the "aesthetic emotion." This emotion by means of which one responds purely to art, that is, to its abstract harmonics, has been regarded with suspicion by eminent investigators unable to separate it from other emotions and unable to admit that man, being what he is, a gross bundle of appetites, memories, and experiences all bound together into a single receiving system, can react purely to any stimulus. But the suspicion, I believe, is ill-founded. The aesthetic emotion is the unique property of those who love only art and not life; whose receptive apparatus, through disuse, has so shrivelled that it is no longer capable of responding to anything but abstractions. Painters possessing this peculiar emotion are really convinced that it is no longer capable of responding to anything but abstractions. Painters possessing this peculiar emotion are really convinced that they have symbolized the grace of the human body, and the dynamic power and movement of modern machines, by abstract combinations of lines and masses bearing no discoverable relation to the objects in question. They maintain that an abstract art is the reflex of a machine age, and that its technique is the organic expression of the scientific trend of the times, a theory echoed by many writers. It happens, however, that the Modernists, by their own confession, are aggressively hostile to our machine age, and that they live as far from it as possible, preferably in the more romantic quarters of Paris. In the ways of contemporary civilization, they are poorly educated, and their pseudo-scientific technique is an arbitrary method deduced from Cézanne, a Provençal recluse for whom the machine age never existed.

Yet, making allowances for all that is excrescential in modernism, I find the movement vastly more interesting than its sworn enemy, the official art of France. Even in its slightest activities—the child's play of the customs house officer, Rousseau, the consumptive art of Modigliani and the smartness of Dufy—there are evidences of creative ability—of a personality moulding materials into new and arresting forms instead of faithfully recording the dimensions and visual appearances of nature. On certain departments of the crafts—costume-designing, weaving, print-cloths, pottery and kitchen wares—the influence of modernism has been gay and beneficial; on the wholesale decoration of interiors its effect has been abominable, largely because the Cubist designers, ignoring the animal and spiritual needs of man, have imposed an eccentric pictorial formula upon utilitarian objects. What the movement will lead to I do not know. In France the more intelligent men, following the example of Lhote, are gradually returning to representational art; the others, professing to symbolize subconscious nightmares by indecipherable diagrams which they call *Super-Realism,* are beyond redemption. Matisse, growing old, turns out pretty sentiments for the American trade; and Picasso, to judge by his prize-winning exhibit at the Carnegie Institute, is a candidate for the Academy. The present condition of French painting is not one to make the heart rejoice. There is more hope in North America.

THOMAS HART BENTON

• The careers of three of the leading artists in America during the thirties, Thomas Hart Benton, Edward Hopper, and Stuart Davis, provide dramatic contrasts in the variety of their responses toward the problem of making art in America.

Benton was only one of many American artists who abandoned abstraction to return to figurative art. The nature of his reversal is best studied by comparing his statement for the 1916 Forum Exhibition with excerpts from his autobiography, published in 1937. Common to both are an anti-intellectualism and a distrust of consistency that run as undercurrents throughout the recent history of American art.

[FROM *Catalogue of the Forum Exhibition,* Anderson Gallery (New York: Hugh Kennerly, 1916).]

My experience has proved the impracticability of depending upon intellectualist formulas for guidance, and I find it therefore impossible to ally myself definitely with any particular school of aesthetics, either in its interpretative or constructive aspects.

I may speak generally of my aim as being toward the achievement of a compact, massive and rhythmical composition of forms in which the tactile sensations of alternate bulgings and recessions shall be exactly related to the force of the line limiting the space in which these activities take place. As the idea of form cannot be grasped without mental action on the part of the beholder; as its comprehension, that is, implies the necessity of a more intense mental state than is requisite for the enjoyment of simple loveliness of color, I value its development, manipulation, etc., by far the most important element entering into the construction of a work of art.

The generation of the idea of form depends upon a comparison of contoural or linear extensions, their force, direction and the like; this generation is caused by attention to boundaries of shapes; the preeminent stimulus to realizing a cubic existence is line—therefore I make the production of interesting line relations the first business in my painting. Color I use simply to reinforce the solidity and spatial position of forms predetermined by line.

I believe the importance of drawing, of line, cannot be overestimated, because of its above-mentioned control of the idea of form, and I believe that no loveliness of color can compensate for deficiency in this respect. While considering color of secondary constructive importance, I realize, nevertheless, its value in heightening the intensity of volume, and am, to a certain extent, in accordance with all those developments which, emanating from Cézanne, tend to accentuate its functioning power.

I believe that particular attention to consistency in method is bad, and for this reason employ any means that may accentuate or lessen the emotive power of the integral parts of my work.

In conclusion I wish to say that I make no distinctions as to the value of subject matter. I believe that the representation of objective forms and the presentation of abstract ideas of form to be of equal artistic value.

[FROM *An Artist in America* (rev. ed.; Kansas City: University of Kansas City Press, Twayne Publishers, 1951).]

John Steuart Curry and Grant Wood rose along with me to public attention in the thirties. They were very much a part of what I stood for and made it possible for me in my lectures and interviews to promote the idea that an indigenous art with its own aesthetics was a growing reality in America. . . .

We were different in our temperaments and many of our ideas but we were alike in that we were all in revolt against the unhappy effects which the Armory Show of 1913 had on American painting. We objected to the new Parisian aesthetics which was more and more turning art away from the living world of active men and women into an academic world of empty pattern. We wanted an American art which was not empty, and we believed that only by turning the formative processes of art back again to meaningful subject matter, in our cases specifically American subject matter, could we expect to get one.

The term [Regionalism] was, so to speak, wished upon us. Borrowed from a group of southern writers who were interested in their regional cultures, it was applied to us somewhat loosely, but with a fair degree of appropriateness. However, our interests were wider than the term suggests. They had their roots in that general and country-wide revival of Americanism which followed the defeat of Woodrow Wilson's universal idealism at the end of World War One and which developed through the subsequent periods of boom and depression until the new internationalisms of the Second World War pushed it aside. This Americanist period had many facets, some dark, repressive, and suggestive of an ugly Neo-Fascism, but on the whole it was a time of general improvement in democratic idealism. After the break of 1929, a new and effective liberalism grew over the country and the battles between that liberalism and the entrenched moneyed groups, which had inherited our post Civil War sociology and were in defense of it, brought out a new and vigorous discussion of the intended nature of our society. This discussion and the political battles over its findings, plus a new flood of historical writing concentrated the thirties on our American image. It was this country-wide concentration more probably than any of our artistic efforts which raised Wood, Curry, and me to prominence in the national scene. We symbolized aesthetically what the majority of Americans had in mind—America itself. Our success was a popular success. Even where some American citizens did not agree with the nature of our images, instanced in the objections to my state-sponsored murals in Indiana and Missouri, they understood them. What ideological battles we had were in American terms and were generally comprehensible to Americans as a whole. This was exactly what we wanted. The fact that our art was arguable in the language of the street, whether or not it was liked, was proof to us that we had succeeded in separating it from the hothouse atmospheres of an imported and, for our country, functionless aesthetics. With that proof we felt that we were on the way to releasing American art from its subservience to borrowed forms. In a heyday of our success, we really believed we had at last succeeded in making a dent in American aesthetic colonialism.

However, as later occurrences have shown, we were well off the beam on that score. As soon as the Second World War began substituting in the public mind a world concern for the specifically American concerns which had prevailed during our rise, Wood, Curry, and I found the bottom knocked out from under us. In a day when the problems of America were mainly exterior, our interior images lost public significance. Losing that, they lost the only thing which could sustain them because the critical world of art had, by and large, as little use for our group front as it had for me as an individual. The coteries of highbrows, of critics, college art professors, and museum boys, the tastes of which had been thoroughly conditioned by the new aesthetics of twentieth-century Paris, had sustained themselves in various subsidized ivory towers, and kept their grip on the journals of aesthetic opinion all during the Americanist period. These coteries, highly verbal but not always notably intelligent or able to see through momentarily fashionable thought patterns, could never accommodate our popularist leanings. They had, as a matter of fact, a vested interest in aesthetic obscurity, in highfalutin symbolisms and devious and indistinct meanings. The entertainment of these obscurities, giving an appearance of superior discernment and extraordinary understanding, enabled them to milk the wealthy ladies who went in for art and the college and museum trustees of the country for the means of support. Immediately after it was recognized that Wood, Curry, and I were bringing American art out into a field where its meanings had to be socially intelligible to justify themselves and where aesthetic accomplishment would depend on an effective representation of cultural ideas, which were themselves generally comprehensible, the ivory tower boys and girls saw the danger to their presumptions and their protected positions. They rose with their supporting groups of artists and highbrowish disciples to destroy our menace. . . .

Now all this anarchic idiocy of the current American art scene cannot be blamed solely on the importation of foreign ideas about art or on the existence in our midst of institutions which represent them. It is rather that our artists have not known how to deal with these. In other fields than art, foreign ideas have many times vastly benefited our culture. In fact, few American ideas are wholly indigenous, nor in fact are those of any other country, certainly not in our modern world. But most of the imported ideas which have proved of use to us were able to become so by intellectual assimilation. They were thoughts which could be thought of. The difficulty in the case of aesthetic ideas is that intellectual assimilation is not enough—for effective production. Effective aesthetic production depends on something beyond thought. The intellectual aspects of art are not art, nor does a comprehension of them enable art to be made. It is in fact the over-intellectualization of modern art and its separation from ordinary life intuitions which have permitted it, in this day of almost wholly collective action, to remain psychologically tied to the "public be damned" individualism of the last century and thus in spite of its novelties to represent a cultural lag.

Art has been treated by most American practitioners as if it were a form of science where like processes give like results all over the world. By learning to carry on the processes by which imported goods were made, the American artist assumed that he would be able to end with their expressive values. This is not perhaps wholly his fault because a large proportion of the contemporary imports he studied were themselves laboratory products, studio experiments in process, with primarily a process evolution. This put inventive method rather than a search for the meaning of one's life at the center of artistic endeavor and made it appear that aesthetic creation was a matter for intellectual rather than intuitive insight. Actually this was only illusory, and art's modern flight from representation to technical invention has only left it empty and stranded in the backwaters of life. Without those old cultural ties which used to make the art of each country so expressive of national and regional character, it has lost not only its social purpose but its very techniques for expression.

EDWARD HOPPER

• In his essay on Burchfield, the American Scene painter Edward Hopper praised in his friend many of the picturesque qualities to be found in his own art.

[FROM "Charles Burchfield, American," *The Arts,* XIV (July, 1928).]

The work of Charles Burchfield is most decidedly founded, not on art, but on life, and the life that he knows and loves best. From what is to the mediocre artist and unseeing layman the boredom of everyday existence in a provincial community, he has extracted a quality that we may call poetic, romantic, lyric, or what you will. By sympathy with the particular he has made it epic and universal. No mood has been so mean as to seem unworthy of interpretation; the look of an asphalt road as it lies in the broiling sun at noon, cars and locomotives lying in God-forsaken railway yards, the steaming summer rain that can fill us with such hopeless boredom, the blank concrete walls and steel constructions of modern industry, midsummer streets with the acid green of close-cut lawns, the dusty Fords and gilded movies—all the sweltering, tawdry life of the American small town, and behind all, the sad desolation of our suburban landscape. He derives daily stimulus from these, that others flee from or pass with indifference.

Through many of these transcriptions are woven humorous anecdotes, which seem to be so firmly kneaded into the picture's plastic qualities that they play only a minor role in one's enjoyment of the intense reality.

Our native architecture with its hideous beauty, its fantastic roofs, pseudo-Gothic, French Mansard, Colonial, mongrel or what not, with eye-searing color or delicate harmonies of faded paint, shouldering one another along interminable streets that taper off into swamps or dump heaps—these appear again and again, as they should in any honest delineation of the American scene. The great realists of European painting have never been too fastidious to depict the architecture of their native lands in their pictures. . . .

There is no fear in any of this of painting, literature, or of making art that is not great art, or of offending good taste. Through all of it runs the courage to do that which the painter has most at heart, a lack of self-consciousness, and an obstinate disregard of that deadly discrimination that blights so often the works of the knowing and well-read.

Is it not the province of work such as Burchfield's to render to us the sensations that form, color, and design refuse to reveal when used too exclusively as an aim in themselves, and which words fail to encompass?

A train rushes on straight and shining rails across our vision, past closed gates, raises clouds of suffocating dust, and rumbles into vague stretches that imagination tries to construct.

IVAN ALBRIGHT

• One of the leading Magic Realists, Ivan Albright had a fascination with the morbid that may date from the period when he made surgical drawings for a medical unit during World War I. With his twin brother, known professionally as Zsissly, he developed a bizarre mixture of the fantastic and the hyper-realistic. Like the Collier brothers, Albright represents a kind of extreme eccentricity that seems characteristically American—in the sense of individuality carried to the limits of a self-expression ultimately bordering on the obsessive. In the contemporary assemblages of Bruce Conner and Edward Kienholz one sees a continuation of Albright's involvement with the more grotesque aspects of the American scene. West Coast "funk art," a kind of buckeye Surrealism, also continues in this direction.

[FROM *American Realists and Magic Realists,* edited by Dorothy C. Miller and Alfred H. Barr, Jr. With statements by the artists and an Introduction by Lincoln Kirstein. (New York: Museum of Modern Art, 1943).]

In the past I have painted herrings that changed from purple to an orange oxide, women whose torrid flesh folds resembled corrugated mush, lemons and imitation fur, purple glazed leaves that exuded a funereal odor, and tawdry costume rings whose size all but covered actor-less hands. My models' idiosyncrasies have varied. Ida munched peanuts and threw the shelled husks on the floor for me to step on. The bearded one who sat on a town bench in the public square of San Diego chose to eat the lordly Judas bean and in so doing conceived himself an unsung Saint John. There was the long-haired flaxen Canadian, a Rosicrucian, in the electrically heated basement which he tended, who extolled his sliding Adam's apple as a mark of great spirituality.

I have painted keys that were of brass and calla lilies that drooped from their overload of paraffin and showed inclinations to become tops to jelly jars. I have pumiced white-clean an old tombstone, eliminating its incised inscription, and used it in a painting for a threshold, when its proper place should have been at the head of the grave lichen-covered rather than under a door. But all things, whether a bluebottle fly or red flying hair, have had their points and counterpoints and it may be that in the wide future I will walk and amuse myself looking at this thing and at that thing through my ill-ground bifocal glasses that make an aberration next to the object I am looking at.

CHARLES BURCHFIELD

• Other artists, including many who worked in the Federal Art Project of the WPA, had a more programmatic social message to embody in their art. Charles Burchfield was one of these, and his description of his painting *The Parade,* written in 1954 to Lawrence A. Fleischman, a Detroit art collector, pungently evokes the spirit of the thirties.

[FROM Correspondence of Mr. and Mrs. Lawrence A. Fleischman (1953–64), in *Art in America,* LIII, No. 4 (August–September, 1965).]

This picture grew out of an experience my wife and I had one day during the Depression of the early thirties.

We had come into Buffalo, on the bus, on some errand, and as we got off the bus, we found our way blocked by an unemployment parade—a group of men on their way to the City Hall to make a protest of their plight. As we watched them go past, sullen and bedraggled (it was a thaw day in winter) we knew that unless something were done, that our society might crumble, and much worse come on us. The mounted police were silently watching, seemed to have a cold sinister air about them.

The incident stuck in my mind and I felt I must get it down on paper. The answer came to me oddly enough at a symphony concert—during the playing of Beethoven's Fifth Symphony (which had nothing to do with the mood)—I suddenly saw the scene clearly in my mind. The parade seen through the arches of a concrete bridge. That seemed to give it a tomb-like character. To further heighten the effect I put in the foreground the vapors arising from a sewer vent, and the crack in the bridge was to symbolize that the foundations of our society were cracking.

The only depression picture I painted. I planned a similar one during World War II, a protest against war—but it never materialized. I felt, I guess, nothing I could do would halt the destruction of young men. (I believed in our participation in the war, but hated war itself.)

I also felt I would get myself and my dealer in trouble if I exhibited such a picture—and to no purpose. So the impulse dissipated into nothing.

EDWARD BRUCE

• The first to suffer from the effects of the Depression, artists were also allowed to share in New Deal pump-priming measures, as employees of the federal government. Edward Bruce, chief of the Section of Fine Arts, Public Buildings Administration, evaluated the first WPA project in 1934.

[FROM "Implications of the Public Works Arts Project," *American Magazine of Art,* March, 1934.]

The reaction of the artists to the project . . . has been that while the economic relief afforded them by the project was enormously appreciated and greatly needed, the spiritual stimulus to them in finding that they were recognized as useful and valuable members of the body politic and that the government desired their work, has been simply amazing. It has, as many of them expressed it, broken down the wall of isolation and brought them in touch and in line with the life of the nation. It has stimulated them to the maximum effort and aroused their excitement and imagination. . . .

The lady in an expensive fur coat who told me it was all right to feed the artists, but why make the public look at their stuff, is in for a shock. I think perhaps the outstanding feature of the work which has been produced so far is its honesty and fine quality of naturalness. It is a native product. While, of course, it shows signs of a definite art tradition and an art background, it is amazingly free from isms and fads and so-called modern influences. Ninety per cent of it is modern in the best sense. . . .

It has been a very exciting experience to discover vigorous local art movements all over the country and talent where we did not know talent existed. Artists who were thought of as having only a moderate talent are producing work far beyond and better than they have ever produced before, and artists who were absolutely unknown are producing some of the best work on the project.

If through the project there comes a demand for a beautiful America, the economic as well as the spiritual and esthetic possibilities are very great.

The backers of this project went into it with their eyes open. They didn't expect a hundred per cent quality and they won't get it, but it is quite apparent from the work already accomplished that this country is going to get a great many works of art of high quality which will show the investment to have been very profitable as well as very fine. Masterpieces and geniuses are not produced from isolated efforts: if the history of art is any criterion they come only from large art movements. A large body of work and a large number of artists are necessary to reproduce the Leonardos, the Piero della Francescas, and the Michelangelos.

REGINALD MARSH

• The American Scene painter Reginald Marsh describes his experience in painting a post office mural in Washington, D.C.

[FROM "Poverty, Politics, and Artists, 1930–45," *Art in America*, LIII, No. 4 (August–September, 1965).]

Having mounted the scaffold without a colored smock and a Tam o'Shanter resulted in many employees asking when the artist was coming along. This happened even after I had completed full length figures. In all the time I was there, no one asked me my name.

One or two had heard of Kent—three or four had heard of Grant Wood, and about a dozen of a Mexican who had trouble with Rockefeller Center. One had heard of Michelangelo.

Many volunteered to tell me that Cubism angered them.

Many wanted to know if there were new jobs in store for me and always looked at me in a pitying way.

Most of them ventured that I must have been born that way.

BURGOYNE DILLER

• Abstract artists, too, were given a chance to work on the Project. Burgoyne Diller, supervisor for the New York City Federal Art Project, was one of the leading American abstractionists of the thirties. In an interview made for the Archives of American Art in 1964, shortly before his death, he recalled the experience shared with many leading New York artists.

[FROM "Poverty, Politics, and Artists, 1930–45," *Art in America*, LIII, No. 4 (August–September, 1965).]

There's something that's unforgettable about that period. There was a sense of belonging to something, even if it was an underprivileged and downhearted time. It was exciting.

We worked day and night and weekends and believe me, we were not paid well for it, but we thought it was the most wonderful thing that could be happening. We were enthusiastic and we were ready and willing to do anything. It was a madhouse.

I was very much interested in abstract painting. They felt that there was no place for it at the time because they felt the project should be a popular program and while they didn't attempt to invalidate or question the validity of the work, abstract art had no place because you did have a great problem of building up public sympathy and understanding. . . .

We made a rather elaborate model of the work to be done for the (Arshile) Gorky mural in the Newark Airport. We did a rather good one for Gorky's presentation to the Art Commission of the City of Newark. The Commission was made up of rather elderly gentlemen. I'm sure they were of some prestige socially and economically. I'm sure they fit into the upper echelons of Newark society—rather cool, forbidding characters. They were the sort of people you would see sitting in the windows of the Princeton Club, or the Yale club. When we presented the mural I deliberately presented it as decoration so they wouldn't quibble about art. But one of them, probably brighter than the rest, said, "Well, that's abstract art, isn't it?" That unleashed the devil. They started, of course, a tirade of questions and cross-questions and accusations and statements about modern art. Beatrice Windsor, who is socially and economically their equal, shamed them into accepting it.

BALCOMB GREENE

• Despite the hostility of the American public toward the budding abstract art movement, there was a growing belief among artists that modernism, born in Europe, might flourish naturally in the United States, the world's most advanced and modern country. Even before the mass exodus of artists from Europe caused by the Nazi invasion, a number of abstract artists, such as Jean Hélion and Fernand Léger, came to New York, hoping to find a reception for their progressive ideas.

On the eve of World War II, Balcomb Greene, a member of the American Abstract Artists, wrote of the difficulties and the possible promise facing the advanced artist in America. In his appraisal, Greene describes the crisis—later called paralyzing by Harold Rosenberg—of social and political values that rocked the artistic and intellectual worlds in the late thirties as artists and intellectuals, disenchanted with politics, viewed the coming war in Europe.

[FROM "American Perspective," *Plastique,* Spring, 1938.]

The opinion is often heard that Europe is too unstable politically for a virile art to subsist there—much less this new art of abstraction which must, ironically, discipline and restrain itself before a public which is neurasthenic. It is hoped America is the acreage not under fire, the plot in which plastic properties may be cultivated within the limitations of the canvas—a country attractive to Nierendorf and the collector Reber, but also pleasing to men less free in their mobility such as Gropius, Moholy-Nagy, and Hélion. If Non-Objectivity is a function of the fine arts, suitable to a practical people who build efficient business and industrial machines, one may well ask what forces confront the new tradition in the United States.

The ablest detractor of any artist's integrity is probably the one on best terms with the artist's ego—a form of self interest, the desire to make a name quickly and sell pictures. For this achievement one must make pictures which are easily understood. Avoiding this, the inclination is to make paintings easier for oneself to understand, which exact less work from one, which basically are formulas, automatic and decorative. Our first concern should be for this opposition which does its damage "internally."

The stricture falls today upon the ambitious abstractionist that he cannot any longer provoke or scandalize by being Non-Objective. His amorphous and geometric forms cannot sing the tunes of home-soil nationalism or of prolitarian discontent—much less combine them as present American "social realists" seem to. Therefore, perhaps in a new sense, our elimination of the subject offers a survival value.

The American abstractionist seems usually to understand that capitalist society hampers the development of his art. But he resents the professional revolutionist's demand for an art immediately comprehensible to the masses which will bolster up sales for a society which in turn is allowed a generation of dictators for its realization. The result in this country is a wary fraternalizing of artist with revolutionist. The "line" followed today by the Marxist is to end his Plekhanovistic attack on abstractionism by commending Hélion and Léger on their balance and their brushwork. Picasso, currently honored for his sadistic venture into Guernica, is honored not for his balance, his brushwork or his content, but for what is viewed as a lapse from individualism.

It is in this world of shaded pragmatisms that the artist as idealist must seek his values. He can hardly avoid visualizing himself laying cornerstones for the city of the future while other men—assisted by his alter ego—train their artillery on an enemy city now flying the Fascist flag. The argument as to how much construction should be suspended while destruction goes on is a tough one. And academic.

The central difficulty for the advanced artist may now be clear. Granted he has the tenacity to turn out his number of canvases, what besides his remote ideal has he to keep his work from becoming a mere brush service to his independence, automatic therefore, often imitative and always decorative? What stimulation?

In the United States he may lack the first essential, a certain public integrity however unenlightened. For a European it is difficult to imagine what adroit agencies for publicity we have developed here, difficult to imagine with what gusto the sensationalist magazines may inflate the vulgar homosexual today, a living primitive tomorrow, a slick master of the streamlined woodblock the next day. The artist witnessing this may well be a cynic.

Certain facts complicate the picture. Largely it is the younger men and women who turn to our tradition. The teachers out of all proportion support and understand our effort. In an unspectacular way the mural division of the Federal Art Project is able to place many abstract murals, and without the expected indignation. And yet the general run of art magazines has fallen to a new low in selling the artist's personality and neglecting his work. That most influential New York museum of "modern art," by name and in its origin progressive, exhibits a craving for popularity which makes impossible any leadership. What abstract work is able to exhibit itself draws encouraging crowds, but seems to have built a following which makes its judgements privately. One might say the validity of the new tradition is established, but that the manipulators see no profit in assisting it.

Opposed by the chaotic temper of the world, and not assisted by the machinery which makes successes easy, the strength of the new tradition and its persistence may be attributed at last to the substance of the paintings and constructions themselves.

JOHN GRAHAM

• In a prophetic but obscure treatise on aesthetics, John Graham, one of the most successful Cubist painters in America in the thirties, spoke of the artist's "handwriting," or *ecriture,* in a manner that would come to characterize the Abstract Expressionist use of gesture, and described the way his friend Gorky would begin to use line.

[FROM "What Is the Relationship of Art to Technique?," in *System and Dialectics of Art* (New York: Delphic Studios, 1937).]

—What is the relationship of art to technique?

Art is the authentic reaction of the artist to a phenomenon observed, set authoritatively to the operating plane. No technical perfection or elegance can produce a work of art. *A work of art* is neither the faithful nor distorted representation, it *is the immediate, unadorned record of an authentic intellecto-emotional REACTION of the artist set in space.* Artist's reaction to a breast differs from his reaction to an iron rail or to hair or to a brick wall. *This authentic reaction recorded within the measurable space immediately and automatically in terms of brush pressure, saturation, velocity, caress or repulsion, anger or desire which changes and varies in unison with the flow of feeling at the moment, constitutes a work of art.*

Cold-blooded calculation and perfect technical execution do not constitute a work of art but a work of industry, and it is harmful and criminal before the public, artists, art students, and posterity to misrepresent such as works of art. Unfortunately about 90% of the holdings of all museums and collections are of this variety.

The difficulty in producing a work of art lies in the fact that artist has to unite at one and the same time three elements: thought, feeling, and *automatic "ecriture."**

When a person talks about different objects which interest him his voice and gestures in their rise and fall and in their velocity, impetuously register his reaction to various aspects of these objects. Drawing or painting or writing is an immediate and organic accumulation of these *spontaneous* gestures set to the operating plane.

People who have never experienced anything deeply or had intense perception of any kind, have no means of differentiating between a work of art and a fraud (a work produced by sheer technique and nothing else).

People who are incapable of deep experiences are those whose emotional equipment is naturally poor as a result of inheritance or those whose emotional equipment has been weakened and stunted in childhood by mild and sterile rearing.

Art is essentially a creative process. Technique, therefore, plays but little part in it, namely the part of discipline and study. It is legitimate to keep on developing one's technique as long as one uses it to learn more and more about the *object* or about the *medium* itself, but the

* By ecriture is understood a personal technique—result of training and improvisation in contradistinction to technique in general which is an accumulation of professional methods.

moment technique begins to be an aim in itself, it serves only the purpose of disguising ignorance and lack of ability. Then technique becomes an impediment to the artist and a dishonest camouflage to the public.

The subject matter, representation, imitation of nature, technique, or trained skill have nothing to do with art. There are people who can paint Picasso's paintings with a greater technical perfection, there are people who can perform all [the] most difficult pirouette steps of Lifar or Nijinsky with greater technical perfection, etc., but the element of art is absent. All this is to say that any artist—painter, poet, dancer or singer—should have something to say first before bothering about technique. In fact, perfect technique makes the thing even more void if it is void, because the process of technique is impedimentary to free delivery of message unless the message is of such grandeur that nothing can impair it. Technique binds one's unconscious and if the messages of the unconscious are weak, the technique will kill them. Only genius can afford a perfect technique.

Children's drawings are frequently delightful by their fresh, unwise point of view and their direct response to space. A gifted child revalorizes the space-point element of the phenomenon observed so as to produce an equivalent of it. However children's drawings have no value because children cannot bring to consciousness their own unconscious understanding of space. The work of technically skilled craftsmen in art has no value because it has only a conscious attempt to understand space. Only the two combined produce a work of art.

STUART DAVIS

• The catalogue of the Whitney Museum's 1935 exhibition, *Abstract Painting in America,* included this important essay by Stuart Davis, the country's leading abstractionist, tracing the development of abstract art in America.

Stuart Davis

[FROM "On Abstract Art," in *Abstract Painting in America* (New York: Whitney Museum of American Art, 1935).]

I begin very, very broadly by saying that the American artist became conscious of abstract art by the impact of the Armory Show in 1913. Previous to this important event in the art education in the United States, there were several American artists working in Europe who were incorporating the abstract viewpoint in their canvases. But it was the Armory Show of 1913 with its huge panorama of the scene of art for the foregoing seventy-five years which brought to the American artist as a whole the realization of the existence of abstract art, along with its immediate artistic historical background.

The abstract portion of the exhibition which consisted of works by European artists, with few exceptions, created a real sensation. Argumentation and dispute were constantly carried on in front of these canvases by laymen as well as artists. Friendships were broken and new friends made in that heat induced by these daily congresses of opinion. There was no American artist who saw this show but was forced to revalue his artistic concepts. The final charge was touched off in the foundations of the Autocracy of the Academy in a blast which destroyed its strangle hold on critical art values forever. Henceforth the American artist realized his right to free expression and exercised that right. This was made very clear in the annual exhibitions of the Society of Independent Artists where all artists could show their works without submission to jury. Henceforth a more acute angularity was imparted to the divergence of approach of the different artist groups.

Among these groups the artists who followed the abstract attitude completely or in appreciable part were relatively small. Why this was so I do not know, I simply state it as a matter of fact for the record. But the function of this small group of abstract painters and sculptors continued to make more clear the special character of the aesthetic divergence among American painters as a whole. They were the leaven implanted in the mass body of the American artists which continued the revolution of aesthetic opinion instigated in February, 1913, by the abstract section of the International Exhibition of Modern Art commonly called the Armory Show.

What is Abstract art? The question will be answered differently by each artist to whom the question is put. This is so because the generative idea of abstract art is alive. It changes, moves, and grows like any other living organism. However, from the various individual answers some basic concordance could doubtless be abstracted. This basic concordance of opinion would be very elementary and would probably run something like this. Art is not and never was a mirror reflection of nature. All efforts at imitation of nature are foredoomed to failure. Art is an understanding and interpretation of nature in various media. Therefore in our efforts to express our understanding of nature we will always bear in mind the limitations of our medium of expression. Our pictures will be expressions which are parallel to nature and parallel lines never meet. We will never try to copy the uncopiable but will seek to establish a material tangibility in our medium which will be a permanent record of an idea or emotion inspired by nature. This being so, we will never again ask the question of a painting, "Is it a good likeness, does it look like the thing it is supposed to represent?" Instead we will ask the question, "Does this painting, which is a defined two-dimensional surface, convey to me a direct emotional or ideological stimulus?" Since we forego all efforts to reflect optical illusions and concentrate on the reality of our canvas, we will now study the material reality of our medium, paint on canvas or whatever it may be. The approach has become scientifically experimental. A painting for example is a two-dimensional plane surface and the process of making a painting is the act of defining two-dimensional space on that surface. Any analogy which is drawn from our two-dimensional expression to three-dimensional nature will only be forceful in the degree to which our painting has achieved a two-dimensional clarity and logic.

The above is my idea of the basic implications in the abstract concept and I think it is implicit in all the various explanations and viewpoints which have been advanced about abstract art. The American artists who from various angles have oriented themselves about the abstract idea have not in all cases been as wholeheartedly scientific as the above considerations would seem to call for. However, I believe that even in those cases where the artistic approach has been almost entirely emotional, the concept of the autonomous existence of the canvas as a reality which is parallel to nature has been recognized. It should also be noted that the ideas suggested above automatically explain the geometric character of many abstract works of art.

The period of greatest activity in abstract art in America was probably from about 1915 to 1927. This in no sense implies that abstract work was not done before and after the above dates nor does it even suggest that the best work in abstract form was done between those two dates. It merely indicates a rough calculation on my part to the effect that between those dates a greater number of American artists were in whole or in part following an abstract point of view in their work.

Abstract art in America as shown in this exhibition, although actively participated in by relatively few artists, has been a vital factor in the sharpening of issues. Its objective and real contributions will not be lost.

• One of the first to appreciate the special flavor and tempo of American life, Davis tried with success to express them in art, both modern and American. In his elevation of the popular, the social, and the commonplace, he is close to Henri and to the "new realism" of pop art.

[FROM Katherine Kuh, *The Artist's Voice* (New York: Harper & Row, 1960).]

The artist sees and feels not only shapes but words as well. We see words everywhere in modern life; we're bombarded by them. But physically words are also shapes. You don't want banal boring words any more than you want banal boring shapes or a banal boring life. You've always got to make a choice. In choosing words I find that the smallest idea is equal to the greatest. I've used insignificant words and drawn insignificant objects because at times these were all that were at hand. By giving them value as experiences and by equating great with little, I discovered that the act of believing was what gave meaning to the smallest idea. For instance, take my paintings that grew out of cigarette packages, or the canvas called Champion. The idea for that picture came from a package of matches—an insignificant inspiration, but what made it work was a great belief in the possibilities of any inspiration. . . .

Some of the things which have made me want to paint, outside of other paintings, are: American wood- and iron-work of the past; Civil War and skyscraper architecture; the brilliant colors on gasoline stations, chain store fronts and taxicabs; the music of Bach; synthetic chemistry; the poetry of Rimbaud; fast travel by train, auto and airplane which brought new and multiple perspectives; electric signs; the landscape and boats of Gloucester, Mass.; five-and-ten-cent-store kitchen utensils; movies and radio; Earl Hines' hot piano and Negro jazz music in general. In one way or another the quality of these things plays a role in determining the character of my paintings.

GEORGE L. K. MORRIS

• Abstract art in America had another voluble defender in the person of George L. K. Morris, an abstractionist himself and art critic for *Partisan Review* in the late thirties. Fond of addressing his opponents directly, his language was often as strong and his tone as argumentative as that of his opposite number in the realists' camp, Thomas Craven. On the occasion of their first group exhibition at the American Fine Arts Galleries in 1937, Morris addressed the radical young group of American Abstract Artists, of which he was a member, on the difficulties they would face as modernists in America.

[FROM "To the American Abstract Artists," *Partisan Review,* March, 1938.]

The strongest public opposition will issue, as always, from the large troupe of perpetual gallery visitors. Like other members of established society, they have become categorically opposed to anything unaccustomed; and the traditions you seek to perpetuate surely require a reorientation. Unable to shake away preconceived notions of what a "work of art" should be, many visitors will continue to suspect that you are artfully concealing representational objects. But this large-scale opposition no longer counts at all. Only a few of the newspaper columnists still give it public utterance.

Another group—and one which should know better—presents a more formidable barrier to recognition. For it contains artists, teachers, critics. The natural function of these should be to lead the public; in America the critics merely confuse and hold the public back. Many of them are of course governed by fear, not merely the conventional bourgeois fear that hungers for conformity with the past, but the more definite fear that an understanding of the abstract processes might suggest that their own years of effort had been misdirected. They have for a century been evolving ingenious arguments to defeat your predecessors in every art form. And now in turn they will pronounce your pictures "dead" (as though the life in a work of art were derived from the liveliness of its subject-matter); that they are imitative (as though all aesthetic innovators had not been likewise dependent on their precursors); that they are purely emotional; that they are not emotional enough; that they are academic; that they are governed by no laws of any kind.

And you must not overlook an opposition that will oppose you on political grounds, that will satirize you as "escapists" who work in a vacuum. They will find in your work no visible connection with the causes of social justice, adding that illustrative propaganda is a natural function of art, that much past culture was essentially propagandist. Surely this reasoning does not delve very far into the esthetic processes. It ignores the long periods before the art-currents of the past had developed, before they were capable of supporting heavy propagandist over-meanings; it overlooks the slow centuries of complete or semi-abstract efforts toward realization, the Greek urn decorations, the Byzantine mosaics, etc. And even the later direct propaganda—humanistic, religious, or social—was the exception; most of it moreover (Fra Angelico, Daumier) will tend to look old-fashioned as it becomes removed by time. The most enduring masters present the opposite approach. Their full weight is thrown into the plastic language, and, being men of their epochs, they could bring to their task only the available contemporary symbols, which they shaped to their individually expressive ends.

You have had your troubles in freeing yourselves from the accepted accessories. Many of you still hang on to representation by the eyelids; bottles, pipes, faces protrude from certain corners. And, in your desire to become grounded in the new tradition, a number of you hide your voices so stiffly behind alien fabrics that no tone can emerge at all. Yet this is as it should be; it is only the second time that you have had mass-connection with an audience. Any talent must close for years upon the problems of expression before the signal can be given for independent advances, before it can exude a genuine distinction of style.

The derogatory charges of European imitation that you will have to face present a purely modern and journalistic brand of criticism. In no other period was the artist expected to appear, fully-armed, as by spontaneous combustion. Can it be imagined that Raphael was derided for imitating Perugino? Dürer, Rubens, or Poussin for incorporating the art of Italy into their own? On the contrary, it is natural and beneficial that you should assimilate at the start whatever implements are available. However, there is no need for you to make these answers to the charge at all. Your exhibition walls resound with a native clarity and color sense that speaks strongly of America. The rest will follow if there is enthusiasm and patience.

This exhibition can teach many things. In our present environment, so full of divergent currents, only discipline and restriction can build up a lasting flexibility. You saw how the artists of the world had gone completely awry with their elaborate campaigns to conquer the visible world (Impressionism), the unconscious world (Surrealism), the political world (Propagandism), the complex texture of a new locality (American Scene). Whereas the shapes themselves—their weight and position and movement—that seemingly unimportant infantry with whom the masters of the past in every climate were accustomed to conquer and maintain their traditions for centuries on end, had been left half-trained and fainting at their tasks. I cannot foresee what your group may be producing in a decade. But in the meantime you qualify as the sole organization in America that is dedicated to the hewing out of an authentic and appropriate cultural expression.

Chapter Six

Art of This Century

HAROLD ROSENBERG AND ROBERT MOTHERWELL

• The decision to accept, as a condition of their art, the divorce of art from society was a difficult, sometimes agonizing one for American artists to make. In opposition to those who felt art should convey a social message, John Sloan issued this statement: "There is also much talk today about socially-conscious painting. My old work was unconsciously very much so, especially before I became a Socialist. After that I felt that such a thing should not be put into painting and I reserved it for my etching. They may say that I am now fiddling while Rome burns, but I question whether social propaganda is necessary to the life of a work of art."

The position of the New York School painters as the country emerged from World War II was articulated by Harold Rosenberg and Robert Motherwell on the title page of the review *Possibilities,* which they edited. It clearly indicates that the separation of art from politics that began in the thirties had become generally accepted.

[FROM *Possibilities,* No. 1 (Winter, 1947–48).]

Naturally the deadly political situation exerts an enormous pressure.

The temptation is to conclude that organized social thinking is "more serious" than the act that sets free in contemporary experience forms which that experience has made possible.

One who yields to this temptation makes a choice among various theories of manipulating the known elements of the so-called objective state of affairs. Once the political choice has been made, art and literature ought of course to be given up.

Whoever genuinely believes he knows how to save humanity from catastrophe has a job before him which is certainly not a part-time one.

Political commitment in our times means logically—no art, no literature. A great many people, however, find it possible to hang around in the space between art and political action.

If one is to continue to paint or write as the political trap seems to close upon him he must perhaps have the extremest faith in sheer possibility.

In his extremism he shows that he has recognized how drastic the political presence is.

ROBERT MOTHERWELL

• The dilemma facing the avant-garde artist in America as he struggled to extract his art from a social context while preserving its radical content was put forth most succinctly by Robert Motherwell, youngest of the first-generation Abstract Expressionists, and often their scholarly spokesman.

[FROM "The Modern Painter's World," *Dyn,* VI (1944).]

The function of the *modern* artist is by definition the felt expression of modern reality. This implies that reality changes to some degree.

It is because reality has a historical character that we feel the need for new art. The past has bequeathed us great works of art; if they were wholly satisfying, we should not need new ones. From this past art, we accept what persists *qua* eternally valuable, as when we reject the specific religious values of Egyptian or Christian art, and accept with gratitude their form. Other values in this past art we do not want. To say this is to recognize that works of art are by nature pluralistic: they contain more than one *class* of values. It is the eternal values that we accept in past art. By eternal values are meant those which, humanly speaking, persist in reality in any space-time, like those of aesthetic form, or the confronting of death.

Not all values are eternal. Some values are historical—if you like, *social,* as when now artists especially value personal liberty because they do not find positive liberties in the concrete character of the modern state. It is the values of our own epoch which we cannot find in past art. This is the origin of our desire for new art. In our case, for *modern art*. . . .

The term "modern" covers the last hundred years, more or less. Perhaps it was Eugène Delacroix who was the first modern artist. But the popular association with the phrase "modern art" like that of mediaeval art, is stronger than its historical denotation. The popular association with mediaeval art is religiousness. The popular association with modern art is its *remoteness* from the symbols and values of the majority of men. There is a break in modern times between artists and other men without historical precedent in depth and generality. Both sides are wounded by the break. There is even hate at times, though we all have a thirst for love.

The remoteness of modern art is not merely a question of language, of the increasing "abstractness" of modern art. Abstractness, it is true, exists, as the result of a long, specialized internal development in modern artistic structure.

But the crisis is the modern artists' rejection, almost *in toto,* of the values of the bourgeois world. In this world modern artists form a kind of *spiritual underground*. . . .

Modern art is related to the problem of the modern individual's freedom. For this reason the history of modern art tends at certain moments to become the history of modern freedom. It is here that there is a genuine rapport between the artist and the working class. At the same time, modern artists have not a social, but an individualist experience of freedom: this is the source of the irreconcilable conflict between the Surrealists and the political parties of the working class.

The social condition of the modern world which gives every experience its form is the spiritual breakdown which followed the collapse of religion. This condition has led to the isolation of the artist from the rest of society. The modern artist's social history is that of a spiritual being in a property-loving world.

No synthesized view of reality has replaced religion. Science is not a view, but a method. The consequence is that the modern artist tends to become the last active spiritual being in the great world. It is true that each artist has his own religion. It is true that artists are constantly excommunicating each other. It is true that artists are not always pure, that sometimes they are concerned with their public standing or their material circumstance. Yet for all that, it is the artists who guard the spiritual in the modern world. . . .

In the spiritual underground the modern artist tends to be reduced to a single subject, his ego. . . . This situation tells us where to expect the successes and failures of modern art. If the artist's conception, from temperament and conditioning, of freedom is highly individualistic, his egoism then takes a romantic form. Hence the Surrealists' love-at-first-sight for the Romantic period, for disoriented and *minor* artists: individualism limits *size*. If the artist, on the contrary, resents the limitations of such subjectivism, he tries to objectify his ego. In the modern world, the way open to the objectivization of the ego is through form. This is the tendency of what we call, not quite accurately, abstract art. Romanticism and formalism both are responses to the modern world, a rejection, or at least a reduction, of modern social values. Hence the relative failure of Picasso's public mural of the Spanish Republic's pavilion in the Paris Exposition, *The Bombing of Guernica*. Hence Picasso's great successes, given his great personal gifts, with the formal and emotional inventions in cubism, the *papier collé,* and even in many of the preliminary drawings for *Guernica:* here it is a question of Picasso's own genius. In the public mural, it is a question of his solidarity with other men. Picasso is cut off from the great social classes, by the decadence of the middle-class and the indifference of the working-class, by his own spirituality in a property-ridden world. *Guernica* is therefore a *tour de force*. It expresses Picasso's indignation, as an individual, at public events. In this it is akin to Goya's *Los Desastres de la Guerra*. The smaller format of etchings, or even of easel paintings is more appropriate. We see this in the greater effective horror of Picasso's *Girl with a Cock*. The mural form, by virtue of its size and public character, must speak for a whole society, or at the very least, a whole class. *Guernica* hangs in an uneasy equilibrium between now disappearing social values, i.e., moral indignation at the character of modern life—what Mondrian called the *tragic,* as opposed to the eternal and the formal, the aesthetics of the *papier collé*.

We admire Picasso for having created *Guernica*. We are moved by its intent. Yet how accurately, though intuitively, art measures the contradictions of life. Here a contradiction exists. So long as the artist does not belong, in the concrete sense, to one of the great historical classes of humanity, so long he cannot realize a social expression in all its public fullness. Which is to say, an expression for, and not against. The artist is greatest in affirmation. This isolation spiritually cripples the artist, and sometimes gives him, at present, a certain resemblance to Dostoyevsky's *idiot*.

The history of Picasso, from one point of view, is that of his effort not to be limited to the strictly aesthetic, not to strip his art bare of a full social content, and contemplate her merely under the eternal aspect of beauty. He would not so impoverish himself. It is an aesthetician's error to suppose that the artist's principal concern is Beauty, any more than the philosopher's principal concern is Truth. Both are technical problems, which the artist and the philosopher must solve, but they do not represent the end in view. To express the felt nature of reality is the artist's principal concern. Picasso *wills* therefore the retention of social values, at any cost, just as Masson strives with a kind of desperation, like Delacroix, to raise modern life to the level of our great humanist past. But since Picasso, no more than any artist, can accept the values of a middle-class world, he must, in retaining them, treat them with a savage mockery, like Joyce. Here somewhere is the ground of Picasso's otherwise unparalleled parody of the history of art.

It was the late Piet Mondrian who accepted the impoverishment of his art involved by the rejection of social values. He was perhaps less opposed to ordinary life than indifferent to its drama. It was the eternal, the "universal," in his terminology, which preoccupied him: he had an affinity with oriental saints, with, say, Mallarmé. Since the aesthetic is the main quality of the eternal in art, it may be that this is why Mondrian's work, along with certain aspects of automatism, was the first technical advance in twentieth century painting since the greatest of our discoveries, the *papier collé*. It was Mondrian who accepted most simply that debased social values provide no social content. . . .

The artist's problem is *with what to identify himself*. The middle-class is decaying, and as a conscious entity the working-class does not exist. Hence the tendency of modern painters to paint for each other. . . .

The preponderance of modern artists come from the middle-class. To this class modern art is always hostile by implication, and sometimes directly so. Even before the socialists, the artists recognized the enemy in the middle-class. But being themselves of middle-class origin, and leading middle-class lives—certainly not the lives of the proletariat—the artist in a certain sense attacks himself. He undermines his own concrete foundation. He is then led to abstract eternal goods from reality. Here begins the rise of abstract art. All art is abstract in character. But it is especially in modern times that after the operation of abstraction so little remains.

The artist's hostility for the middle-class is reciprocated. This period, more than other[s], has detested its greatest creations, even when made by extremely conventional beings, like Cézanne. In the face of this hostility, there have been three possible attitudes of which the artist was not always conscious; to ignore the middle-class and seek the eternal, like Delacroix, Seurat, Cézanne, the cubists, and their heirs; to support the middle-class by restricting oneself to the decorative, like Ingres, Corot, the Impressionists in general, and the fauves; or to oppose the middle-class, like Courbet, Daumier, Pissarro, Van Gogh, and the Dadaists. The last class tends to be destroyed by the struggle. Some artists like Picasso, have had all three relations to the middle-class.

Actually, nearly all modern painters have been rejected by the middle-class until their works gained a property-value. Henri Matisse had to resist a career as a Salon painter; Manet and Degas were involved in the impressionist's fight; Rouault is not mentioned in a recent comprehensive work on modern Catholic painting. The sentimental and academic painting which the middle-class really likes disappears with its patrons.

The right-wing Surrealists and "neo-romantics" have been the first modern painters to be accepted from the beginning by the middle-class. . . .

The argument of this lecture is that the materialism of the middle-class and the inertness of the working-class leave the modern artist without any vital connection to society, save that of the *opposition;* and that modern artists have had, from the broadest point, to replace other social values with the strictly aesthetic. Even where the Surrealists have succeeded, it has been on technical grounds. This formalism has led to an intolerable weakening of the artist's ego; but so long as modern society is dominated by the love of property—and it will be, so long as property is the only source of freedom—the artist has no alternative to formalism. He strengthens his formalism with his other advantages, his increased knowledge of history and modern science, his connections with the eternal, the aesthetic, his relations with the folk (e.g., Picasso and Miró), and, finally his very opposition to middle-class society gives him a certain strength. Until there is a radical revolution in the values of modern society, we may look for a highly formal art to continue. We can be grateful for its extraordinary technical discoveries, which have raised modern art, plastically speaking, to a level unreached since the earlier Renaissance. When a revolution in values will take place, no one at present can tell. The technical problems which stand before us I must speak of some other time.

JOHN FERREN

• Although the obituary may have been premature, John Ferren's postmortem on the development of Abstract Expressionism provides a clear account of its origin and subsequent rise to a position of international preeminence.

[FROM "Epitaph for an Avant-garde," *Arts,* XXXII (November, 1958).]

The present avant-garde coalesced as a movement in the years immediately following World War II, but the major figures shared a rebellion against the intellectual climate, not to speak of the privations, of the thirties. This took the specific form of a reaction against, first, American Regional painting.

By this I mean the Benton-Curry-Wood School and the Rivera-derived WPA murals of the time. These painters seemed to us inexcusably blind to the pictorial discoveries of the School of Paris and therefore to be painting retrogressively. We disliked the subservience of art to political propaganda which their art represented. We found that, even on their own terms, the Regional painters did not present a picture of America that corresponded to our own experience either as social fact or in its emotional meaning. The Iowa farms painted by Grant Wood seemed to us—and still seem—like dream fantasies of the ideal, immaculately clean farm owned by the most prosperous, happy farmer. (Maybe Grant Wood was the most Surrealist painter of the period.) Strangely enough, America in the thirties seemed to be uniquely the Middle West; nothing bordering the two oceans was admitted into the museums, the art magazines or the popular press—perhaps out of a fear of contamination with foreign parts. Somehow, "social significance" left us cold, as an aesthetic and as a credo. Not all of us at the same time. Some were converted early and some late, but by 1940 it was understood.

Our second rebellion was against the School of Paris; in particular, against Cubism and Surrealism. And this particular rebellion requires explanation, for it was double-edged. Finding so little artistic nourishment here, we looked abroad as so many American artists had once in the past. The native attempts to imitate European styles did not satisfy us. When we looked at our American Cubists, it seemed to us that they had taken only the manner of a great intellectual discipline and used it to jazz up the same factories and farms and bridges as the Regional painters used, adding no more than a certain basic dryness and sterility. (It is still a shibboleth of American art criticism that to be dry is to be American.) We later rejected Cubism totally, or at least we think we did, but for very different and serious reasons. We came to see it as the modern academy, the new province of the industrial arts, more suitable perhaps to the flood of mass-produced interior decoration. Cubism was a body of intellectual precepts concerning reality which showed us how and why to make a picture we no longer wanted to make.

Surrealism made its inroads in the late thirties and early forties and quickly won official support and acclaim, only to end up in hosiery advertisements. Here again, we rejected it and for one of the same reasons we rejected the Regional painters: its practitioners used a retrograde technique, this time mainly from the seventeenth century.

Also, our local practitioners were a little "specialized" in their subconscious drives.

But the *idea* of the subconscious, the techniques of chance, and a concern for the depths of the inner life: these took hold as a powerful influence. They remained a part of our thinking, soon to join other ideas in the general ferment of a new point of view. These other ideas were: the two-dimensional surface of Cubism, the free form of Miró and Kandinsky, the primitivism of Klee, the end-all of Mondrian, the color of Matisse and Bonnard, the genius pure and simple of Picasso. We are all the sons of our fathers, and there is no denying that most of our fathers were European. However brutal it may be, rejection is part of revolution. Each of us, in some way or manner, and in varying degrees, has rejected the father we may still love: the intellectual, decorative discipline of Cubism; the bourgeois, seductive, indoor stuffiness of Matisse, Bonnard, and Vuillard; the cliché dream of Surrealism. In the end we reacted against the awful shadow of the School of Paris. Abstract Expressionism managed to step out of that shadow. That is why the Europeans are now following us; that is why we now have a little shadow of our own.

It has been said that Abstract Expressionism was a marriage of Abstraction and Surrealism. It is a half-truth, and as such, a misleading one. For one thing, it was a three-way marriage. The fact that Jackson Pollock was a pupil of Benton, then influenced by the abstract Picasso and then by the Surrealist André Masson, is not without meaning here. The stubborn temper that made Benton deny Europe and paint the Middle West which he knew is present in Abstract Expressionism. And the essential principles of Abstraction, that "pure form and color have emotional significance," and of Surrealism, "that human experience of life goes inwardly in depth as well as outwardly," were adopted by us—but in their fusion they were radically altered and became something else.

World War II—or rather, the situation brought on by the war—created an atmosphere in which these elements of revolt were turned into a body of work different in kind and quality from anything that had come before. Some of us went to war; others, for whatever reasons, did not. In New York, the war cut off the French imports, and the galleries and museums suffered the loss of their staple product. Some French artists came here, and our contact with them did two things. It removed the aura of Olympus which still surrounded Parisian art for many of us, and it produced a direct and fecund influence on certain artists. Pollock was definitely influenced by the exhibited works of Masson, and Arshile Gorky, by Surrealist doctrine in the person of André Breton.

At the end of the war, certain artists had already established a foothold in the galleries, and others returned to their studios with a more sober feeling and a stand-offish attitude toward the clichés of American life. Behind them was an experience which gave a new and different meaning and stature to the profession of being an artist. They founded a Club where loud and vital arguments were held. They took over abandoned lofts, painted them white, and began to work again. It is not accident that contemporary painting used lots of black and white. It didn't come from the sunlit fields—it came from white lofts in dirty buildings on dirty streets and from the inner resources of the mind. Its beginning was urban, of the city. It was an art of the individual, lonely and in rebellion, even if the rebellion was muted.

It was not a question of knocking over other gods. It was a question of finding your own reality, your own answers, your own experience. . . . We discovered a simple thing, yet far-reaching in its effects: "The search is the discovery." Picasso had said, "I don't search, I find." We lacked the confidence for such an arrogant remark. We discovered instead that searching was itself a way of art. Not necessarily a final way, but a way. I remember that around the Club in the late forties the word "evaluation" was taboo. We looked, and we liked it or did not; we did not give it a value. We took it as part of the search. Our feeling was the reverse of the motto "I don't know anything about art, but I know what I like." We knew something about art, but we didn't know what we liked. . . .

ARSHILE GORKY

• Arshile Gorky's murals of the thirties were perhaps the first indication that American art could fully assimilate, in order to recast in its own terms, the fundamentals of European modernism. Here Gorky describes his goals in the creation of these large-scale public works. In his use of stylized airplane parts as "plastic symbols" he imitated Stuart Davis' manner of transforming symbolic objects into stylized flat shapes, although in his emphasis on fantasy, Gorky reveals himself, like his contemporaries, to be moving away from the impersonal world of Cubism toward Surrealism's private world of the dream.

[FROM "Aviation: Evolution of Forms under Aerodynamic Limitations," in Ethel K. Schwabacher, *Arshile Gorky* (New York: Whitney Museum of American Art, 1957).]

The architectonic two-dimensional surface plane of walls must be retained in mural painting. How was I to overcome this plastic problem when the subject of my murals was that of the unbounded space of the sky-world of aviation? How keep the walls from flying away or else crushing together as they would be sure to do in a pictorial narrative? The problem resolved itself when I considered the new vision that flight has given to the eyes of man. The isle of Manhattan with all its skyscrapers from the view of an aeroplane five miles up becomes but a geographical map, a two-dimensional surface plane. This new perception simplifies the form and shapes of earth objects. The thickness of objects is lost and only the space occupied by the object remains. Such simplification removes all decorative details and leaves the artist with limitations which become a style, a plastic invention, particular to our time. How was I to utilize this new concept for my murals?

In the popular idea of art, an aeroplane is painted as it might look in a photograph. But such a hackneyed concept has no architectural unity in the space that it is to occupy nor does it truthfully represent an aeroplane with all its ramifications. An operation was imperative, and that is why in the first panel of *Activities on the Field,* I had to dissect an aeroplane into its constituent parts. An aeroplane is composed of a variety of shapes and forms and I have used such elemental forms as a rudder, a wing, a wheel, a searchlight, etc., to create not only numerical interest, but also to include within a given wall space, plastic symbols of aviation. These plastic symbols are the permanent elements of aeroplanes that will change with the change of design. These symbols, these forms, I have used in paralyzing disproportions in order to impress upon the spectator the miraculous new vision of our time.

To add to the intensity of these shapes, I have used such local colors as are to be seen on the aviation field, red, blue, yellow, black, gray, brown, because these colors were used originally to sharpen the objects against neutral backgrounds so that they could be seen clearly and quickly.

The second panel of the same wall contains objects commonly used around a hangar, such as a ladder, a fire extinguisher, a gasoline truck, scales, etc. These objects I have dissected and reorganized in the same homogeneous arrangement as in the previous panel.

In the panel, *Early Aviation,* I sought to bring into elemental terms the sensation of the passengers in the first balloon to the wonder of the sky around them and the earth beneath. Obviously this conception entails a different problem than those previously cited. In fact each of the walls presents a different problem concerning aviation and to solve each one, I had to use different concepts, different plastic qualities, different colors. Thus, to appreciate my panel of the first balloon, the spectator must seek to imaginatively enter into the miraculous sense of wonder experienced by the first balloonists. In the shock of surprise everything changes. The sky becomes green. The sun is black with astonishment on beholding an invention never before created by the hand of God. And the earth is spotted with such elliptical brown forms as had never been seen before.

The image of wonder I continued in the second panel. From the first balloon of Montgolfier, aviation developed until the wings of the modern aeroplane, figuratively speaking, stretch across the United States. The sky is still green for the wonders of the sky never cease, and the map of the United States takes on a new geographical outline because of the illusion of change brought about by the change in speed.

The first three panels of *Modern Aviation* contain the anatomical parts of autogyros in the process of soaring into space, and yet with the immobility of suspension. The fourth panel is a modern aeroplane simplified to its essential form and so spaced as to give a sense of flight.

In the last three panels I have used arbitrary colors and shapes; the wing is black, the rudder yellow, so as to convey the sense that these modern gigantic toys of men are decorated with the same fanciful play as children have in coloring their kites. In the same spirit the engine becomes in one place like the wings of a dragon, and in another the wheels, propeller, and motor take on the demonic speed of a meteor cleaving the atmosphere.

In *Mechanics of Flying* I have used morphic shapes. The objects portrayed, a thermometer, hygrometer, anemometer, an aeroplane map of the United States, all have a definitely important usage in aviation, and to emphasize this, I have given them importance by detaching them from their environment.

• By 1941, the year in which he painted *Garden in Sochi,* the subject of the poem below, Gorky's lyric and poetic gifts had reached their full flowering, opening new possibilities for expression that had consequences not only for Gorky but for his younger contemporaries, on whom he exerted considerable influence. Attempting to approximate the content of the painting in the poem, Gorky demonstrates the difficulty of finding satisfactory verbal equivalents for visual phenomena, which would plague art writers of the forties and fifties. As themes and motifs are freely associated in the painting, Gorky allows free association to carry him spontaneously from one image to another, perhaps in imitation of the "automatic" techniques of Surrealist poetry, which he admired.

[FROM "Garden in Sochi," poem written in June, 1942 (Collections Archives, Museum of Modern Art).]

I like the heat the tenderness the edible the lusciousness the song
of a single person the bathtub full of water to bathe myself beneath
the water. I like Uccello Grünewald Ingres the drawings and sketches
for paintings of Seurat and that man Pablo Picasso.
I measure all things by weight.
I love my Mougouch. What about Papa Cézanne.
I hate things that are not like me and all the things I haven't got
are god to me.
Permit me—
I like the wheatfields the plough the apricots the shape of apricots

those flirts of the sun. And bread above all.
My liver is sick with the purple.

About 194 feet away from our house on the road to
the spring my father had a little garden with a
few apple trees which had returned from giving fruit.
There was a ground constantly in shade where grew
incalculable amounts of wild carrots and porcupines
had made their nests. There was a blue rock half
buried in the black earth with a few patches of moss
placed here and there like fallen clouds. But from
where came all the shadows in constant battle like
the lancers of Paolo Uccello's painting? The garden
was identified as the Garden of Wish Fulfillment
and often I had seen my mother and other
village women opening their bosoms and taking their
soft and dependable breasts in their hands to rub
them on the rock. Above all this stood an enormous
tree all bleached under the sun the rain the cold
and deprived of leaves. This was the Holy Tree.
I myself do not know why this tree was holy
but I had witnessed many people whoever did pass
by that would tear voluntarily a strip of their clothes
and attach this to the tree. Thus through many
years of the same act like a veritable parade
of banners under the pressure of the wind all these
personal inscriptions of signatures very softly to my
innocent ear used to give echo to the sh-h-h of
silver leaves of the poplars.

WILLIAM BAZIOTES

• The wish to find a universally meaningful subject often led American painters in the forties to look to ancient myths for inspiration. In these passages and those by Rothko, Newman, and Gottlieb that follow, some of the attitudes of leading Abstract Expressionists toward content in art are set forth.

[FROM *Personal Statement,* David Porter Gallery, 1945.]

There is always a subject that is uppermost in my mind. Sometimes I am aware of it. Sometimes not. I work on my canvas until I think it is finished. Often I recognize my subject at completion of the picture and again I may wait a long time before I know what it is about.

[FROM *Possibilities,* No. 1 (Winter, 1947–48).]

I work on many canvases at once. In the morning I line them up against the wall of my studio. Some speak; some do not. They are my mirrors. They tell me what I am like at the moment.

MARK ROTHKO

[FROM *Possibilities,* No. 1 (Winter, 1947–48).]

The romantics were prompted to seek exotic subjects and to travel to far off places. They failed to realise that, though the transcendental must involve the strange and unfamiliar, not everything strange or unfamiliar is transcendental.

The unfriendliness of society to his activity is difficult for the artist to accept. Yet this very hostility can act as a lever for true liberation. Freed from a false sense of security and community, the artist can abandon his plastic bankbook, just as he has abandoned other forms of security. Both the sense of community and of security depend on the familiar. Free of them, transcendental experiences become possible.

I think of my pictures as dramas; the shapes in the pictures are the performers. They have been created from the need for a group of actors who are able to move dramatically without embarrassment and execute gestures without shame.

Neither the action nor the actors can be anticipated or described in advance. They begin as an unknown adventure in an unknown space.

It is at the moment of completion that in a flash of recognition, they are seen to have the quantity and function which was intended. Ideas and plans that existed in the mind at the start were simply the doorway through which one left the world in which they occur.

The great Cubist pictures thus transcend and belie the implications of the Cubist program.

The most important tool the artist fashions through constant practice is faith in his ability to produce miracles when they are needed. Pictures must be miraculous: the instant one is completed, the intimacy between the creation and the creator is ended. He is an outsider. The picture must be for him, as for anyone experiencing it later, a revelation, an unexpected and unprecedented resolution of an eternally familiar need.

On shapes:

They are unique elements in a unique situation.

They are organisms with volition and a passion for self-assertion.

They move with internal freedom, and without need to conform with or to violate what is probable in the familiar world.

They have no direct association with any particular visible experience, but in them one recognizes the principle and passion of organisms.

The presentation of this drama in the familiar world was never possible, unless everyday acts belonged to a ritual accepted as referring to a transcendent realm.

Even the archaic artist, who had an uncanny virtuosity found it necessary to create a group of intermediaries, monsters, hybrids, gods and demigods. The difference is that, since the archaic artist was living in a more practical society than ours, the urgency for transcendent experience was understood, and given an official status. As a consequence, the human figure and other elements from the familiar world could be combined with, or participate as a whole in, the enactment of the excesses which characterize this improbable hierarchy. With us the disguise must be complete. The familiar identity of things has to be pulverized in order to destroy the finite associations with which our society increasingly enshrouds every aspect of our environment.

Without monsters and gods, art cannot enact our drama: art's most profound moments express this frustration. When they were abandoned as untenable superstitions, art sank into melancholy. It became fond of the dark, and enveloped its objects in the nostalgic intimations of a half-lit world. For me the great achievements of the centuries in which the artist accepted the probable and familiar as his subjects were the pictures of the single human figure—alone in a moment of utter immobility.

But the solitary figure could not raise its limbs in a single gesture that might indicate its concern with the fact of mortality and an insatiable appetite for ubiquitous experience in face of this fact. Nor could the solitude be overcome. It could gather on beaches and streets and in parks only through coincidence, and, with its companions, form a *tableau vivant* of human incommunicability.

I do not believe that there was ever a question of being abstract or representational. It is really a matter of ending this silence and solitude, of breathing and stretching one's arms again.

BARNETT NEWMAN

[FROM *The Ideographic Picture,* Betty Parsons Gallery, January 20–February 8, 1947.]

The Kwakiutl artist painting on a hide did not concern himself with the inconsequentials that made up the opulent social rivalries of the Northwest Coast Indian scene, nor did he, in the name of a higher purity, renounce the living world for the meaningless materialism of design. The abstract shape he used, his entire plastic language, was directed by a ritualistic will towards metaphysical understanding. The everyday realities he left to the toymakers; the pleasant play of non-objective pattern to the women basket weavers. To him a shape was a living thing, a vehicle for an abstract thought-complex, a carrier of the awesome feelings he felt before the terror of the unknowable. The abstract shape was, therefore, real rather than a formal "abstraction" of a visual fact, with its overtone of an already-known nature. Nor was it a purist illusion with its overload of pseudo-scientific truths.

The basis of an aesthetic act is the pure idea. But the pure idea is, of necessity, an aesthetic act. Here then is the epistemological paradox that is the artist's problem. Not space cutting nor space building, not construction nor Fauvist destruction; not the pure line, straight and narrow, nor the tortured line, distorted and humiliating; not the accurate eye, all fingers, nor the wild eye of dream, winking; but the idea-complex that makes contact with mystery—of life, of men, of nature, of the hard, black chaos that is death, or the grayer, softer chaos that is tragedy. Everything else has everything else.

Spontaneous, and emerging from several points, there has arisen during the war years a new force in American painting that is the modern counterpart of the primitive art impulse. As early as 1942, Mr. Edward Alden Jewell was the first publicly to report it. Since then, various critics and dealers have tried to label it, to describe it. It is now time for the artist himself, by showing the dictionary, to make clear the community of intention that motivates him and his colleagues. For here is a group of artists who are not abstract painters, although working in what is known as the abstract-style.

ADOLPH GOTTLIEB

[FROM "The Ides of Art," *Tiger's Eye,* No. 2 (December, 1947).]

Certain people always say we should go back to nature. I notice they never say we should go forward to nature. It seems to me they are more concerned that we should go back, than about nature.

If the models we use are the apparitions seen in a dream, or the recollection of our prehistoric past, is this less part of nature or realism, than a cow in a field? I think not.

The role of the artist, of course, has always been that of image maker. Different times require different images. Today when our aspirations have been reduced to a desperate attempt to escape from evil, and times are out of joint, our obsessive, subterranean, and pictographic images are the expression of the neurosis which is our reality. To my mind, certain so-called abstraction is not abstraction at all. On the contrary, it is the realism of our time.

HANS HOFMANN

• Of the artists who emigrated to New York during the thirties and forties, none was more important than Hans Hofmann. Bringing with him one of the most sophisticated minds and painting techniques in Europe, Hofmann played a role in elevating the painting culture of America that cannot be overestimated. Stressing both instinct and awareness, he was able to strike a balance between spontaneity and formal coherence that would serve as a model for several generations of American painters. His emphasis on the primacy of color was later adopted by the new abstractionists of the sixties.

[FROM *Catalogue of the Hans Hofmann Exhibition,* Kootz Gallery, New York, 1955.]

The genuine value of a painting is greatly determined through its basic concept.

In painting we differentiate between "pure painting" and "tonal painting." Pure painting is the antithesis of tonal painting.

We deal with tonal painting where color is degraded to a tonal gradation from the highest light down into the deepest tonal shades. Tonal gradation can be produced by any kind of color mixture.

In pure painting color serves simultaneously a plastic and a psychological purpose. We deal, in the achievement of this purpose, with a formal problem and with a color problem in parallel occurrence, the synchronization of which constitutes the pictorial synthesis of the work. Color has in itself a sovereign function on the basis of its intrinsic qualities. Color in itself is Light. *In nature, light creates the color; in the picture color creates light.* Every color shade emanates a very characteristic light—no substitute is possible.

The luminous quality of a work depends not only upon the light-emanating quality of every color but predominantly upon the relation of these qualities. *Relation is the product of a hypersensitive creative mind. Relation produces a new quality of a higher order through a created actuality*, either in the form of tension, when we deal with the compositional demand of integrated form, or in the form of intervals, when we deal with color relations. *We must always distinguish between form in a physical sense (nature) and form in an aesthetical sense (the form of the work itself as a creation of the mind).*

Color undergoes in this process still another metamorphosis, in the textural progression of the work. Texture is the consequence of the general pigmentary development of the work, and becomes in this way an additional light-producing factor, capable of altering the luminosity of the colors in the pace of their development towards a color-totality.

Basically and technically the color problem is dual conditioned: it is a formal problem in its inevitable structural relation to the pictorial surface, and it is—*per se*—a problem of color development which must respect its own inherent laws. Since each of these laws operates in a rhythm entirely its own, their interplay leads to a pictorial consonance comparable to harmony and counterpoint in music.

The magic of painting, however, can never be fully, rationally explained. It is the harmony of heart and mind in the capacity of *feeling into things* that plays the instrument. The instrument answers the throb of the heart in every instance. Painting is always intuitively conditioned. Theoretically it is a process of metabolism, whereby color transubstantiates into vital forces that *become the real sources of painterly life*. These sources are not of a physical but rather of a hyperphysical nature—the product of a sensitive mind. . . .

Whereas in tonal painting neighborhood relations are achieved through dark-and-light transitions, in pure painting the rhythmic interweaving of the color scales brings the color into an "open" neighborhood relationship in which colors are compositionally in accordance with a color development upon which their formal grouping ultimately depends. The colors meet now in neighborly relation in the sense of *tensional difference*—that is to say, in the sense of *simultaneous contrast.* The finest difference in color shades can achieve powerful contrasts. Although tonal development may lead to an overall pictorial harmony, it sacrifices simultaneous contrast, which is the predominant quality of pure painting.

A painting has an immediate impact, but is conceived sequentially. The process of development is made invisible in the synthesis of the completed work.

Looking at a picture is a spontaneous act that reveals at once the quality or non-quality of the work.

But what is quality? Quality is the essence resulting from convincingly established felt-relationships. It can only be produced through an act of empathy, that is, the power to feel *into* the nature of things. . . .

Pictorial life is a created reality. Without it, pictorial communication —the appeal to the sense and the mind—is nonexistent. Color, in nature as well as in the picture, is an agent to give the highest aesthetic enjoyment. The emotion-releasing faculty of the color related to the formal aspect of the work becomes a means to awaken in us the feelings to which the medium of expression responds analogously when we attempt to realize our experiences creatively. Upon it will depend the formal and psychic appeal of the created image which is finally achieved through an absolute synchronization, in which a multitude of seemingly incompatible developments have been firmly interwoven—molded in the synthesis of the work.

[FROM "Statement by Hans Hofmann," *IT IS,* Winter–Spring, 1959.]

America is at present in a state of cultural blossoming. I am supposed to have contributed my share as teacher and artist by the offering of a multiple awareness. This awareness I consider to constitute a visual experience and a pictorial creation.

"Seeing" without awareness, as a visual art, is just short of blindness. "Seeing" with awareness is a visual experience; it is an art.

We must learn to see. The interpretation in pictorial terms of what we see is "another" art.

Every act of pictorial creation has, therefore, a dual conceptual approach.

The origin of creation is, therefore, a reflection of nature on a creative mind:

We are nature

What surrounds us is nature

Our creative means are nature

Nothing, however, will happen without the creative faculties of our conscious-and-unconscious mind.

One of these faculties is an awareness of space in every form of manifestation: either

a) in the form of movement and counter-movement, with the consequence of rhythm and counter-rhythm; or
b) in the form of force and counter-force in a two-dimensional play in every direction; or
c) in the form of tension as a result of these forces.

The pictorial life as a pictorial reality results from the aggregate of two-and-three-dimensional tensions: a combination of the effect of simultaneous expansion and contraction with that of push and pull.

The nature of the light-and-color problem in the plastic arts cannot be fully understood without an awareness of the foregoing considerations. Color and light are to a very great extent subjected to the formal problems of the picture surface.

The color problem follows a development that makes it a life-and-light-emanating plastic means of first order. Like the picture surface, color has an inherent life of its own. A picture comes into existence on the basis of the interplay of this dual life. In the act of predominance and assimilation, colors love or hate each other, thereby helping to make the creative intention of the artist possible.

Talent is, in general, common—original talent is rare. A teacher can only accompany a talent over a certain period of time—he can never make one. As a teacher, I approach my students purely with the human desire to free them from all scholarly inhibitions. And I tell them, "Painters must speak through paint—not through words."

Chapter Seven

The New American Painting

• The following statements by Jackson Pollock, Willem de Kooning, and Franz Kline provide information on their working methods and attitudes toward their own art, and art in general, which may be taken as typical of those painters who used gesture as their primary expressive means.

JACKSON POLLOCK

[FROM *Arts and Architecture,* February, 1944.]

Living is keener, more demanding, more intense and expansive in New York than in the West; the stimulating influences are more numerous and rewarding. At the same time, I have a definite feeling for the West: the vast horizontality of the land, for instance; here only the Atlantic gives you that.

I have always been very impressed with the plastic qualities of American Indian art. The Indians have the true painter's approach in their capacity to get hold of appropriate images, and in their understanding of what constitutes painterly subject-matter. Their color is essentially Western, their vision has the basic universality of all real art. Some people find references to American Indian art and calligraphy in parts of my pictures. That wasn't intentional; probably it was the result of early memories and enthusiasms.

I accept the fact that the important painting of the last hundred years was done in France. American painters have generally missed the point of modern painting from beginning to end. (The only American master who interests me is Ryder.) Thus the fact that good European moderns are now here is very important, for they bring with them an understanding of the problems of modern painting. I am particularly impressed with their concept of the source of art being the unconscious. This idea interests me more than these specific painters do, for the two artists I admire most, Picasso and Miró, are still abroad. . . .

The idea of an isolated American painting, so popular in this country during the thirties, seems absurd to me, just as the idea of creating a purely American mathematics or physics would seem absurd. . . . And in another sense, the problem doesn't exist at all; or, if it did, would solve itself. An American is an American and his painting would naturally be qualified by that fact, whether he wills it or not. But the basic problems of contemporary painting are independent of any one country.

[FROM "My Painting," *Possibilities,* No. 1 (Winter, 1947–48).]

My painting does not come from the easel. I hardly ever stretch my canvas before painting. I prefer to tack the unstretched canvas to the hard wall or the floor. I need the resistance of a hard surface. On the floor I am more at ease. I feel nearer, more a part of the painting, since this way I can walk around it, work from the four sides and literally be *in* the painting. This is akin to the method of the Indian sand painters of the West.

I continue to get further way from the usual painter's tools such as easel, palette, brushes, etc. I prefer sticks, trowels, knives, and dripping fluid paint or a heavy impasto with sand, broken glass, and other foreign matter added.

When I am *in* my painting, I'm not aware of what I am doing. It is only after a sort of "get acquainted" period that I see what I have been about. I have no fears about making changes, destroying the image, etc., because the painting has a life of its own. I try to let it come through. It is only when I lose contact with the painting that the result is a mess. Otherwise there is pure harmony, an easy give and take, and the painting comes out well.

WILLEM DE KOONING

[FROM "What Abstract Art Means to Me," *Museum of Modern Art Bulletin,* XVIII, No. 3 (Spring, 1951).]

The word "abstract" comes from the lighttower of philosophers, and it seems to be one of their spotlights that they have particularly focussed on "Art." So the artist is always lighted up by it. As soon as it—I mean the "abstract"—comes into painting, it ceases to be what it is as it is written. It changes into a feeling which could be explained by some other words, probably. But one day, some painter used "Abstraction" as a title for one of his paintings. It was a still life. And it was a very tricky title. And it wasn't really a very good one. From then on the idea of abstraction became something extra. Immediately it gave some people the idea that they could free art from itself. Until then, Art meant everything that was in it—not what you could take out of it sometime when you were in the right mood—that abstract and indefinable sensation, the aesthetic part—and still leave it where it was. For the painter to come to the "abstract" or the "nothing," he needed many things. Those things were always things in life—a horse, a flower, a milkmaid, the light in a room through a window made of diamond shapes maybe, tables, chairs, and so forth. The painter, it is true, was not always completely free. The things were not always of his own choice, but because of that he often got some new ideas.

The aesthetics of painting were always in a state of development parallel to the development of painting itself. They influenced each other and vice versa. But all of a sudden, in that famous turn of the century, a few people thought they could take the bull by the horns and invent an aesthetic beforehand. After immediately disagreeing with each other, they began to form all kinds of groups, each with the idea of freeing art, and each demanding that you should obey them. Most of these theories have finally dwindled away into politics or strange forms of spiritualism. The question, as they saw it, was not so much what you *could* paint but rather what you could *not* paint. You could *not* paint a house or a tree or a mountain. It was then that subject came into existence as something you ought *not* to have.

This pure form of comfort became the comfort of "pure form."

Kandinsky understood "Form" as *a* form, like an object in the real world; an object, he said, was a narrative—and so of course, he disapproved of it. He wanted his "music without words." He wanted to be "simple as a child." He intended, with his "inner self," to rid himself of "philosophical barricades" (he sat down and wrote something about all this). But in turn his own writing has become a philosophical barricade, even if it is a barricade full of holes. It offers a kind of Middle-European idea of Buddhism or, anyhow, something too theosophic for me.

The sentiments of the Futurists were simpler. No space. Everything ought to keep on going! That's probably the reason they went themselves. Either a man was a machine or else a sacrifice to make machines with.

The moral attitude of Neo-Plasticism is very much like that of Constructivism, except that the Constructivists wanted to bring things out in the open and the Neo-Plasticists didn't want anything left over.

I have heard a lot from all of them and they have confused me plenty too. One thing is certain, they didn't give me my natural aptitude for drawing. I am completely weary of their ideas now.

The only way I still think of these ideas is in terms of the individual artists who came from them or invented them. . . .

The point they all had in common was to be both inside and outside at the same time. A new kind of likeness! The likeness of the group instinct.

Personally, I do not need a movement. What was given to me, I take for granted. Of all movements, I like Cubism the most. It had that wonderful unsure atmosphere of reflection—a poetic frame where something could be possible, where an artist could practise his intuition. It didn't want to get rid of what went before. Instead it added something to it. The parts that I can appreciate in other movements came out of Cubism. Cubism *became* a movement, it didn't set out to be one. It has force in it, but it was no "force-movement." And then there is that one-man movement, Marcel Duchamp—for me a truly modern movement because it implies that each artist can do what he thinks he ought to—a movement for each person and open for everybody.

FRANZ KLINE

[FROM David Sylvester, "Interview with Franz Kline," *Living Arts,* Spring, 1963.]

On Black and White Paintings

It wasn't a question of deciding to do a black-and-white painting. I think there was a time when the original forms that finally came out in black and white were in color, say, and then as time went on I painted them out and made them black and white. And then, when they got that way, I just liked them, you know. . . .

I didn't have a particularly strong desire to use color, say, in the lights or darks of a black-and-white painting, although what happened is that accidentally they look that way. Sometimes a black, because of the quantity of it or the mass or the volume, looks as though it may be a blue-black, as if there were blue mixed in with the black, or as though it were a brown-black or a red-black. The whites the same way; the whites of course turned yellow, and many people call your attention to that, you know; they want white to stay white forever. It doesn't bother me whether it does or not. It's still white compared to the black.

On Calligraphy

You don't make the letter "C" and then fill the white in the circle. When people describe forms of painting in the calligraphic sense they really mean the linear, that painting was the equalization of the proportions of black, or the design of black against a form of white; but, in a lot of cases, apparently it does look that way. I rather imagine as people have come from the tradition of looking at drawing, they look at the lines, until you go to art school and then some drawing teacher tells you to look at the white spaces in it; but I didn't think about the black-and-white paintings as coming that way. I thought about it in a certain sense of the awkwardness of "not-balance," the tentative reality of lack of balance in it. The unknown reason why a form would be there and look just like that and not meaning anything particularly, would, in some haphazard way, be related to something else that you didn't plan either.

On Paint-handling

I don't like to manipulate the paint in any way in which it doesn't normally happen. In other words, I wouldn't paint an area to make texture, you see? And I wouldn't decide to scumble an area to make it more interesting to meet another area which isn't interesting enough. I love the idea of the thing happening that way and through the painting of it, the form of the black or the white comes about in exactly that way, plastically.

On Composition as Process

Paint never seems to behave the same. Even the same paint doesn't, you know. In other words, if you use the same white or black or red, through the use of it, it never seems to be the same. It doesn't dry the same. It doesn't stay there and look at you the same way. Other things seem to affect it. There seems to be something that you can do so much with paint and after that you start murdering it. There are moments or periods when it would be wonderful to plan something and do it and have the thing only do what you planned to do, and then, there are other times when the destruction of those planned things becomes interesting to you. So then, it becomes a question of destroying—of destroying the planned form; it's like an escape, it's something to do; something to begin the situation. You yourself, you don't decide, but if you want to paint you have to find out some way to start this thing off, whether it's painting it out or putting it in, and so on.

It can at times become like the immediate experience of beginning it; in other words, I can begin a painting if I decide it would be nice to have a large triangle come up and meet something that goes across like this. Now, on other occasions, I can think the whole thing through. The triangle needs an area that goes this way and then at the top something falls down and hits about here and then goes over there. So I try and rid my mind of anything else and attack it immediately from that complete situation. Other times, I can begin it with just the triangle meeting a large form that goes over that way, and when I do it, it doesn't seem like anything. When this series of relationships that go on in the painting relate—I don't particularly know what they relate to—I, in some way, try to form them in the original conception of what I rather imagined they would look like. Well then, at times, it's a question of maybe making them more than that. You see what I mean. It'd be a question of, say, eliminating the top or the bottom. Well, I can go through and destroy the whole painting completely without even going back to this original situation of a triangle and a long line, which seems to appear somewhere else in the painting. When it appears the way I originally thought it should, boy, then it's wonderful.

On Seeing Images in His Work

If someone says, "That looks like a bridge," it doesn't bother me really. Naturally, if you title them something associated with that, then when someone looks at it in the literary sense, he says, "He's a bridge painter." . . .

There are forms that are figurative to me, and if they develop into a figurative image it's all right if they do. I don't have the feeling that something has to be completely non-associative as far as figure form is concerned.

I think that if you use long lines, they become—what could they be? The only thing they could be is either highways or architecture or bridges.

On Emotional Content

It is nice to paint a happy picture after a sad one. I think that there is a kind of loneliness in a lot of them which I don't think about as the fact that I'm lonely and therefore I paint lonely pictures, but I like kind of lonely things anyhow; so if the forms express that to me, there is a certain excitement that I have about that. Any composition—you know, the overall reality of that does have something to do with it; the impending forms of something, do maybe have a brooding quality, whereas in other forms, they would be called or considered happier.

On Painting as Drawing

I rather feel that painting is a form of drawing and the painting that I like has a form of drawing to it. I don't see how it could be dissociated from the nature of drawing. I find that in many cases a drawing has been the subject of the painting—that would be a preliminary stage to that particular painting.

BARNETT NEWMAN

• "Abstract sublime" was the phrase critic Robert Rosenblum chose to denote the simplified, reduced, static abstractions of Barnett Newman and Mark Rothko. In this passage Newman states his views on the sublime in art, and, in the one following, Rothko gives his reasons for painting environmental, mural-sized pictures.

[FROM *Tiger's Eye,* No. 6 (December, 1948).]

The invention of beauty by the Greeks, that is, their postulate of beauty as an ideal, has been the bugbear of European art and European aesthetic philosophies. Man's natural desire in the arts to express his relation to the Absolute became identified and confused with the absolutisms of perfect creations—with the fetish of quality—so that the European artist has been continually involved in the moral struggle between notions of beauty and the desire for sublimity. . . .

Michaelangelo [*sic*] knew that the meaning of the Greek humanities for his time involved making Christ—who is God; that his plastic problem was neither the medieval one, to make a cathedral, nor the Greek one, to make a man like a god, but to make a cathedral out of man. In doing so, he set a standard for sublimity that the painting of his time could not reach. Instead, painting continued on its merry quest for a voluptuous art until in modern times, the Impressionists, disgusted with its inadequacy, began the movement to destroy the established rhetoric of beauty by the Impressionist insistence on a surface of ugly strokes.

The impulse of modern art was this desire to destroy beauty. However, in discarding Renaissance notions of beauty, and without an adequate substitute for a sublime message, the Impressionists were compelled to preoccupy themselves, in their struggle, with the culture values of their plastic history so that instead of evoking a new way of experiencing life they were able only to make a transfer of values. . . .

So strong is the grip of the *rhetoric* of exaltation as an attitude in the large context of the European culture pattern that the elements of sublimity in the revolution we know as modern art, exist in its effort and energy to escape the pattern rather than in the realization of a new experience. Picasso's effort may be sublime but there is no doubt that his work is a preoccupation with the question of what is the nature of beauty. Even Mondrian, in his attempt to destroy the Renaissance picture by his insistence on pure subject matter, succeeded only in raising the white plane and the right angle into a realm of sublimity, where the sublime paradoxically becomes an absolute of perfect sensations. The geometry (perfection) swallowed up his metaphysics (his exaltation).

The failure of European art to achieve the sublime is due to this blind desire to exist inside the reality of sensation (the objective world, whether distorted or pure) and to build an art within a framework of pure plasticity (the Greek ideal of beauty, whether that plasticity be a romantic active surface, or a classic stable one). In other words, modern art, caught without a sublime content, was incapable of creating a new sublime image, and unable to move away from the Renaissance imagery of figures and objects except by distortion or by denying it completely for an empty world of geometric formalisms—a pure rhetoric of abstract mathematical relationships, and became enmeshed in a struggle over the nature of beauty; whether beauty was in nature or could be found without nature.

I believe that here in America, some of us, free from the weight of European culture, are finding the answer, by completely denying that art has any concern with the problem of beauty and where to find it. The question that now arises is how, if we are living in a time without a legend or mythos that can be called sublime, if we refuse to admit any exaltation in pure relations, if we refuse to live in the abstract, how can we be creating a sublime art?

We are reasserting man's natural desire for the exalted, for a concern with our relationship to the absolute emotions. We do not need the obsolete props of an outmoded and antiquated legend. We are creating images whose reality is self-evident and which are devoid of the props and crutches that evoke associations with outmoded images, both sublime and beautiful. We are freeing ourselves of the impediments of memory, association, nostalgia, legend, myth, or what have you, that have been the devices of Western European painting. Instead of making *cathedrals* out of Christ, man, or "life," we are making it out of ourselves, out of our own feelings. The image we produce is the self-evident one of revelation, real and concrete, that can be understood by anyone who will look at it without the nostalgic glasses of history.

MARK ROTHKO

[FROM *Interiors,* May, 1951.]

I paint very large pictures. I realize that historically the function of painting large pictures is painting something very grandiose and pompous. The reason I paint them, however—I think it applies to other painters I know—is precisely because I want to be very intimate and human. To paint a small picture is to place yourself outside your experience, to look upon an experience as a stereopticon view or with a reducing glass. However you paint the larger picture, you are in it. It isn't something you command.

AD REINHARDT

• Although a member of the first generation of Abstract Expressionists, Ad Reinhardt was often referred to as the "black monk" of the movement because of his constant refusal to interest himself in either Expressionist paint handling or emotional content. Yet his calls for impersonality, aloofness, and asceticism have been heeded by many of the younger American artists. Reinhardt's insistence on the separation of art from life led him to propagandize from the thirties onward for a pure art-for-art's sake in a most persuasive, if dogmatic, manner. A source for the new cool reductive abstraction, Reinhardt has influenced both painters and the "minimal" sculptors.

[FROM "Art-as-Art," *Art International,* VI, No. 10 (December 20, 1962).]

The one thing to say about art and life is that art is not life and life is not art. A "slice-of-life" art is no better or worse than a "slice-of-art" life. Fine art is not a "means of making a living" or a "way of living a life," and an artist who dedicates his life to his art, or his art to his life, burdens his art with his life and his life with his art. Art that is a matter of life and death is neither fine nor free.

The one assault on fine art is the ceaseless attempt to subserve it as a means to some other end or value. The one fight in art is not between art and non-art but between true art and false art, between pure art and Action-Assemblage art, between abstract art and Surrealist-Expressionist–anti-art, between free art and servile art. Abstract art has its own integrity, not some other "integration" with something else. Any combining, mixing, adding, diluting, exploiting, vulgarizing or popularizing abstract art deprives art of its essence and depraves the artist's artistic consciousness. Art is free, but it is not a free-for-all.

The one struggle in art is the struggle of artists against artists, of artist against artist, of the artist-as-artist within and against the artist-as-man, -animal, or -vegetable. Artists who claim that their art-work comes from nature, life, reality, earth, or heaven, are subjectively and objectively rascals or rustics. The art of "figuring" or "picturing" is not a fine art. "New images of man"—figures and "nature-in-abstraction"—pictures are fakes. An artist who is lobbying as a "creature of circumstances" or logrolling as a "victim of fate" is not a fine master-artist. No one ever forces an artist to be pure.

The one meaning in art comes from art-working and the more an artist works, the more there is to do. Artists come from artists, art-forms come from art-forms, painting comes from painting. The one direction in fine or abstract art today is in the painting of the same one form over and over again. The one intensity and the one perfection comes only from long and lonely routine attention and repetition. The one originality exists only where all artists work in the same tradition and master the same convention. The one freedom is realized only through the most conscious art-discipline and through the most regular studio ritual. Only a standardized, prescribed form can be imageless, only a stereotyped image can be formless, only a formula-ized art can be formula-less. A painter who does not know what or how or where to paint is not a fine artist.

The one work for the fine artist, the one painting, is the painting of the one-size canvas—the single-scheme, one formal device, one color-monochrome, one linear-division in each direction, one symmetry, one texture, one free-hand-brushing, one rhythm, one working everything into one dissolution and one indivisibility, each painting into one over-all uniformity and non-irregularity. Everything into irreducibility, un-reproducibility, imperceptibility. Nothing "usable," "manipulatable," "salable," "dealable," "collectable," "graspable." No art as a commodity or a jobbery. Art is not the spiritual side of business.

STUDIO 35

• Round-table discussions at the Artist's Club and elsewhere gave the Abstract Expressionists an opportunity to clarify mutual concerns. At the third meeting of Studio 35, the discussion group that met in the spring of 1950, preceding the Club's formation, the following remarks were made on finishing a painting and on the relationship of the artist to tradition—crucial issues to the participants.

[FROM *Modern Artists in America,* edited by Robert Motherwell and Ad Reinhardt (New York: Wittenborn, Schultz, 1952).]

MODERATOR MOTHERWELL: The question then is, *"How do you know when a work is finished?*

BAZIOTES: I consider my painting finished when my eye goes to a particular spot on the canvas. But if I put the picture away about thirty feet on the wall and the movements keep returning to me and the eye seems to be responding to something living, then it is finished.

NEWMAN: I think the idea of a "finished" picture is a fiction. I think a man spends his whole lifetime painting one picture or working on one piece of sculpture. The question of stopping is really a decision of moral considerations. To what extent are you intoxicated by the actual act, so that you are beguiled by it. To what extent are you charmed by its inner life? And to what extent do you then really approach the intention or desire that is really outside of it? The decision is always made when the piece has something in it that you wanted.

DE KOONING: I refrain from "finishing" it. I paint myself out of the picture, and when I have done that, I either throw it away or keep it. I am always in the picture somewhere. The amount of space I use I am always in, I seem to move around in it, and there seems to be a time when I lose sight of what I wanted to do, and then I am out of it. If the picture has a countenance, I keep it. If it hasn't, I throw it away. I am not really very much interested in the question.

REINHARDT: It has always been a problem for me—about "finishing" a painting. Among modern artists there is a value placed upon "unfinished" work. Disturbances arise when you have to treat the work as a finished and complete object, so that the only time I think I "finish" a painting is when I have a deadline. If you are going to present it as an "unfinished" object, how do you "finish" it?

HOFMANN: To me a work is finished when all parts involved communicate themselves, so that they don't need me.

MOTHERWELL: I dislike a picture that is too suave or too skilfully done. But, contrariwise, I also dislike a picture that looks too inept or blundering. I noticed in looking at the Carré exhibition of young French painters who are supposed to be close to this group, that in "finishing" a picture they assume traditional criteria to a much greater degree than we do. They have a real "finish" in that the picture is a real object, a beautifully made object. We are involved in "process" and what is a "finished" object is not so certain.

HOFMANN: Yes, it seems to me all the time there is the question of a heritage. The American painter of today approaches things without a basis. The French approach things on the basis of a cultural heritage—one feels that in all their work. It is a working towards a refinement and quality rather than working toward new experiences, and painting out these experiences that may finally become tradition. The French have it easier. They have it in the beginning.

DE KOONING: I am glad you brought up this point. It seems to me that in Europe every time something new needed to be done it was because of traditional culture. Ours has been a striving to come to the same point that they had—not to be iconoclasts.

GOTTLIEB: There is a general assumption that European—specifically French—painters have a heritage which enables them to have the benefits of tradition, and therefore they can produce a certain type of painting. It seems to me that in the last fifty years the whole meaning of painting has been made international. I think Americans share that heritage just as much, and that if they deviate from tradition it is just as difficult for an American as for a Frenchman. It is a mistaken assumption in some quarters that any departure from tradition stems from ignorance. I think that what Motherwell describes is the problem of knowing what tradition is, and being willing to reject it in part. This requires familiarity with his past. I think we have this familiarity, and if we depart from tradition, it is out of knowledge, not innocence.

DE KOONING: I agree that tradition is part of the whole world now. The point that was brought up was that the French artists have some "touch" in making an object. They have a particular something that makes them look like a "finished" painting. They have a touch which I am glad not to have.

BAZIOTES: We are getting mixed up with the French tradition. In talking about the necessity to "finish" a thing, we then said American painters "finish" a thing that looks "unfinished," and the French, they "finish" it. I have seen Matisses that were more "unfinished" and yet more "finished" than any American painter. Matisse was obviously in a terrific emotion at the time, and it was more "unfinished" than "finished."

Chapter Eight

After Abstract Expressionism

• Just as the new abstraction separates art rrom life, so is pop art interested in reintroducing the stuff of life into art. Statements by Jasper Johns and Robert Rauschenberg, whose early use of mass-culture images helped other artists break with Abstract Expressionism, as well as statements from pop artists Claes Oldenburg and Roy Lichtenstein, indicate a set of common attitudes toward art and life and their possible reintegration in an imagistic style.

JASPER JOHNS

[FROM *Sixteen Americans,* edited by Dorothy C. Miller (New York: Museum of Modern Art, 1959).]

Sometimes I see it and then paint it. Other times I paint it and then I see. Both are impure situations, and I prefer neither.

At every point in nature there is something to see. My work contains similar possibilities for the changing focus of the eye.

Three academic ideas which have been of interest to me are what a teacher of mine (speaking of Cézanne and Cubism) called "the rotating point of view" (Larry Rivers recently pointed to a black rectangle, two or three feet away from where he had been looking in a painting, and said ". . . like there's something happening over there too."); Marcel Duchamp's suggestion "to reach the Impossibility of sufficient visual memory to transfer from one like object to another the memory imprint"; and Leonardo's idea ("Therefore, O painter, do not surround your bodies with lines . . .") that the boundary of a body is neither a part of the enclosed body nor a part of the surrounding atmosphere.

Generally, I am opposed to painting which is concerned with conceptions of simplicity. Everything looks very busy to me.

ROBERT RAUSCHENBERG

[FROM *Sixteen Americans,* edited by Dorothy C. Miller (New York: Museum of Modern Art, 1959).]

Any incentive to paint is as good as any other. There is no poor subject.

Painting is always strongest when in spite of composition, color, etc., it appears as a fact, or an inevitability, as opposed to a souvenir or arrangement.

Painting relates to both art and life. Neither can be made. (I try to act in that gap between the two.)

A pair of socks is no less suitable to make a painting with than wood, nails, turpentine, oil and fabric.

A canvas is never empty.

CLAES OLDENBURG

[FROM Claes Oldenburg, "Environments Situations Spaces," *Exhibition Catalog,* Martha Jackson Gallery, 1961.]

I am for an art that takes its form from the lines of life, that twists and extends impossibly and accumulates and spits and drips, and is sweet and stupid as life itself. I am for an artist who vanishes, turning up in a white cap, painting signs or hallways.

I am for an art that comes out of a chimney like black hair and scatters in the sky. I am for an art that spills out of an old man's purse when he is bounced off a passing fender. I am for the art out [of] a doggy's mouth, falling five floors from the roof. I am for the art that a kid licks, after peeling away the wrapper. I am for an art that is smoked, like a cigarette, smells, like a pair of shoes. I am for art that flaps like a flag, or helps blow noses, like a handkerchief. I am for art that is put on and taken off, like pants, which develops holes, like socks, which is eaten, like a piece of pie. . . .

I am for art you can sit on. . . . I am for art that is flipped on and off with a switch. I am for art that unfolds like a map, that you can squeeze, like you your sweety's arm, or kiss, like a pet dog. Which expands and squeaks, like an accordion, which you can spill your dinner on, like an old tablecloth. I am for an art you can hammer with, stitch with, sew with, paste with, file with. I am for an art that tells you the time of day and which helps old ladies across the street.

I am for the art of red and white gasoline pumps and blinking biscuit signs. I am for the art of old plaster and new enamel. I am for the art of slag and black coal and dead birds. I am for the art of scratchings in the asphalt. I am for the art of bending and kicking things and breaking them and by pulling on them making them fall down. I am for the art of sat-on bananas.

I am for the art of underwear and the art of taxicabs. I am for the art of ice cream cones dropped on concrete. I am for the blinking arts, lighting up the night. I am for falling, splashing, wiggling, jumping, going on and off. I am for the art of fat truck-tires and black eyes. I am for Kool Art, 7-Up Art, Pepsi Art, Sunkist Art, Dro-bomp Art, Vam Art, Pamryl Art, San-O-Med Art, 39 cents Art and 9.99 Art.

I am for the white art of refrigerators and their muscular openings and closings. . . . I am for the art of decapitated teddy bears, exploded umbrellas, chairs with their brown bones broken, burning Xmas trees, firecracker ends, pigeon bones, and boxes with men sleeping in them. I am for the art of hung, bloody rabbits and wrinkly chickens, tambourines and plastic phonographs, and abandoned boxes tied like pharaohs.

ROY LICHTENSTEIN

[FROM an interview by G. Swenson with Roy Lichtenstein, *Art News,* November, 1963.]

(What is Pop Art?)

I don't know—the use of commercial art as subject matter in painting, I suppose. It was hard to get a painting that was despicable enough so that no one would hang it—everybody was hanging everything. It was almost acceptable to hang a dripping paint rag, everyone was accustomed to this. The one thing everyone hated was commercial art; apparently they didn't hate that enough either.

(Are you anti-experimental?)

I think so, and anti-contemplative, anti-nuance, anti-getting-away-from-the-tyranny-of-the-rectangle, anti-movement-and-light, anti-mystery, anti-paint-quality, anti-Zen, and anti all of those brilliant ideas of preceding movements which everyone understands so thoroughly.

We like to think of industrialization as being despicable. I don't really know what to make of it. There's something terribly brittle about it. I suppose I would still prefer to sit under a tree with a picnic basket rather than under a gas pump, but signs and comic strips are interesting as subject matter. There are certain things that are usable, forceful and vital about commercial art. We're using those things—but we're not really advocating stupidity, international teenagerism and terrorism.

CLEMENT GREENBERG

• Organized by Clement Greenberg in 1963 for the Los Angeles County Museum, the exhibition "Post-Painterly Abstraction" included thirty-one artists. Among them were Helen Frankenthaler, Kenneth Noland, Morris Louis, Ray Parker, Jules Olitski, Sam Francis, Ellsworth Kelly, Paul Feeley, John Ferren, Frank Stella, and Nicolas Krushenick. Mr. Greenberg's catalogue essay, excerpted below, gave his reasons for feeling that a reaction against the painterly aspects of Abstract Expressionism had set in.

[FROM *Post-Painterly Abstraction,* Catalogue of the Los Angeles County Museum, 1964.]

The great Swiss art historian, Heinrich Woelfflin, used the German word, *malerisch,* which his English translators render as "painterly," to designate the formal qualities of Baroque art that separate it from High Renaissance or Classical art. Painterly means, among other things, the blurred, broken, loose definition of color and contour. The opposite of painterly is clear, unbroken, and sharp definition, which Woelfflin called "linear." The dividing line between the painterly and the linear is by no means a hard and fast one. There are many artists whose work combines elements of both, and painterly handling can go with linear design, and vice versa. This still does not diminish the usefulness of these terms or categories. With their help—and keeping in mind that they have nothing to do with value judgments—we are able to notice all sorts of continuities and significant differences, in the art of the present as well as of the past, that we might not notice otherwise.

The kind of painting that has become known as Abstract Expressionism is both abstract and painterly. Twenty years ago this proved a rather unexpected combination. Abstract art itself may have been born amid the painterliness of Analytical Cubism, Léger, Delaunay, and Kandinsky thirty years earlier, but there are all kinds of painterliness, and even Kandinsky's seemed restrained by comparison with Hofmann's and Pollock's. The painterly beginnings of abstract and near-abstract art would appear, anyhow, to have been somewhat forgotten, and during the 1920's and 1930's abstract art had become almost wholly identified with the flat silhouettes and firm contours of Synthetic Cubism, Mondrian, the Bauhaus, and Miró. (Klee's art was an exception, but the smallness of his works made their painterly handling relatively unobtrusive; one became really aware of Klee's painterliness only when it was "blown up" later on by artists like Wols, Tobey, and Dubuffet.) Thus the notion of abstract art as something neatly drawn and smoothly painted, something with clean outlines and flat, clear colors, had become pretty well ingrained. To see this all disappear under a flurry of strokes, blotches, and trickles of paint was a bewildering experience at first. It looked as though all form, all order, all discipline, had been cast off. Some of the labels that became attached to Abstract Expressionism, like the *"informel"* and "Action Painting," definitely implied this; one was given to understand that what was involved was an utterly new kind of art that was no longer art in any accepted sense.

This was, of course, absurd. What was mostly involved was the disconcerting effect produced by wide-open painterliness in an abstract context. That context still derived from Cubism—as does the context of every variety of sophisticated abstract art since Cubism, despite all appearances to the contrary. The painterliness itself derived from the tradition of form going back to the Venetians. Abstract Expressionism—or Painterly Abstraction, as I prefer to call it—was very much art, and rooted in the past of art. People should have recognized this the moment they began to be able to recognize differences of *quality* in Abstract Expressionism. . . .

Abstract Expressionism was, and is, a certain style of art, and like other styles of art, having had its ups, it had its downs. Having produced art of major importance, it turned into a school, then into a manner, and finally into a set of mannerisms. Its leaders attracted imitators, many of them, and then some of these leaders took to imitating themselves. Painterly Abstraction became a fashion, and now it has fallen out of fashion, to be replaced by another fashion—Pop Art—but also to be continued, as well as replaced, by something as genuinely new and independent as Painterly Abstraction itself was ten or twenty years ago.

The most conspicuous of the mannerisms into which Painterly Abstraction has degenerated is what I call the "Tenth Street touch" (after East Tenth Street in New York), which spread through abstract painting like a blight during the 1950's. The stroke left by a loaded brush or knife frays out, when the stroke is long enough, into streaks, ripples, and specks of paint. These create variations of light and dark by means of which juxtaposed strokes can be graded into one another without abrupt contrasts. (This was an automatic solution for one of the crucial technical problems of abstract painting: that of asserting the continuity of the picture plane when working more or less "in the flat"—and it's one of the reasons why the "Tenth Street touch" caught on the way it did.) Out of these close-knit variations or gradations of light and dark, the typical Abstract Expressionist picture came to be built, with its density of accents and its packed, agitated look.

In all this there was nothing bad in itself, nothing necessarily bad as art. What turned this constellation of stylistic features into something bad as art was its standardization, its reduction to a set of mannerisms, as a dozen, and then a thousand, artists proceeded to maul the same viscosities of paint, in more or less the same ranges of color, and with the same "gestures," into the same kind of picture. And that part of the reaction against Painterly Abstraction which this show tries to document is a reaction more against an attitude than against Painterly Abstraction as such.

As far as style is concerned, the reaction presented here is largely against the mannered drawing and the mannered design of Painterly Abstraction, but above all against the last. By contrast with the interweaving of light and dark gradations in the typical Abstract Expressionist picture, all the artists in this show move towards a physical openness of design, or towards linear clarity, or towards both. They continue, in this respect, a tendency that began well inside Painterly Abstraction itself, in the work of artists like Still, Newman, Rothko, Motherwell, Gottlieb, Mathieu, the 1950–1954 Kline, and even Pollock. A good part of the reaction against Abstract Expressionism is, as I've already suggested, a continuation of it. There is no question, in any case, of repudiating its best achievements. . . .

Some of the artists in this exhibition look "hard-edged," but this by itself does not account for their inclusion. They are included because they have won their "hardness" from the "softness" of Painterly Abstraction; they have not inherited it from Mondrian, the Bauhaus, Suprematism, or anything else that came before.

Another thing the artists in this show, with two or three exceptions, have in common is the high keying as well as lucidity of their color. They have a tendency, many of them, to stress contrasts of pure hue, rather than contrasts of light and dark. For the sake of these, as well as in the interests of optical clarity, they shun thick paint and tactile effects. Some of them dilute their paint to an extreme and soak it into unsized and unprimed canvas (following Pollock's lead in his black and white paintings of 1951). In their reaction against the "hand-writing" and "gestures" of Painterly Abstraction, these artists also favor a relatively anonymous execution. This is perhaps the most important motive behind the geometrical regularity of drawing in most of the pictures in this show. It certainly has nothing to do with doctrine, with geometrical form for its own sake. These artists prefer trued and faired edges simply because these call less attention to themselves as drawing—and by doing that they also get out of the way of color.

JULES OLITSKI

• The following statement by Jules Olitski illustrates the degree to which the new abstractionists are equally absorbed by the problems of color and those of structure.

[FROM *Catalogue of the International Biennial Exhibition of Art,* Venice, 1966.]

Painting is made from inside out. I think of painting as possessed by a structure—i.e. shape and size, support and edge—but a structure born of the flow of color feeling. Color *in* color is felt at any and every place of the pictorial organization; in its immediacy—its particularity. Color is felt throughout.

What is of importance in painting is paint. Paint can be color. Paint becomes painting when color establishes surface. Where edge exists within the structure, it must be felt as an integral and necessary outcome of the color structure. Outer edge cannot be thought of as being in some way within—it is the outermost extension of the color structure. The decision as to *where* the outer edge is, is final, not initial. The focus in recent painting has been on the lateral—a flat and frontal view of the surface. This has tended toward the use of flat color areas bounded, inevitably, by edges. Edge is drawing and drawing is *on* the surface. The color areas take on the appearance of overlay, and if the conception of form is governed by edge—no matter how successfully it possesses the surface—paint, even when stained into raw canvas remains on or above the surface. I think, on the contrary, of color as being seen *in,* not *on,* the surface.

JOSEF ALBERS

• The theoretical work and experiments in color contrast of Josef Albers, one of the outstanding abstract painters of the century, have provided the basis for much of the research in optical art. In addition, his simple geometric compositions and use of high-intensity color must be considered as part of the context in which the "new abstraction" was developed.

[FROM *Homage to the Square* (New York: Museum of Modern Art, 1964).]

The colors in my paintings are juxtaposed for various and changing effects. They are to challenge or to echo each other, to support or oppose one another. The contrasts, respectively boundaries, between them may vary from soft to hard touches, may mean pull and push besides clashes, but also embracing, intersecting, penetrating.

Despite an even and mostly opaque application, the colors will appear above or below each other, in front or behind, or side by side on the same level. They correspond in concord as well as in discord, which happens between both, groups and singles.

Such action, reaction, interaction—or interdependence—is sought in order to make obvious how colors influence and change each other: that the same color, for instance—with different grounds or neighbors—looks different. But also, that different colors can be made to look alike. It is to show that 3 colors can be read as 4, and similarly as 2, and also 4 as 2.

Such color deceptions prove that we see colors almost never related to each other and therefore unchanged; that color is changing continually: with changing light, with changing shape and placement, and with quantity which denotes either amount (a real extension) or number (recurrence). And just as influential are changes in perception depending on changes of mood, and consequently of receptiveness.

All this will make [one] aware of an exciting discrepancy between physical fact and psychic effect of color.

But besides relatedness and influence I should like to see that my colors remain, as much as possible, a "face"—their own "face," as it was achieved—uniquely—and I believe consciously—in Pompeian wall paintings—by admitting coexistence of such polarities as being dependent and independent—being dividual and individual.

Often, with paintings, more attention is drawn to the outer, physical, structure of the color means than to the inner, functional, structure of the color action as described above. Here now follow a few details of the technical manipulation of the colorants which in my painting usually are oil paints and only rarely casein paints.

Compared with the use of paint in most painting today, here the technique is kept unusually simple, or more precisely, as uncomplicated as possible.

[FROM Katherine Kuh, *The Artist's Voice* (New York: Harper & Row, 1960).]

I think art parallels life; it is not a report on nature or an intimate disclosure of inner secrets. Color, in my opinion, behaves like man—in two distinct ways: first in self-realization and then in the realization of relationships with others. In my paintings I have tried to make two polarities meet—independence and interdependence, as for instance, in Pompeian art. There's a certain red the Pompeians used that speaks in both these ways, first in its relation to other colors around it, and then as it appears alone, keeping its own face. In other words, one must combine both being an individual and being a member of society. That's the parallel. I've handled color as man should behave. With trained and sensitive eyes, you can recognize this double behavior of color. And for all this, you may conclude that I consider ethics and aesthetics as one.

QUESTION: When your colors vibrate, are you trying to suggest movement?

ALBERS: I don't accept your term "vibrate," because in my understanding, vibration of color happens only rarely. What I'm after, in a broader term, is interaction. If I can refer again to the parallel with life, the job is to make the unbearable, bearable, or to make that which doesn't behave, behave. This means a different organization of conditions for every color and every situation. A color can be placed among other colors so that it loses its identity. Red looks green or looks like a gas—dematerialized. Gray can look black, depending on what surrounds it. This I call "acting color." I work with the same painting, the same colors over and over—innumerable times. As a rule, I use either three or four colors in a painting. Merely by changing one color, a totally different climate is produced, though all the other colors in the work remain identical in area and hue. With two separate colors in no way overlapping, three are produced through interaction. Each borrows from and gives to the other. Where they meet, where they intersect, a new color results. In science, one plus one is two, but in art it can be three. Often I have to paint ten different times before I reach a realization. I usually start with a very small sketch; then comes painting after painting until I realize what I'm after. What I want is to play staccato and legato—and all the other musical terms, but not for the purpose of expressing myself.

QUESTION: If you're not expressing yourself, what are you doing?

ALBERS: I'm pleasing myself and educating others to see. If these paintings are me, this is an unavoidable result—not calculated. What I'm calculating is the interaction of color. . . . In my paintings, line doesn't amount to much, but in my linear constructions I use line for the purpose of interaction. According to most color systems, harmony depends on the constellation of colors with a system. I go further in saying that, first, harmony is not the main aim of color. Disharmony is just as important in color as in music. And second, I say that every color goes with every other color if the quantities are right. This, of course, leads to a new seeing of color.

SIDNEY TILLIM

• In a review of "The Responsive Eye" exhibition at the Museum of Modern Art, which introduced optical art, Sidney Tillim clarified the relationship of "optical art" to the European tradition of geometric art and to American post-painterly abstraction.

[FROM "Optical Art: Pending or Ending?" *Arts,* XXXIX (January, 1965).]

The general tendency of Post-Abstract Expressionist art in the United States, exclusive of the painterly Neo-Dadaists Rauschenberg and Johns and the assemblage school, has been toward hard-edged forms, a corresponding simplicity of structure and a greater emphasis on color. These "hard" qualities are present not only in abstractionist art but in

Pop art and some realism as well, though far less self-evidently. And while it now seems that Ellsworth Kelly has failed to move very far off the bridge he represents between hard-edge art and a convincingly Post-Abstract Expressionism abstraction, Louis and Noland, staining liquid bars of color across huge canvases, and, in an even less painterly idiom, Stella, with his shaped canvases have extended the "new" American painting into the sixties. . . .

European abstractionist art, on the other hand, has not had, at least until now, an equivalent "hard-edge" reaction of such clarity partly because that need has been partially filled by the greater tolerance on the Continent for traditional geometric art, partly because painterly abstraction never achieved the violence and the pervasive influence there that it achieved here and consequently did not require as clean-cut a reaction, and, finally, partly because of the persistence of doctrinaire habits implied in the first two reasons. . . .

To the extent that it is optical at all, the American style is far more color-oriented than percept-oriented—which implies structual differences as well. American-type "opticality" is conscious of a field which expands rather than contracts from the deposition of dry waves, lines and spots of translucent hues. A distinguishing feature of the paintings by Noland, Louis, and Poons is that traditional dark-and-light contrasts have been exchanged for the contrasts of hues which are usually of equal value and intensity. Thus the entire field becomes a chiaroscuro-less "positive" form, "bulked space" as it were, rather than space that has been carved into traditional, structured figure-ground relationships.

FRANK STELLA AND DONALD JUDD

• In a recent article, critic Sidney Tillim singled out Frank Stella and Donald Judd as the leading figures of the "new avant-garde," the youngest generation of American painters and sculptors. Reacting against the metaphysical *angst* of Abstract Expressionism, these young artists are producing an apodictic, impersonal abstraction that is, nonetheless, derived from Abstract Expressionism rather than from European geometric art.

[FROM Bruce Glaser, "Questions to Stella and Judd," *Art News,* September, 1966.]

STELLA: The European geometric painters really strive for what I call relational painting. The basis of their whole idea is balance. You do something in one corner and you balance it with something in the other corner. Now the "new painting" is being characterized as symmetrical. Ken Noland has put things in the center and I'll use a symmetrical pattern, but we use symmetry in a different way. It's nonrelational. In the newer American painting we strive to get the thing in the middle, and symmetrical, but just to get a kind of force, just to get the thing on the canvas. The balance factor isn't important. We're not trying to jockey everything around.

GLASER: What is the "thing" you're getting on the canvas?

STELLA: I guess you'd have to describe it as the image, either the image or the scheme. Ken Noland would use concentric circles; he'd want to get them in the middle because it's the easiest way to get them there, and he wants them there in the front, on the surface of the canvas. If you're that much involved with the surface of anything you're bound to find symmetry the most natural means. As soon as you use any kind of relational placement for symmetry, you get into a terrible kind of fussiness which is the one thing that most of the painters now want to avoid. When you're always making these delicate balances, it seems to present too many problems; it becomes sort of arch.

GLASER: An artist who works in your vein has said he finds symmetry extraordinarily sensuous; on the other hand, I've heard the comment that symmetry is very austere. Are you trying to create a sensuous or an austere effect? Is this relevant to your surfaces?

JUDD: No, I don't think my work is either one. I'm interested in spareness, but I don't think it has any connection to symmetry. . . . I don't have any ideas as to symmetry. My things are symmetrical because, as you said, I wanted to get rid of any compositional effects, and the obvious way to do it is to be symmetrical.

GLASER: Why do you want to avoid compositional effects?

JUDD: Well, those effects tend to carry with them all the structures, values, feelings of the whole European tradition. It suits me fine if that's all down the drain. When Vasarely has optical effects within the squares, they're never enough, and he has to have at least three or four squares, slanted, tilted inside each other, and all arranged. That is about five times more composition and juggling than he needs.

GLASER: You've written about the predominance of chance in Robert Morris' work. Is this element in your pieces too?

JUDD: Yes. Pollock and those people represent actual chance; by now it's better to make that a foregone conclusion—you don't have to mimic chance. You use a simple form that doesn't look like either order or disorder. We recognize that the world is ninety per cent chance and accident. Earlier painting was saying that there's more order in the scheme of things than we admit now, like Poussin saying order underlies nature. Poussin's order is anthropomorphic. Now there are no preconceived notions. Take a simple form—say a box—and it does have an order, but it's not so ordered that that's the dominant quality. The more parts a thing has, the more important order becomes, and finally order becomes more important than anything else.

STELLA: The artist's tools or the traditional artist's brush and maybe even oil paint are all disappearing very quickly. We use mostly commercial paint, and we generally tend toward larger brushes. In a way, Abstract-Expressionism started all this. De Kooning used house painter's brushes and house painter's techniques.

GLASER: Pollock used commercial paint.

STELLA: Yes, the aluminum paint. What happened, at least for me, is that when I first started painting I would see Pollock, de Kooning, and the one thing they all had that I didn't have was an art school background. They were brought up on drawing and they all ended up painting or drawing with the brush. They got away from the smaller brushes and, in an attempt to free themselves, they got involved in commercial paint and house-painting brushes. Still it was basically drawing with paint, which has characterized almost all twentieth-century painting. The way my painting was going, drawing was less and less necessary. It was the one thing I wasn't going to do. I wasn't going to draw with the brush.

GLASER: What induced this conclusion that drawing wasn't necessary any more?

STELLA: Well, you have a brush and you've got paint on the brush, and you ask yourself why you're doing whatever it is you're doing, what inflection you're actually going to make with the brush and with the paint that's on the end of the brush. It's like handwriting. And I found out that I just didn't have anything to say in those terms. I didn't want to make variations; I didn't want to record a path. I wanted to get the paint out of the can and onto the canvas. I knew a wise guy who used to make fun of my painting, but he didn't like the Abstract-Expressionists either. He said they would be good painters if they could only keep the paint as good as it is in the can. And that's what I tried to do. I tried to keep the paint as good as it was in the can.

GLASER: Are you implying that you are trying to destroy painting?

STELLA: It's just that you can't go back. It's not a question of destroying anything. If something's used up, something's done, something's over with, what's the point of getting involved with it?

GLASER: Are you suggesting that there are no more solutions to, or no more problems that exist in painting?

STELLA: I always get into arguments with people who want to retain the old values in painting—the humanistic values that they always find on the canvas. My painting is based on the fact that only what can be seen there *is* there. It really is an object. Any painting is an object and anyone who gets involved enough in this finally has to face up to the objectness of whatever it is that he's doing. He is making a thing. All that should be taken for granted. If the painting were lean enough, accurate enough or right enough, you would just be able to look at it. All I want anyone to get out of my paintings, and all I ever get out of them, is the fact that you can see the whole idea without any confusion. . . . What you see is what you see.

GLASER: But some would claim that the visual effect is minimal, that you're just giving us one color or a symmetrical grouping of lines. A nineteenth-century landscape painting would presumably offer more pleasure, simply because it's more complicated.

JUDD: I don't think it's more complicated.

STELLA: No, because what you're saying essentially is that a nineteenth-century landscape is more complicated because there are two things working—deep space and the way it's painted. You can see how it's done and read the figures in the space. Then take Ken Noland's painting, for example, which is just a few stains on the ground. If you want to look at the depths, there are just as many problematic spaces. And some of them are extremely complicated technically; you can worry and wonder how he painted the way he did.

JUDD: Old master painting has a great reputation for being profound, universal and all that, and it isn't, necessarily.

STELLA: But I don't know how to get around the part that they just wanted to make something pleasurable to look at, because even if that's what I want, I also want my painting to be so you can't *avoid* the fact that it's supposed to be entirely visual.

GLASER: You've been quoted, Frank, as saying that you want to get sentimentality out of painting.

STELLA: I hope I didn't say that. I think what I said is that sentiment wasn't necessary. I didn't think then, and I don't now, that it's necessary to make paintings that will interest people in the sense that they can keep going back to explore painterly detail. One could stand in front of any Abstract-Expressionist work for a long time, and walk back and forth, and inspect the depths of the pigment and the inflection and all the painterly brushwork for hours. But I wouldn't particularly want to do that and also I wouldn't ask anyone to do that in front of my paintings. To go further, I would like to prohibit them from doing that in front of my painting. That's why I make the paintings the way they are, more or less. . . . I don't go out of my way to be economical. It's hard to explain what exactly it is I'm motivated by, but I don't think people are motivated by reduction. It would be nice if we were, but actually, I'm motivated by the desire to make something, and I go about it in the way that seems best. . . .

I make the canvas deeper than ordinarily, but I began accidentally. I turned one-by-threes on edge to make a quick frame, and then I liked it. When you stand directly in front of the painting it gives it just enough depth to hold it off the wall; you're conscious of this sort of shadow, just enough depth to emphasize the surface. In other words, it makes it more like a painting and less like an object, by stressing the surface.

Chapter Nine

Toward a Sculptural Renaissance

GASTON LACHAISE

• Born in France, Gaston Lachaise, creator of voluptuous nudes and intricately locked couples, was among the first artists in America openly to defy Puritanism in all its aspects, shamelessly proclaiming the sovereignty of the erotic. In the following reminiscence, he describes his meeting with the young Boston matron, his future wife, Isabel Dutard Nagle, who was to inspire his art for the next thirty years.

[FROM "A Comment on My Sculpture," *Creative Art,* III (August, 1928).]

At twenty, in Paris, I met a young American person who immediately became the primary inspiration which awakened my vision and the leading influence that had directed my force. Throughout my career as an artist, I refer to this person by the word "Woman." . . .

"Woman," as a vision sculptured, began to move, vigorously, robustly, walking, alert, lightly, radiating sex and soul. Soon she came to forceful repose, serene, massive as earth, soul turned towards heaven. "La Montagne"! The feet almost disappeared. Mountains neither jump nor walk, but have fertile rolling pastures, broad and soft as fecund breasts.

Then "Woman" rose again, upstanding, noble, bountiful, poised on her toes, with closed self-absorbed eyes, nearly detached from earth. Still later, after communion with the universe and cosmic realization, "Woman,"—spheroid, planetary, radiative—was entirely projected beyond the earth, as protoplasm, haunted by the infinite, thrust forth man, by means of art, towards the eternal.

On certain occasions I have made use of animals, sea gulls, sea lions, dolphins, peacocks, penguins, to translate spiritual forces. I have enjoyed doing portraits. My interest in portraiture has always been keen, for a portrait of an individual is synthesis of the prevalent forces within the individual, and in this process there is expansion for the creator. Of late a vision of the form of "Man" is growing more clear and precise to me. I must begin to attempt to realize it. Undoubtedly he will be the son of "Woman."

Whenever an American artist is led to speak of his achievement in art he is, necessarily, on account of the violent intensity and fabulous wealth of this land, anchored to certain cold facts which in the United States are stressed, fantastically, beyond the reality of art.

The path to achievement, though cleared of a few stumps and morasses, is as bare and dangerous as the trail over the plains, across the Rockies, to the Far West in 1828. Financial strain from all sides, no genuine support for the better part of a lifetime are yours. Will power, tenacity, pride that can disregard all humiliations conceivable, aggressiveness, essential on occasions, long stretches of labor—day and night—twenty hours out of twenty-four, are your only assets. Hardships for all concerned. Artists' wives are assuredly the pioneer women of this era. Artists' wives will go to heaven, let me tell you....

Yet it cannot be overlooked, that at present, even though neglected, the American artist "living and true"—creative and bearer of fruit, has begun to grow roots and function in the rocky soil of America. At wide intervals artists do meet individuals who possess the ability to render vital support to them in addition to holding tremendous enthusiasm for them. This is marvelously refreshing. Response from the artists is never lacking. Curiously, in the United States, this individual of discernment, taste and character strong enough to both appreciate and cooperate with an artist is rare, whereas artists who contain untold potentialities increase rapidly whatever the hardships their choice of life offers. . . .

What some twelve years ago I declared, I repeat emphatically, "The most favorable ground for the continuity of art is here."

JOHN FLANNAGAN

• Applying for a Guggenheim Fellowship in 1939, John Flannagan made the statement below, in which he shows his aims to be close to Brancusi's. Later, in a letter to his dealer, Curt Valentin, Flannagan gave clues to the meaning of his work. Like the early Abstract Expressionists, Flannagan searched for the archetypes Jung had located in the collective unconscious.

[FROM *Art in America,* LIII, No. 4 (August–September, 1965).]

My aim is to continue the purpose of twenty years of working in sculpture—to create a plastic idiom alive as the spoken word; sculpture as direct and swift in feeling as a drawing, sculpture with such ease, freedom and simplicity that it hardly seems carved but to have endured always. Fulfilled, it should mean the development of an instrument so sensitive as to record the human psyche in all its various moods and reactions to life instead of the usual banal platitudes and worn clichés.

This is an austere art which compels a clear perception of its scope and limitations. Therefore it seems that it should be of a generalized universal symbolic nature . . . man, woman, child, animal. The fusion of abstract design with feeling and representational values is one of the major problems of art expression. The design, the sculptural form is of course fundamental but it is necessary to vitalize this through emotion and verisimilitude, else the work becomes cold and remote. Over and above the tactile organization of lines, planes and masses should brood the mystery of a living thing.

[FROM *Letters of John B. Flannagan* (New York: Curt Valentin, 1942).]

"The Stone-Cutter" is timeless and *haunted* by the *old human* dreams so old-prehistoric; yet the Artist does *remember*. The Alligator called the "Dragon Motif" carved by a chisel that *thinks* and *feels* fascinated by the *wonder* and terror that must have made the fearsome phantasy that was the *"Monster Motif Phantasy."* The great longing of the *wishful-rebirth phantasy* that is in "Jonah." These things are not *conscious,* may be *unconscious,* thought only *by hand* and just now I realize the *fish* (as in Jonah) is the very ancient symbol of the Female Principle so "Jonah and the Whale the Rebirth Motif."

ALEXANDER CALDER

• In an interview, Alexander Calder, a pioneer of Kinetic Sculpture, explains the origin and significance of his mobiles.

[FROM Katherine Kuh, *The Artist's Voice* (New York: Harper & Row, 1960).]

QUESTION: Which has influenced you more, nature or modern machinery?

CALDER: Nature. I haven't really touched machinery except for a few elementary mechanisms like levers and balances. You see nature and then you try to emulate it. But, of course, when I met Mondrian I went home and tried to paint. The basis of everything for me is the universe. The simplest forms in the universe are the sphere and the circle. I represent them by disks and then I vary them. My whole theory about art is the disparity that exists between form, masses and movements. . . . Even my triangles and spheres, but they are spheres of a different shape.

QUESTION: How do you get that subtle balance in your work?

CALDER: You put a disk here and then you put another disk that is a triangle at the other end and then you balance them on your finger and keep on adding. I don't use rectangles—they stop. You can use them; I have at times but only when I want to block, to constipate movement.

QUESTION: How did the mobiles start?

CALDER: The mobiles started when I went to see Mondrian. I was impressed by several colored rectangles he had on the wall. Shortly after that I made some mobiles; Mondrian claimed his paintings were faster than my mobiles.

QUESTION: What role does color play in your sculpture?

CALDER: Well, it's really secondary. I want things to be differentiated. Black and white are first—then red is next—and then I get sort of vague. It's really just for differentiation, but I love red so much that I almost want to paint everything red. I often wish that I'd been a *fauve* in 1905.

QUESTION: Do you think that your early training as an engineer has affected your work?

CALDER: It's made things simple for me that seem to confound other people, like the mechanics of the mobiles. I know this, because I've had contact with one or two engineers who understood my methods. I don't think the engineering really has much to do with my work; it's merely the means of attaining an aesthetic end.

QUESTION: How do your mobiles differ from your stabiles in intention?

CALDER: Well, the mobile has actual movement in itself, while the stabile is back at the old painting idea of implied movement. You have to walk around a stabile or through it—a mobile dances in front of you. You can walk through my stabile in the Basle museum. It's a bunch of triangles leaning against each other with several large arches flying from the mass of triangles.

QUESTION: How did you begin to use sound in your work?

CALDER: It was accidental at first. Then I made a sculpture called Dogwood with three heavy plates that gave off quite a clangor. Here sound was just another variation. You see, you have weight, form, size, color, motion, and then you have noise.

DAVID SMITH

• Nonconformist in both his art and his opinions, America's greatest sculptor, David Smith, spoke eloquently of his own art and of the place of sculpture in modern culture.

[FROM "A Symposium on Art and Religion," *Art Digest,* December 15, 1953.]

It is a little late even to toy with the idea that art has any chance with ideologies better served by plaster saints, television, radio and Tin Pan Alley. Whole segments of Christianity still shun art which was part of the aggrandizement, pomp, and corruption of the Roman church before the Reformation. The association of art with the graven and golden image likewise makes art taboo.

The truly creative art of our time cannot play an important part in organized religion because the traditions are diametrically opposed. The artist is not involved with translation. He is not dedicated to a program or a faith other than his work, which for him is a different kind of faith from religious faith. His profundities and philosophy are himself, delicately hidden from verbalizers and proselytizers. His freedom to conceive in visual terms is greater than any other freedom of our time. To produce at his highest, he cannot be harnessed to any doctrine.

There is a particular sense of rightness which inspiration and conviction give to the work of art, wholly personal and individual, which organized religion does not understand.

The artist's tradition antedates Christianity by 30,000 years and encompasses pagan cultures which Christianity has attempted to destroy.

[FROM "Thoughts on Sculpture," *College Art Journal,* Winter, 1954.]

I do not believe that any two people see the same sculpture, simply because no two people see each other.

In the same way, no two people see the same apple. The reality of an apple is not a mono image of stopped action, nor a photo view. The reality is actually all apples and all views; it is an associative image. The red apple may be green, or yellow, or black, spotted or striped. It may be halved with the core, or against the core, or segmented. It may be sweet, sour, rotten, sensuously felt, hanging, rolling, crushed to juice, the blossom flower or a bud. The recording of the apple image can go on indefinitely, interlocked with associations until it becomes personal history.

In sculpture or painting, if the artist chooses to depict the image denoting apple, the eye sees and the spirit knows, but the knowing is not all the same. The artist has presented the form for perceptual response. The definition is selected from the experience of the beholder. The apple and its mode of presentation are only the spark to fire the viewer's imagination.

There were no words in the artist's creation; no words are involved in understanding. No judgment, no logic, no conclusion, no set of values outside of man's world, no form involved which the eye of man has not seen. The mind records everything the eye sees. In spirit, or more technically, in perception, all men are potentially equal. Man's lack of visual perception does not represent a lack of ability. Instead, it may be a case of censoring, originating in the doubt that that which cannot be verbally explained, cannot be perceived.

Perception through vision is a highly accelerated response, so fast, so free that it is too complex to tabulate, but nevertheless a natural reaction since the origin of man. The comparatively recent mode of word communication cannot act as a substitute for the perception of form. There are not enough words in the language, nor can the relatively slow conscious mind keep up to record the vision.

As an example, based on the most simple element in use by both sculptor and painter, let me pose a question to black. Is it white? Is it day or night? Good or evil? Positive or negative? Is it life or death? Is it the superficial scientific explanation about the absence of light? Is it a solid wall or is it space? Is it paint, a man, a father? Or does black mean nothing? Did it come out blank having been censored out by some unknown or unrecognizable association? There is no one answer. Black is no one thing. It is many things. The answer depends upon individual reaction. The importance of black depends upon the conviction and the artistic projection of black, the mytho-poetic view, the myth of black. And to the creative mind, the dream and the myth of black is the truth of black, not the scientific theory or dictionary explanation or the philosopher's account of black. Black, as a word, or as an image recall, flashes in the mind as a dream, too fast for any rational word record. But its imagery is all involved by the artist when he uses black on a brush.

From the artist there is little accent on moral judgment, no conscious involvement with his historic position, no conscious effort to find universal truth or beauty, no analyzing of other men's minds in order to speak for them. His act in art is an act of personal conviction and identity. If there is truth in art, it is his own truth.

It is doubtful if aesthetics has any value to the creative artist, except as reading matter. It is doubtful if it has any value to his historic understanding of art, because his history of art is built upon the visual record of art and not written accounts made on a basis of speculation.

From the philosophic-aesthetic point of view, at the time of creation the contemporary work of art is a vulgarization. By vulgar I mean the Oxford definition, "offending against refinement of good taste." This describes where the advance schools of art rate with most critical opinion now, and how Van Gogh, Cézanne and Cubism were regarded by the critics of their time. The work of art does not change. The mellow of time, the pedant's talk, only legitimize it in the minds of the audience who may wish to hear, but refuse to see.

The influential majority of aestheticians are at present a quarter of a century or more behind art. Thus the contemporary artist cannot be impressed by the written directives on art. His directives are emotional and intuitive, arising from contemporary life. To make art the artist must deal with unconscious controls, the intuitive forces which are his own convictions. Those especial and individual convictions that set his art apart from that of other men are what permit him to project beyond the given art history. This takes blind conviction, for if his contribution is original, it stands little chance of acceptance from the reactionary or status quo authorities.

Aesthetics usually represent the judgments which lesser minds hold as rules to keep the creative artist inside the verbal realm and away from his visual world. Actually the philosophy of art and the history of art have nothing to do with creative artist's point of view. Both are in entirely different fields. But the layman is apt to become confused if he is not able to make this differentiation. He often expects the artist to perform according to the philosopher's truth theorems or the didactic historian's speculations.

When we speak of the creative artist we must speak of affection—intense affection which the artist has for his work. An affection, along with belligerent vitality and conviction. Can the critics, the audience, the art philosophers ever possess the intensity of affection which the creator possessed? Do they extend affection and vitality into the effort of understanding? Can they project this intense affection to the work of art? Or do they miss it?

In his regard for nature the contemporary artist stands in much the same position as primitive man. He accepts nature, intuitively. He becomes a part of nature. He is not the superman, the pseudo-scientist in nature. He accepts it for its own statement as existence. He marvels. Nature is beauty. Beauty becomes the point of departure—for celebration to produce the work of art. The work of art can have subject to any degree of abstracting or the artist himself is the subject for celebration or identification.

Often the artist is asked to explain his work. Naturally he cannot, but in one instance I have recalled a few motivations in the procedure of a sculpture. This work, later called *Hudson River Landscape,* has been exhibited at the University of Illinois and elsewhere.

This sculpture came in part from dozens of drawings made on a train between Albany and Poughkeepsie, a synthesis of ten trips over a 75 mile stretch. Later, while drawing, I shook a quart bottle of India ink and it flew over my hand. It looked like my river landscape. I placed my hand on paper. From the image that remained, I travelled with the landscape, drawing other landscapes and their objects, with additions, deductions, directives, which flashed unrecognized into the drawing, elements of which are in the sculpture. Is my sculpture the Hudson River? Or is it the travel and the vision? Or does it matter? The sculpture exists on its own; it is an entity. The name is an affectionate designation of the point prior to travel. My object was not a word justification or the Hudson River but it may travel on any river—rivers are much the same—or on a higher level, the viewer may travel through his own form response arrived at through his own recall.

I have identified only part of the related clues. The sculpture possesses nothing unknown to any man. I want the viewer to travel by perception the path I travelled in creating it. The viewer always has the privilege of rejecting it. He can like it, or almost like it. He may feel hostile toward it, if it demands more than he is capable of extending. But its understanding can only come by affection and visual perception, which were the elements in its making. My own words cannot make it understood and least of all, the words of others.

[FROM "Second Thoughts on Sculpture," *College Art Journal,* Spring, 1954.]

When the artist starts to make his own statement, he must recognize that he is a product of his time, that what has gone before is his heritage, and from his particular vantage point, his purpose is to project beyond. He will identify himself with his filial epoch, which is only his present history, probably not many decades back, possibly only as far back as the oldest artists of his time. But whatever distance back he accepts as his filial heritage, his concept must press beyond the art of his time and in this sense he must always work towards that which he doesn't know. Many artists of my generation feel that Cézanne is the beginning of their filial epoch.

In the 20th century, Cézanne used the room still life ratio of viewing for the distant landscape. The Cubist views were from all distances—the room, far away, in equal stature and in actual identification with the artist. It may have been Kandinsky during Cubism's first decade, who moved farthest, paralleled by Mondrian, but here the move was not only in distance but in identity. Both painters were moving independently farther from the object identity.

The contemporary artist has not only inherited the feeling of moving and distance on the earth plane but also possesses the newly found distance element of viewing vertically down, from which view the current mode of travel gives him the working tenet.

Poetically he has known that pattern is form. That chiaroscuro is not his age. That no area can be indicated without man's intuitive vision projecting the dimension. Practically he sees the fallacy of any two-dimensional supposition. This two-dimensional reference which critics have used to distinguish painting from sculpture seems to be the most abstract kind of thought. Especially when he reflects that the thicknesses of some of Van Gogh and Cézanne's paintings have been equal or greater than the dimensional contrasts of Han dynasty tomb carving.

And yet the work of the advanced artist is not influenced so much by his physical position in distance or the contradictions in rationale but by the poetic position, that irrational creative state upon which his whole approach depends.

Most important in this poetic point of viewing has been his moving and the lengthening of distance between the artist and the object. He has moved so far away from the object that he meets it from the other side, consumes it, and becomes the object himself, leaving only two factions involved, the artist and his work. The artist is now his own nature, the work is the total art. There is no intermediary object. The artist has now become the point of departure. Like many changes in art critically termed revolutions, this position is not wholly new, it has occurred in art before to some degree. This represents a closer position to the total or ultimate degree. His new position is somewhat that of primitive man. He is not the scientific viewer of nature. He is a part of nature. He is the nature in the work of art.

Art history is one thing to the art historian and another to the creative artist. Art history to the artist is visual. His art is not made up of historian's words of judgments. His choices are made the same way he makes the work of art—by the visual, irrational, creative. His history is a selection of his own preferences. His visionary reconstruction goes farther back in the history of man than the evidence. His history may even leave a few openings for mythical reconstruction or epochs destroyed or lying still buried. Actually the artist by his working reference to art of the past is often the discoverer of new value, in historically unimportant epochs, and the first to pick out the art value in work which was previously viewed as ethnographic only.

The artist sees a wholly different set of masterpieces than those the art historians have chosen to acclaim. He first sees the forms of the Venus of Willendorf before those of Melos. He sees the structures of Braccelli before the ripples of Michelangelo. A Cameroon head, a sepik mask before a Mona Lisa. Using his visual art references he will go to an earlier and perhaps neglected period and pick out an approach that is sympathetic to his own time. In Chinese Rei Sho character writing, the graphic aim was to show force as if carved or engraved in steel. In Japanese painting the power intent was suggested by conceiving a stroke outside the paper, continuing through the drawing space to project beyond, so that the included part possessed both power origin and projection. Even accident—which is never accident but intuitive fortune—was explained. If drops fall, they become acts of providence. If the brush flows dry into hairmarks, such may be greater in energy. And that in the painting certain objects possessing force, the sentiment of strength must be evoked and felt [*sic*]. I do not cite these tenets to show that we are direcly influenced by oriental art. The forces involved have occurred in art without declaration. The visual aesthetic the artist retains by memory of an Assyrian wounded lion frieze is still more his aesthetic on the power stroke than the oriental statement.

In contemporary work, force, power, ecstasy, structure, intuitive accident, statements of action dominate the object. Or they power the object with belligerent vitality. Probably the fact that man the artist can make works of art direct without the object meets opposition by its newness. Possibly this direct approach is a gesture of revolt representing the new freedom, unique in our time. Possibly there is a current ecstasy in the artist's new position much like that of 1910–12 Cubism.

From the artist there is no conscious effort to find universal truth or beauty, no effort to analyze other men's minds in order to speak for them. His act in art is an act of personal conviction and identity. If there is truth in art, it is his own truth. If beauty is involved, it is only the metaphor of imagination.

Chapter Ten

Toward an American Architecture

LOUIS SULLIVAN

• Louis Sullivan and his pupil Frank Lloyd Wright were prolific writers, keenly aware of the problems of the fine artist, particularly the architect, in a democracy. Outraged by eclecticism, Sullivan maintained, "when we ask an architect to build a memorial to the Great Lakes, the primeval forests and the hardy voyageurs—and he gives us a Doric column, he is not a scholar, he is a faker!" Urging the creation of a distinctly American functionalist architecture, independent of European models, Sullivan advocated an art expressive both of the democratic spirit and the modern age. In a series of lectures ("Kindergarten Chats") published serially in 1901 in the *Interstate Architect of Cleveland, Ohio,* Sullivan sought for architecture a new foundation on the "formation of a plastic alphabet." Revised in 1918, "Kindergarten Chats" analyze and redefine the most basic and rudimentary concepts of structure and ornament; they provide a source not only for Wright's ideas on organic architecture, but for many of the soundest principles still active in American architecture.

As Henri had done in painting, Sullivan rejected academic methods and urged individual self-expression. And as Henri insisted on the social role of art, Sullivan emphasized the social function of architecture. Even more poetic and Whitmanesque in his prose than the less articulate Henri, Sullivan stressed the role of the artist in a democracy as the thinker, the inquirer, the seeker, and above all, the worker. When, in 1939, the address Sullivan delivered to the Architectural League of America in 1900 was reprinted in a magazine, the editor concluded that the "Burning and true words in 1900 [are] burning and true in 1939." Some might even hold that they are still burning and true.

Toward an American Architecture

[FROM "The Young Man in Architecture," *Twice a Year,* Spring–Summer, 1939.]

It is my premise that the Architectural League of America has its being in a sense of discontent with conditions now prevailing in the American malpractice of the architectural art; in a deep and wide sense of conviction that no aid is to be expected from the generation now representing that malpractice; and in the instinctive feeling that, through banding together, force, discretion and coherence may be given to the output of these feelings which are, in themselves, for the time being, vague and miscellaneous, however intensely they may be felt.

Did I not believe that this statement substantially represents the facts, I should be the last to take an interest in your welfare; I would be indifferent concerning what you did or what you did not.

That you have abundant reason for discontent needs no proof: Let him read who runs through the streets.

That you have cause for discontent is evident. That you should *feel* discontent gives one a delightfully cynical sense of shock, and a newborn desire to believe in the good, the true, the beautiful, and the young.

American architecture is composed, in the hundred, of ninety parts aberration, eight parts indifference, one part poverty, and one part Little Lord Fauntleroy. You can have the prescription filled at any architectural department store, or select architectural millinery establishment.

In truth the American architecture of today is the offspring of an illegitimate commerce with the mongrel styles of the past.

Do not deceive yourselves for a moment as to this.

It is a harsh indictment.

But it is warranted by the facts.

Yet let us not be too severe. Let us remember and make what allowance we may for the depressing, stultifying, paralyzing influence of an unfortunate education.

After all, every American man has had to go to school. And everything that he has been taught over and above the three R's has been in essence for his mental undoing.

I cannot possibly emphasize this lamentable fact too strongly.

And the reason, alas, is so clear, so forcible, so everpresent, as you will see.

We live under a form of government called Democracy. And we, the people of the United States of America constitute the most colossal instance known in history of a people seeking to verify the fundamental truth that self-government is Nature's law for Man.

It is of the essence of Democracy that the individual man is free in his body and free in his soul.

It is a corollary therefrom, that he must govern or restrain himself, both as to bodily acts and mental acts; that in short he must set up a responsible government within his own individual person.

It implies that highest form of emancipation, of liberty physical, mental, and spiritual, by virtue whereof man calls the gods to judgment, while he needs the divinity of his own soul.

It is the ideal of Democracy that the individual man should stand self-centered, self-governing, an individual god.

• A pioneer of multistory architecture, Sullivan in his analysis of the problems of the skyscraper wrote in 1896 a classic essay in American architecture.

[FROM *Kindergarten Chats and Other Writings* (New York: Wittenborn, Schultz, 1947).]

The architects of this land and generation are now brought face to face with something new under the sun—namely, that evolution and integration of social conditions, that special group of them, that results in a demand for the erection of tall office buildings.

It is not my purpose to discuss the social conditions; I accept them as the fact, and say at once that the design of the tall office building must be recognized and confronted at the outset as a problem to be solved—a vital problem, pressing for a true solution.

Let us state the conditions in the plainest manner. Briefly, they are these; offices are necessary for the transaction of business; the invention and perfection of the high-speed elevators make vertical travel, that was once tedious and painful, now easy and comfortable; development of steel manufacture has shown the way to safe, rigid, economical constructions rising to a great height; continued growth of population in the great cities, consequent congestion of centers and rise in value of ground, stimulate an increase in number of stories; these successfully piled one upon another, react on ground values—and so on, by action and reaction, interaction and inter-reaction. Thus has come about that form of lofty construction called the "modern office building." It has come in answer to a call, for in it a new group of social conditions has found a habitation and a name.

Up to this point all in evidence is materialistic, an exhibition of force, of resolution, of brains in the keen sense of the word. It is the joint product of the speculator, the engineer, the builder.

Problem: How shall we impart to this sterile pile, this crude, harsh, brutal agglomeration, this stark, staring exclamation of eternal strife, the graciousness of those higher forms of sensibility and culture that rest on the lower and fiercer passions? How shall we proclaim from the dizzy height of this strange, weird, modern housetop the peaceful evangel of sentiment, of beauty, the cult of a higher life?

This is the problem; and we must seek the solution of it in a process analogous to its own evolution—indeed, a continuation of it—namely, by proceeding step by step from general to special aspects, from coarser to finer considerations.

It is my belief that it is of the very essence of every problem that it contains and suggests its own solution. This I believe to be natural law. Let us examine, then, carefully the elements, let us search out this contained suggestion, this essence of the problem.

The practical conditions are, broadly speaking, these:

Wanted—First, a story below-ground, containing boilers, engines of various sorts, etc.—in short, the plant for power, heating, lighting, etc. Second, a ground floor, so called, devoted to stores, banks, or other establishments requiring large area, ample spacing, ample light, and great freedom of access. Third, a second story readily accessible by stairways—this space usually in large subdivisions, with corresponding liberality in structural spacing and expanse of glass and breadth of external openings. Fourth, above this an indefinite number of stories of offices piled tier upon tier, one tier just like another tier, one office just like all the other offices—an office being similar to a cell in a honeycomb, merely a compartment, nothing more. Fifth, and last, at the top of this pile is placed a space of story that, as related to the life and usefulness of the structure, is purely physiological in its nature —namely, the attic. In this the circulatory system completes itself and makes its grand turn, ascending and descending. The space is filled with tanks, pipes, valves, sheaves, and mechanical etcetera that supplement and complement the force-originating plant hidden below-ground in the cellar. Finally, or at the beginning rather, there must be on the ground floor a main aperture or entrance common to all the occupants or patrons of the building. . . .

[The imperative voice of emotion] demands of us, what is the chief characteristic of the tall office building? And at once we answer, it is lofty. This loftiness is to the artist-nature its thrilling aspect. It is the very open organ tone in its appeal. It must be in turn the dominant chord in his expression of it, the true excitant of his imagination. It must be tall, every inch of it tall. The force and power of altitude must be in it, the glory and pride of exaltation must be in it. It must be every inch a proud and soaring thing, rising in sheer exultation that from bottom to top it is a unit without a single dissenting line—that it is the new, the unexpected, the eloquent peroration of most bald, most sinister, most forbidding conditions. . . .

All things in nature have a shape, that is to say, a form, an outward semblance that tells us why they are, that distinguishes them from ourselves and from each other.

Unfailingly in nature these shapes express the inner life, the native quality of the animal, tree, bird, fish, that they present to us; they are so characteristic, so recognizable, that we say, simply, it is "natural" it should be so. Yet the moment we peer beneath this surface of things, the moment we look through the tranquil reflection of ourselves and the clouds above us, down into the clear, fluent, unfathomable depth of nature, how startling is the silence of it, how amazing the flow of life, how absorbing the mystery. Unceasingly the essence of things is taking shape in the matter of things, and this unspeakable process we call birth and growth. Awhile the spirit and the matter fade away together, and it is this that we call decadence, death. These two happenings seem jointed and interdependent, blended into one like a bubble and its iridescence, and they seem borne along upon a slowly moving air. This air is wonderful past all understanding.

Yet to the steadfast eye of one standing upon the shore of things, looking chiefly and most lovingly upon that side on which the sun shines and that we feel joyously to be life, the heart is ever gladdened by the beauty, the exquisite spontaneity, with which life seeks and takes on its forms in an accord perfectly responsive to its needs. It seems ever as though the life and the form were absolutely one and inseparable, so adequate is the sense of fulfillment.

Whether it be the sweeping eagle in his flight or the open apple blossom, the toiling work horse, the blithe swan, the branching oak, the winding stream at its base, the drifting clouds, over all the coursing sun, form ever follows function, and this is the law. Where function does not change form does not change. The granite rocks, the ever-brooding hills, remain for ages; the lightning lives, comes into shape, and dies in a twinkling.

It is the pervading law of all things organic, and inorganic, of all things physical and metaphysical, of all things human and all things superhuman, of all true manifestations of the head, of the heart, of the soul, that the life is recognizable in its expression, that form ever follows function. This is the law.

Shall we, then, daily violate this law in our art? Are we so decadent, so imbecile, so utterly weak of eyesight, that we cannot perceive this truth so simple, so very simple? Is it indeed a truth so transparent that we see through it but do not see it? Is it really then, a very marvelous thing, or is it rather so commonplace, so everyday, so near a thing to us, that we cannot perceive that the shape, form, outward expression, design or whatever we may choose, of the tall office building should in the very nature of things follow the functions of the building, and that where the function does not change, the form is not to change?

Does this not readily, clearly, and conclusively show that the lower one or two stories will take on a special character suited to the special needs, that the tiers of typical offices, having the same unchanging function, shall continue in the same unchanging form, and that as to the attic, specific and conclusive as it is in its very nature, its function shall equally be so in force, in significance, in continuity, in conclusiveness of outward expression? From this results, naturally, spontaneously, unwittingly, a three-part division, not from any theory, symbol or fancied logic.

And thus the design of the tall office building takes its place with all other architectural types made when architecture, as has happened once in many years, was a living art. Witness the Greek temple, the Gothic cathedral, the medieval fortress.

And thus, when native instinct and sensibility shall govern the exercise of our beloved art; when the known law, the respected law, shall be that form ever follows function; when our architects shall cease struggling and prattling handcuffed and vainglorious in the asylum of a foreign school; when it is truly felt, cheerfully accepted, that this law opens up the airy sunshine of green fields, and gives to us a freedom that the very beauty and sumptuousness of the outworking of the law itself as exhibited in nature will deter any sane, any sensitive man from changing into license, when it becomes evident that we are merely speaking a foreign language with a noticeable American accent, whereas each and every architect in the land might, under the benign influence of this law, express in the simplest, most modest, most natural way that which it is in him to say; that he might really and would surely develop his own characteristic individuality, and the architectural art with him would certainly become a living form of speech, a natural form of utterance, giving surcease to him and adding treasures small and great to the growing art of his land; when we know and feel that Nature is our friend, not our implacable enemy—that an afternoon in the country, an hour by the sea, a full open view of one single day, through dawn, high noon, and twilight, will suggest to us so much that is rhythmical, deep, and eternal in the vast art of architecture, something so deep, so true, that all the narrow formalities, hard and fast rules, and strangling bonds of the schools cannot stifle it in us—then it may be proclaimed that we are on the high-road to a natural and satisfying art, an architecture that will soon become a fine art in the true, the best sense of the word, an art that will live because it will be of the people, for the people, and by the people.

FRANK LLOYD WRIGHT

• Eloquent and implacable, Frank Lloyd Wright represents the extreme type of individualist—the individualist as genius. The first American artist profoundly to influence European art, Wright shared with Stieglitz a concern with quality in place of quantity, and a disgust with compromise and mediocrity that meant he had flatly to reject most of what he saw around him. Wright's criticism of the skyscraper and urban centralization are prophetic of the greatest achievements of twentieth-century architecture.

[FROM "The New Architecture: Principles," in *Writings and Buildings* (New York: Horizon Press, 1960). Copyright Frank Lloyd Wright Foundation.]

I—The Earth Line

Principle one: Kinship of building to ground. This basic inevitability in organic architecture entails an entirely new sense of proportion. The human figure appeared to me, about 1893 or earlier, as the true *human* scale of architecture. Buildings I myself then designed and built—Midwest—seemed, by means of this new scale, to belong to man and at the moment especially as he lived on rolling Western prairie. Soon I had occasion to observe that every inch of height there on the prairie was exaggerated. All breadths fell short. So in breadth, length, height, and weight, these buildings belonged to the prairie just as the human being himself belonged to it with his gift of speed. The term "streamlined" as my own expression was then and there born.

As result, the new buildings were rational: low, swift, and clean, and were studiously adapted to machine methods. The quiet, intuitional, horizontal line (it will always be the line of human tenure on this earth) was thus humanly interpreted and suited to modern machine performance. Machine methods and these new streamlined, flat-plane effects first appeared together in our American architecture as expression of new ways to reach true objectives in building. The main objective was gracious appropriation of the art of architecture itself to the Time, the Place, and Modern Man.

What now is organic "design"? Design appropriate to modern tools, the machine, and this new human scale. Thus, design was opportune, and well within the architect's creative hand if his mind was receptive to these relatively new values: moving perception at this time with reverential spirit toward the understanding of the "nature of nature." The nature of the machine, studied by experiment and basically used in structural design, was still to be limited to a tool, and proved to be a powerful new medium of expression. Buildings before long were evidencing beautiful simplicity, a fresh exuberance of countenance. Originality.

Never did I allow the machine to become a "motif"—always machine for man and never man for machine. Ever since, in organic architecture I have used the machine and evolved a system of building from the inside out, always according to the nature of both man and machine—as I could see it—avoiding the passing aspects now characteristic of urban architecture. The machine I found a better means to broaden the humane interest in modern architecture. Nor, in point of style, have I once looked upon the machine as in itself an end, either in planning or building or style. Quantity has never superseded quality.

II—Impulse To Grow

Principle two: Decentralization. The time for more individual spaciousness was long past due. In 1893 I saw urban-decentralization as inevitable because of a growing necessity, seeking more space everywhere, by whatever steps or stages it was obtainable. Space, short of breath, was suffocating in an airless situation, a shameful imposition upon American life. Then, as now, the popular realtor with his "lot" was the enemy of space; he was usually busy adding limitation to limitation, rounding up the herd and exploiting the ground for quick profit.

Indigestible competition, thus added to the big city, despoiled the villages. Overextended verticality then congested to hold the profits of congestion was added to the congestion already fashioned on the ground.

To offset the senselessness of this inhuman act, I prepared the Broadacre City models at Taliesin in 1932. The models proposed a new space concept in social usage for individual and community building. But the whole establishment was laid out in accordance with the conditions of land tenure already in effect. Though the centers were kept, a new system of subdivision was proposed.

Later, this model of the broader use of ground for a new idea of a new city was carefully studied in detail in a series of smaller tributary models, all as described in *When Democracy Builds,* a book I later wrote on the suggestion of Robert Hutchins. Buildings, roads, planting, habitation, cultivation, decoration, all became as architectural as they were in Umbria in Italy in the Middle Ages; qualities of ancient sort in modern form for modern times, considered in terms of modern humane utility. Thus broadened, the view of architecture as basic now in service to society came as relief and gave a preview of primary form facing the law of the changes inevitable.

Therefore quantity—the machine source—was in no way, nor anywhere, at any time, to be used to hinder the quality of new resources for human profit and delight in living. Living was to be a quality of man's own spirit.

III—Character Is a Natural

Three: Appropriate "character" is inevitable to all architecture if organic. Significance of any building would clearly express its objective, its purpose—whether store, apartment building, bank, church, hotel, or pie club, factory, circus, or school. Fundamental requirement, this should apply to all building, in ground-planning and, especially, relative to human life and its site. This means sane appropriation of imaginative design to specific human purposes, by the natural use of nature-materials or synthetics, and appropriate methods of construction. Our new resources already evolved by science, especially glass and steel wrought by the machine, are bound continually to develop new forms. Continually new ways and shapes of building will continue to give fresh character and true significance to all modern structure.

Poetic tranquility instead of a more deadly "efficiency," should be the consequence in the art of Building: concordant, sane, exuberant, and appropriate to purpose. Durable, serviceable, economical. Beautiful. In the ever-changing circumstances of complex modern existence all this is not too easy to accomplish and the extent of these evolving changes may not yet be fully seen but as architects we may thus reconstitute architecture in our hearts and minds and act to rewrite our dated "codes" and refrain from disfiguring our American landscape by buildings or "service" systems.

IV—Tenuity plus Continuity

Four: Completely new character by these simple means came to architecture; came to view, not by haphazard use, but by organic interpretation, of steel and glass. Steel gave rise to a new property: I call it *tenuity*. Tenuity is simply a matter of tension (pull), something never before known in the architecture of this world. No building could withstand a pull. Push it you might and it would stay together but pull on it and it would fall apart. With tensile strength of steel, this pull permits free use of the cantilever, a projectile and tensile at the same time, in building design. The outstretched arm with its hand (with its drooping fingers for walls) is a cantilever. So is the branch of a tree.

The cantilever is essentially steel at its most economical level of use. The principle of the cantilever in architecture develops tenuity as a wholly new human expression, a means, too, of placing all loads over central supports, thereby balancing extended load against opposite extended load. This brought into architecture for the first time another principle in construction—I call it *continuity*—a property which may be seen as a new, elastic, cohesive *stability*. The creative architect finds here a marvelous new inspiration in design. A new freedom involving far wider spacings of more slender supports. Thus architecture arrived at construction from within outward rather than from outside inward; much heightening and lightening of proportions throughout all building is now economical and natural, space extended and utilized in a more liberal planning than the ancients could ever have dreamed of. This is now prime characteristic of the new architecture called organic.

Rigid box shapes, outsides steel-framed, belong strictly to the nineteenth century. They cannot be twentieth century architecture. Support at rigid corners becomes mere obstruction: corners themselves now insignificant become extravagant waste, mere accents of enclosure. Construction lightened by means of cantilevered steel in tension, makes continuity a most valuable characteristic of architectural enlightenment. Our new architectural freedom now lies within this province. In the character of this new circumstance buildings now may proceed *from within outward:* Because push or pull may be integral to building design.

V—The Third Dimension: Interpretation

Five: To sum up, organic architecture sees the third dimension never as weight or mere thickness but always as *depth*. Depth an element of space; the third (or thickness) dimension transformed to a *space* dimension. A penetration of the inner depths of space in spaciousness becomes architectural and valid motif in design. With this concept of depth interpenetrating depths comes flowering a freedom in design which architects have never known before but which they may now employ in their designs as a true liberation of life and light within walls; a new structural integrity; outside coming in; and the space within, to be lived in, going out. Space outside becomes a natural part of space *within* the building. All building design thus actually becomes four-dimensional and renders more static than ever the two-dimensional effects of the old static post and girder, beam and box frame type of construction, however novel they seem to be made. Walls are now apparent more as humanized screens. They do define and differentiate, but never confine or obliterate space. A new sense of reality in building construction has arrived.

Now a new liberation may be the natural consequence in every building exterior. The first conscious expression of which I know in modern architecture of this *new reality*—the "space within to be lived in"—was Unity Temple in Oak Park. True harmony and economic elements of beauty were consciously planned and belong to this new sense of space-within. The age-old philosophy of Laotze is alive in architecture. In every part of the building freedom is active. Space [is] the basic element in architectural design.

This affirmation, due to the new sense of "the space within" as reality, the original affirmative negation (the great protestant) 1904, the Larkin Building of Buffalo—now demolished. Here came the poetic principle of freedom itself as a new revelation in architecture. This new freedom that was first consciously demonstrated in Unity Temple, Oak Park (1906) as written in 1927 for AN AUTOBIOGRAPHY. With this new principle at work in our American architecture came a new sense of style as innate. A quality natural to the act and art of modern habitation: no longer applied by "taste" (Again: "such as the life is such is the form"—Coleridge gives us perhaps a better slogan that Form Follows Function.) For American as for all shades and shapes of human beings everywhere "style" becomes generic: poetic expression of character. Style is intrinsic—or it is false. As a characteristic of the "space within to be lived in"—the life of style is perpetually fresh.

VI—Space

Six: Space, elemental to architecture, has now found architectural expression. Glass: air in air, to keep air out or keep it in. Steel, a strand slight and strong as the thread of the spider spinning, is able now to span extraordinary spaces. By new products of technology and increased inventive ingenuity in applying them to building construction many superlative new space-forms have already come alive: and, because of them, more continually in sight. Some as a matter of course will be novel but insignificant; some will be significant and really new. But more important, modern building becomes the solid creative art which the poetic principle can release and develop. Noble, vital, exuberant forms are already here. Democracy awakes to a more spiritual expression. Indigenous culture will now awaken. Properly focused upon needs of twentieth century life, new uses of livable space will continually evolve, improved; more exuberant and serene. A new security and a new tranquility. Enlightened enjoyment of fresh beauty is here or due.

VII—Form

Seven: Anyone anything of an architect will never be content to design a building merely (or chiefly) for the picture it makes—any more than a man would buy a horse merely by its color. What kind of intellect must the critic have who seeing a building judges it by "the look of it," ignorant of the nature of its construction?

For the first time in 500 years a sense of architectural form appears as a new spiritual integrity.

Heavy walls, senseless overheads, and overloads of every sort, vanish —let us be glad. Light and thin walls may now depend from cantilever slabs supported from the interior on shallow, dry-wall footings, walls themselves becoming slender screens, entirely independent of use as support. Centralized supports may stand isolated, balancing load against load—seen not as walls at all, but as integral pattern; walls may be slender suspension from point to point, in fascinating pendant forms. In general, structure now becomes an affair from the inside outward instead of from the outside inward. Various geometrical forms (circular especially) in planning structure become more economical than the square of the box. Building loads may be suspended, suspension supported by slender, isolated uprights. Glass or light plastics may be used to fill in and make the whole habitable. Sheet metal and light metal castings afford a permanent material for the exteriors of such structures. Enclosures extremely light in weight combined with such structural elements relieve all modern building of surplus static; structure no longer an obesity or likely to fall of its own weight. Walls require little or no floor space. Spaces hitherto concealed or wasted or made impossible by heavy walls are revealed and made useful. Arrangements for human occupation in comfort may be so well aimed that spaciousness becomes economical as well as beautiful, appearing where it was never before thought to exist. . . .

Organic Unit

Thus environment and building are one: Planting the grounds around the building on the site as well as adorning the building take on new importance as they become features harmonious with the space-within-to-be-lived-in. Site, structure, furnishing—decoration too, planting as well—all these become as one in organic architecture. What was once called "decorating"—landscaping, lighting, etc.—and modern gadgetry (mechanical fixtures like air conditioning) all are within the building structure as features of the building itself. Therefore all are elements of this synthesis of features of habitation and harmonious with environment. This is what *posterity* will call "modern architecture."

VIII—Shelter: Inherent Human Factor

Eight: As interior space to be lived in becomes the reality of building so shelter thus emphasized becomes more than ever significant in character and important as a feature. Shelter is still a strange disorder when reduced to a flat lid—though a common desire on account of economy. *To qualify this common-sense desire for shelter* as most significant feature of architecture is now in organic architecture of greatly increased importance. Witness, for instance: The new sense of spaciousness requires, as inherent human factor, significant cover as well as shade. Cover therefore now becomes in itself a feature more important as architectural form: Solidity of walls vanishing to reappear as imaginative screens involving light, and as inevitable consequence leaving more responsibility to the shapes and shaping of the whole building "overhead" with direct reference to the elements. Radical structural changes too now make the overhead lighter, less an imposition, more graceful, more harmonious feature of environment. Organic architecture sees shelter not only as a quality of space but of spirit, and the prime factor in any concept of building man into his environment as a legitimate feature of it. Weather is omnipresent and buildings must be left out in the rain. Shelter is dedicated to these elements. So much so that almost all other features of design tend to lead by one another to this important feature, shelter, and its component shade. In order to complete the building, protecting all within it from every changing circumstance of light, of cold and heat, wear and tear and usage, we require shelter. The occupants of a building readily discover greater opportunity for comfort and more gracious, expanded living wherever shelter is becoming shade. By shade, charm has been added to character; style to comfort; significance to form.

• Wright's extraordinary grasp of the interaction of aesthetic, social, and economic conditions led him to make some of the most incisive general criticisms of American culture that our literature contains.

[FROM "World Architecture," quoted from *A Testament* (1957), in *Writings and Buildings* (New York: Horizon Press, 1960).]

Machine standardization is apparently growing to mean little that is inspiring to the human spirit. We see the American workman himself becoming the prey of gangsterism made official. Everything as now professionalized, in time dies spiritually. Must the innate beauty of American life succumb or be destroyed? Can we save truth as beauty and beauty as truth in our country only if truth becomes the chief concern of our serious citizens and their artists, architects and men of religion, independent of established authority?

Nevertheless I realize that if all false or unfriendly forces (due to ignorance or so conditioned as here described) inimical to culture, were to become less and less, many long years would still be needed to overcome the deep habituations that have been built into the American scene by inroads upon the American character; wholly against natural grain and against our glorious original aim. If this twentieth century architecture, true to the principles of construction and more in line with our democratic faith, were to be more widely acknowledged by established authority; even if it were to be proclaimed from the housetops by cinema, television, press, politics, government, and society as "the right thing" to be studied and practiced—there would still be controversy. Controversy would, even then, continue for the coming half-century at least, would perhaps never cease. Democracy knows only too well the senseless weight and conflicts of irresponsible public opinion, the chronic oralism, the dead weight of ignorance, the prejudices of conditioned minds siding right or left with selfish interests of hearts hardened—instead of the deep faith in Man necessary to inspire enlightenment by generosity of motive, which democracy meant to our forefathers and must yet mean to us. The common sense of the simple truth in this new-old philosophy, *from within outward,* if awakened in our society as now in our architecture, would ensure the true uses of technology for human shelter and reverential harmonious environment, both socially and politically. It would soon get into politics.

Meanwhile we continue to hope that the Comic Spirit in which we as a people do excel may survive long enough to salt and savor life among us long enough for our civilization to present us to the world as a culture, not merely as an amazing civilization. The basic distinction between the curious and the beautiful, in which culture really consists, will make all the difference between a society with a creative soul and a society with none.

Bibliography

Most works cited in the source notes are not included in the Bibliography.

GENERAL

Art in America, LIII, No. 4 (August–September, 1965). Archives of American Art issue.

BARKER, VIRGIL. "Americanism in Painting," *Yale Review* (Summer, 1936).

———. *A Critical Introduction to American Painting.* New York: Whitney Museum of American Art, 1931.

———. *From Realism to Reality in Recent American Painting.* Lincoln, Neb.: University of Nebraska Press, 1959.

BAUR, JOHN I. H. *Revolution and Tradition in Modern American Art.* New York: Frederick A. Praeger, 1967.

CAHILL, HOLGER, and BARR, ALFRED H., JR. *Art in America in Modern Times.* New York: Reynal & Hitchcock, 1934.

CORTISSOZ, ROYAL. *American Artists.* New York: Scribner's, 1923.

GELDZAHLER, HENRY. *American Painting in the Twentieth Century.* New York: Metropolitan Museum of Art, 1965.

GOODRICH, LLOYD. *American Genre.* New York: Whitney Museum of American Art, 1935.

———. *Three Centuries of American Art.* New York: Frederick A. Praeger, 1966.

GOODRICH, LLOYD, and BAUR, JOHN I. H. *American Art of Our Century.* New York: Frederick A. Praeger, 1961. Catalogue of the Whitney Museum Collection.

HARTMANN, SADAKICHI. *A History of American Art.* 2 vols. Rev. ed. Boston: Page, 1932.

HUNTER, SAM. *Modern American Painting and Sculpture.* New York: Dell Publishing Co., 1959.

Index of Twentieth-Century Artists. New York: College Art Association, 1933–37. A bibliography on American artists.

LARKIN, OLIVER W. *Art and Life in America.* Rev. ed. New York: Holt, Rinehart & Winston, 1964.

MCCAUSLAND, ELIZABETH. "A Selected Bibliography on American Painting and Sculpture," in *Who's Who in American Art.* Washington, D.C.: American Federation of Arts, 1947, IV, 611–53. Originally appeared in the *Magazine of Art,* XXXIX (November, 1946), 329–49.

MCCOUBREY, JOHN W. *American Tradition in Painting.* New York: George Braziller, 1963.

MATHER, FRANK J., JR., *et al. The American Spirit in Art.* New Haven, Conn.: Yale University Press, 1927.

PACH, WALTER. *Modern Art in America.* New York: Kraushaar Galleries, 1928.

ROSE, BARBARA. *American Art Since 1900: A Critical History.* New York: Frederick A. Praeger, 1967.

ROSENBERG, BERNARD, and FLIEGEL, NORRIS E. "The Vanguard Artist in New York," *Social Research,* XXXII, No. 2 (Summer, 1965), 141 ff.

WHEELER, MONROE. *Painters and Sculptors of Modern America.* New York: Thomas Y. Crowell, 1942.

CHAPTER ONE

"Artists of the Philadelphia Press," *Philadelphia Museum Bulletin,* XLI (November, 1945).

BAUR, JOHN I. H. *The Eight.* New York: Brooklyn Museum, 1934.

BROOKS, VAN WYCK. *John Sloan: A Painter's Life.* New York: E. P. Dutton, 1955.

GLACKENS, IRA. *William Glackens and the Ashcan Group.* New York: Grosset & Dunlap, 1957.

GOODRICH, LLOYD. *Thomas Eakins: His Life and Work.* New York: Whitney Museum of American Art, 1933.

HENRI, ROBERT. *The Art Spirit.* Compiled by Margery A. Reyerson. Philadelphia: J. B. Lippincott, 1960.

———. "My People," *Craftsman,* XXVII (February, 1915).

———. "Review of the Independent Show, 1910," *Craftsman,* XVIII (May, 1910).

HOPPER, EDWARD. "John Sloan and the Philadelphians," *The Arts,* XI (April, 1927).

KATZ, LESLIE. "The Centenary of Maurice Prendergast," *Arts,* XXXIV (November, 1960).

———. "The Eight," *Arts Yearbook,* No. 1 (1957).

New York Realists, 1900–1914. New York: Whitney Museum of American Art, 1937.

PACH, WALTER. "The Eight Then and Now," *Art News,* XLII (January 1–14, 1944).

PERLMAN, BENNARD P. *The Immortal Eight: American Painting from Eakins to the Armory Show.* New York: Exposition Press, 1962.
POTTER, MARGARET. *George Bellows.* New York: Gallery of Modern Art, 1965.
READ, HELEN A. *Robert Henri.* New York: Whitney Museum of American Art, 1931.
SHINN, EVERETT. "Recollections of the Eight," in *The Eight.* Brooklyn: Brooklyn Institute of Arts and Sciences, 1943. Catalogue of the Brooklyn Museum Exhibition, November 24, 1943–January 16, 1944.
SLOAN, JOHN. *The Gist of Art.* New York: American Artists Group, 1939.
———. *John Sloan's New York Scene.* Ed. Bruce St. John, with an Introduction by Helen Farr Sloan. New York: Harper & Row, 1965.

CHAPTER TWO

America and Alfred Stieglitz. Ed. W. Frank, L. Mumford, D. Norman, P. Rosenfeld, H. Rugg. New York: Doubleday, Doran & Co., 1934.
"An American Collection," *Philadelphia Museum Bulletin,* XL (May, 1945).
BENSON, EMANUEL M. *John Marin, The Man and His Work.* New York: Museum of Modern Art, 1935.
BENTON, THOMAS HART. "America and/or Alfred Stieglitz," *Common Sense,* IV (January, 1935).
CAHILL, HOLGER. *Max Weber.* New York: Downtown Gallery, 1930.
Camera Work, 1902–17.
COKE, VAN DEREN. *Taos and Santa Fe: The Artist's Environment, 1882–1942.* Albuquerque: University of New Mexico, 1963.
DOW, A. W. "Talks on Art Appreciation," *The Delineator* (January, 1915).
GREENBERG, CLEMENT. "John Marin," in *Art and Culture.* Boston: Beacon Press, 1961.
HARTLEY, MARSDEN. *Adventures in the Arts: Informal Chapters on Painters, Vaudeville and Poets.* New York: Boni and Liveright, 1921.
———. "Art—and the Personal Life," *Creative Art,* II (June, 1928).
HARTMANN, SADAKICHI. "The Photo-Secession, A New Pictorial Movement," *Craftsman,* VI (April, 1904).
HELM, MACKINLEY. *John Marin.* New York: Pellegrini & Cudahy, 1948.
History of an American, Alfred Stieglitz: 291 and After. Exhibition Catalogue.
MCCAUSLAND, ELIZABETH. *A. H. Maurer.* New York: A. A. Wyn, 1951.
———. *Marsden Hartley.* Minneapolis, Minn.: University of Minnesota Press, 1952.
MARIN, JOHN. "A Few Notes," *Twice a Year,* No. 2 (1939).
———. "John Marin by Himself," *Creative Art,* III (October, 1928).
———. *Letters of John Marin.* Ed. H. J. Seligmann. New York: Pellegrini & Cudahy, 1931.
———. *Selected Writings of John Marin.* Ed. and with an Introduction by Dorothy Norman. New York: Pellegrini & Cudahy, 1949.

MELLQUIST, JEROME. *The Emergence of an American Art.* New York: Scribner's, 1942.
MILLER, DOROTHY C. *Lyonel Feininger and Marsden Hartley.* New York: Museum of Modern Art, 1944.
RICH, DANIEL CATTON. *Georgia O'Keeffe.* Chicago: Art Institute of Chicago, 1943. Exhibition Catalogue.
———. *Georgia O'Keeffe.* Worcester, Mass.: Worcester Art Museum, 1960. Exhibition Catalogue.
ROSENFELD, PAUL. *Port of New York: Essays on Fourteen American Moderns.* New York: Harcourt, Brace and Co., 1924.
STEIN, GERTRUDE. *The Autobiography of Alice B. Toklas.* New York: Modern Library, 1933.
STIEGLITZ, ALFRED. "Modern Pictorial Photography," *Century,* LXIV (October, 1902).
———. "Six Happenings," *Twice a Year,* Nos. 14–15 (1946–47).
———. "Stories, Parables and Correspondence," *Twice a Year,* Nos. 8–9 (1942).
291. Ed. Alfred Stieglitz. Nos. 1–12 (1915–16).
WEBER, MAX. "Chinese Dolls and Modern Colorists," *Camera Work,* No. 31 (July, 1910).
———. "The Fourth Dimension from a Plastic Point of View," *Camera Work,* No. 31 (July, 1910).
WIGHT, FREDERICK S. *Arthur G. Dove.* Berkeley: University of California Press, 1958.
WILLIAMS, W. C., PHILLIPS, D., and NORMAN, D. *John Marin.* Los Angeles, Calif.: University of California Press, 1955. Memorial Exhibition.
ZAYAS, MARIUS DE, and HAVILAND, PAUL. *A Study of the Modern Evolution of Plastic Expression.* New York: "291" Gallery, 1913.

CHAPTER THREE

BLASHFIELD, EDWARD. "The Painting of Today," *Century,* LXXXVII (April, 1914).
BRINTON, CHRISTIAN. "American Painting at the Panama-Pacific Exposition," *International Studio,* LXI (August, 1915).
———. "Evolution Not Revolution in Art," *International Studio,* XLIX (April, 1913).
BROWN, MILTON. *American Painting from the Armory Show to the Depression.* Princeton, N.J.: Princeton University Press, 1955.
———. *The Story of the Armory Show.* New York: Joseph H. Hirshhorn Foundation, 1963.
Catalogue of the Forum Exhibition. Anderson Gallery. New York: Hugh Kennerly, 1916.
Collection of the Société Anonyme. New Haven, Conn.: Yale University Art Gallery, 1950.

DU BOIS, GUY PÈNE. *Artists Say the Silliest Things.* New York: American Artists Group, 1940.
EDDY, ARTHUR J. *Cubists and Post-Impressionists.* Chicago: McClurg, 1914.
HAMBIDGE, J., and HAMBIDGE, G. "The Ancestry of Cubism," *Century,* LXXXVII (April, 1914).
KUHN, WALT. *The Story of the Armory Show.* New York: Privately printed, 1938. Supplemented by a similar article in the *Art News Annual* (1939).
MACCALL, W. D. "The International Exhibition of Modern Art," *Forum,* L (July–December, 1913).
MATHER, FRANK J., JR. "Newest Tendencies in Art," *The Independent,* LXXIV (March, 1913).
MELLQUIST, JEROME. "The Armory Show Thirty Years Later," *Magazine of Art,* XXXVI (December, 1943).
MEYERS, JEROME. *An Artist in Manhattan.* New York: American Artists Group, 1940.
PACH, WALTER. *Queer Thing, Painting.* New York: Harper & Bros., 1938.
PHILLIPS, DUNCAN. "Fallacies of the New Dogmatism in Art," *American Magazine of Art,* IX (January, 1918).
———. "Revolution and Reaction," *International Studio,* LI (November–December, 1913).
ROOSEVELT, THEODORE. "A Layman's Views of an Art Exhibition," *The Outlook,* XXIX (March 9, 1913).
SCHAPIRO, MEYER. "Rebellion in Art," in *America in Crisis.* Ed. Daniel Aaron. New York: Alfred A. Knopf, 1952.
TILLIM, SIDNEY. "Dissent on the Armory Show," *Arts,* XXXVII (May–June, 1963).
WRIGHT, WILLARD H. "An Abundance of Modern Art," *Forum,* LV (January–June, 1916).
———. "The Aesthetic Struggle in America," *Forum,* LV (January–June, 1916).

CHAPTER FOUR

AGEE, WILLIAM C. *Synchromism and Color Principles in American Painting.* New York: M. Knoedler & Co., 1965.
ANDREWS, EDWARD D., and ANDREWS, FAITH. "Sheeler and the Shakers," *Art in America,* LIII, No. 1 (February, 1965).
BAUR, JOHN I. H. *Joseph Stella.* New York: Whitney Museum of American Art, 1963.
———. "The Machine and the Subconscious: Dada in America," *Magazine of Art,* XLIV (October, 1951).
BREESKIN, ADELYN. *Roots of Abstract Art in America, 1910–1950.* Washington, D.C.: National Collection of Fine Arts, 1965.
BRINTON, CHRISTIAN. *Modern Art at the Sesqui-Centennial Exhibition.* New York: Société Anonyme, 1926.

BROWN, MILTON. "Cubist-Realism: An American Style," *Marsyas,* III (1943–45).

BUFFET-PICABIA, GABRIELLE. "Some Memories of Pre-Dada: Picabia and Duchamp," in *Dada Painters and Poets.* Ed. Robert Motherwell. New York: Wittenborn, Schultz, 1951.

BURCHFIELD, CHARLES. "On the Middle Border," *Creative Art,* III (September, 1928).

DASBURG, ANDREW. "Cubism—Its Rise and Influence," *The Arts,* IV (November, 1923).

DOCHTERMAN, LILLIAN. *The Quest of Charles Sheeler.* Iowa City: State University of Iowa Press, 1963.

FALSON, S. LANE. "Fact and Art in Charles Demuth," *Magazine of Art,* XLIII (April, 1950).

FRIEDMAN, MARTIN. *The Precisionist View in American Art.* Minneapolis, Minn.: Walker Art Center, 1960.

GOODRICH, LLOYD. *Pioneers of Modern Art in America: The Decade of the Armory Show, 1910–1920.* New York: Frederick A. Praeger, 1963.

GORDON, JOHN. *Geometric Abstraction in America.* New York: Frederick A. Praeger, 1962.

HAMBIDGE, J., and HAMBIDGE, G. "The Ancestry of Cubism," *Century,* LXXXVII (April, 1914).

HAMILTON, GEORGE HEARD. "John Covert, Early American Modern," *College Art Journal,* XII, No. 1 (Fall, 1952), 37–42.

LANGSNER, JULES. *Man Ray.* Los Angeles, Calif.: Los Angeles County Art Museum, 1966.

LEBEL, ROBERT. *Marcel Duchamp.* New York: Grove Press, 1939.

MCBRIDE, HENRY. "A Hero Worshipped," *The Dial,* LXIX (July–December, 1920).

PACH, WALTER. *Modern Art in America.* New York: Kraushaar Galleries, 1928.

RITCHIE, ANDREW C. *Abstract Painting and Sculpture in America.* New York: Museum of Modern Art, 1951.

———. *Charles Demuth.* New York: Museum of Modern Art, 1950.

ROURKE, CONSTANCE. *Charles Sheeler: Artist in the American Tradition.* New York: Harcourt, Brace and Co., 1938.

RUBIN, WILLIAM. "Man Ray," *Art International,* VII, No. 6 (June, 1963).

SIMONSON, LEE. "No Embargos," *Creative Art,* VIII (April, 1931).

STELLA, JOSEPH. "The Brooklyn Bridge (A Page of My Life)," *transition,* Nos. 16–17 (June, 1929).

WOLF, BEN. *Morton Livingston Schamberg.* Philadelphia: University of Pennsylvania Press, 1963.

WRIGHT, WILLARD H. *American Painting and Sculpture.* New York: Museum of Modern Art, 1932.

———. *The Future of Painting.* New York: B. W. Huebsch, 1923.

———. *Modern Painting.* New York: John Lane, 1915.

CHAPTER FIVE

ABELL, WALTER. "The Limits of Abstraction," *Magazine of Art,* XXVIII (December, 1935).

American Abstract Artists. Annual Exhibition Catalogue and checklist from 1937.

ARNASON, H. H. *Stuart Davis.* Washington, D.C.: National Collection of Fine Arts, 1965.

BALDINGER, W. S. "Formal Change in Recent American Painting," *Art Bulletin,* XIX (December, 1937).

BARR, ALFRED H., JR. *Cubism and Abstract Art.* New York: Museum of Modern Art, 1936.

BAUR, JOHN I. H. *Charles Burchfield.* New York: Whitney Museum of American Art, 1956.

BENTON, THOMAS HART. *An Artist in America.* Rev. ed. Kansas City: University of Kansas City Press, Twayne Publishers, 1951.

BLUME, PETER. "After Surrealism," *The New Republic,* LXXX (October 3, 1934).

BREESKIN, ADELYN. *Milton Avery.* New York: American Federation of Arts, 1960.

BURROUGHS, ALAN. *Kenneth Hayes Miller.* New York: Whitney Museum of American Art, 1931.

CAHILL, HOLGER. *Art as a Function of Government.* Washington, D.C.: Federal Art Project, 1937.

———. *New Horizons in American Art.* New York: Museum of Modern Art, 1936.

CAMPBELL, LAWRENCE. "Paintings from WPA," *Art News* (September, 1961).

CHENEY, MARTHA C. *Modern Art in America.* New York: McGraw-Hill Book Co., 1939.

CRAVEN, THOMAS. *Men of Art.* New York: Simon & Schuster, 1931.

———. *Modern Art—the Men, the Movements, the Meaning.* New York: Simon & Schuster, 1934.

———. "Naturalism in Art," *Forum,* XCV (January–June, 1936).

———. *Thomas Hart Benton.* New York: Associated American Artists, 1939.

DAVID, STUART. "Abstract Art in the American Scene," *Parnassus,* XIII (March, 1941).

———. "Abstract Painting," *Art of Today* (April, 1935).

———. "Arshile Gorky in the 1930's, A Personal Recollection," *Magazine of Art,* XLIV (February, 1951).

FARBER, MANNY. "Jack Levine," *Art News* (March, 1955).

GALLATIN, A. E. *Museum of Living Art.* New York: George Grady Press, 1940. A. E. Gallatin Collection.

GEIST, SIDNEY. "Prelude: The 1930's," *Arts,* XXX (September, 1956).
GOODRICH, LLOYD. *Edward Hopper.* New York: Whitney Museum of American Art, 1964.
———. *Pioneers of Modern Art in America.* New York: Whitney Museum of American Art, 1946.
GOOSSEN, E. C. *Stuart Davis.* New York: George Braziller, 1959.
GORKY, ARSHILE. "Stuart Davis," *Creative Art,* IX (September, 1931).
GRAHAM, JOHN D. *System and Dialectics of Art.* New York: Delphic Studios, 1937.
GREENBERG, CLEMENT. "Milton Avery," in *Art and Culture.* Boston: Beacon Press, 1961.
———. "New York Painting Only Yesterday," *Art News* (Summer, 1957).
HOPPER, EDWARD. "Charles Burchfield, American," *The Arts,* XIV (July, 1928).
KIRSTEIN, LINCOLN, and LEVY, J. *Murals by American Painters and Photographers.* New York: Museum of Modern Art, 1932.
KOOTZ, SAMUEL. *Modern American Painters.* New York: Brewer and Warren, 1930.
KRAMER, HILTON. "The Legendary John Graham," *The New York Times,* May 29, 1966, Sec. 2, p. 13.
LARKIN, OLIVER. *Twenty Years of Paintings by Philip Evergood.* New York: Whitney Museum of American Art, 1947.
MILLER, DOROTHY C., and BARR, ALFRED H., JR. (eds.). *American Realists and Magic Realists.* With Statements by the Artists and an Introduction by Lincoln Kirstein. New York: Museum of Modern Art, 1943.
MORRIS, GEORGE L. K. *American Abstract Art.* New York: St. Etienne Galerie, May 22–June 12, 1940. Exhibition Catalogue.
MORRIS, GEORGE L. K., and KIRSTEIN, LINCOLN. "Life or Death for Abstract Art?," *Magazine of Art,* XXXVI (March, 1943).
O'CONNOR, FRANCIS V. *Federal Art Patronage, 1933–1943.* College Park, Md.: University of Maryland Press, 1966.
O'DOHERTY, BRIAN. "Portrait: Edward Hopper," *Art in America,* LII, No. 6 (December, 1964).
PEARSON, RALPH. "The Failure of the Art Critics," *Forum and Century,* XCIV (November, 1935–January, 1936).
Plastique (Paris), No. 3 (1938). Special number dedicated to American Art.
SCHAPIRO, MEYER. "The Nature of Abstract Art," *Marxist Quarterly,* I (January–March, 1937).
———. "Populist Realism," *Partisan Review,* IV (December, 1937–May, 1938). Review of Thomas Hart Benton autobiography.
SOBY, JAMES T. *Ben Shahn.* New York: Museum of Modern Art, 1947.
The 30's: Painting in New York. New York: Poindexter Gallery, 1957. Text by Edwin Denby. Exhibition Catalogue.
WHEELER, MONROE. *Painters and Sculptors of Modern America.* New York: Museum of Modern Art, 1942.

WIGHT, FREDERICK S. *Hyman Bloom.* Boston: Institute of Contemporary Art, 1954.
WILSON, EDMUND. *The American Earthquake.* New York: Doubleday & Co., 1958.

CHAPTER SIX

BAUR, JOHN I. H. *Bradley Walker Tomlin.* New York: Whitney Museum of American Art, 1957.
———. *Nature in Abstraction.* New York: Whitney Museum of American Art, 1958.
BLESH, RUDI. *Modern Art USA.* New York: Alfred A. Knopf, 1956.
DAVENPORT, RUSSELL (ed.). "A *Life* Round Table on Modern Art," *Life* (October 11, 1948).
"Eleven Europeans in America," *Museum of Modern Art Bulletin,* XIII, Nos. 4–5 (1946).
GREENBERG, CLEMENT. "The Present Prospects of American Painting and Sculpture," *Horizon* (October, 1947).
GUGGENHEIM, PEGGY. *Confessions of an Art Addict.* New York: The Macmillan Co., 1960.
———. *Out of This Century.* New York: Dial Press, 1946.
HUNTER, SAM. "Jackson Pollock," *Museum of Modern Art Bulletin,* XXIV, No. 2 (1956–57).
"The Ides of Art: The Attitude of Ten Artists," *Tiger's Eye,* No. 2 (December, 1947).
Jackson Pollock. New York: Marlborough-Gerson Gallery, 1964. Exhibition Catalogue.
JANIS, SIDNEY. *Abstract and Surrealist Art in America.* New York: Reynal & Hitchcock, 1944.
KOOTZ, SAMUEL, and ROSENBERG, HAROLD. *The Intrasubjectives.* New York: Kootz Gallery Exhibition Catalogue, September 14–October 3, 1949.
MOTHERWELL, ROBERT. "The Modern Painter's World," *Dyn,* VI (1944).
———. "Painter's Objects," *Partisan Review,* XI (Winter, 1944).
O'CONNOR, FRANCIS K. "The Genesis of Jackson Pollock: 1912 to 1943." Unpublished Ph.D. dissertation, Johns Hopkins University, 1965.
O'HARA, FRANK. *Jackson Pollock.* New York: George Braziller, 1959.
The Peggy Guggenheim Collection. London: British Arts Council, 1964. Exhibition at the Tate Gallery, December 31, 1964–March 7, 1965.
"La Peinture aux Etats-Unis," *Art d'aujourd'hui* (June, 1951). Special number.
PEREIRA, I. R. "An Abstract Painter on Abstract Art," *American Contemporary Art* (October, 1944).
POLLOCK, JACKSON. *Jackson Pollock.* Ed. Bryan Robertson. New York: Harry N. Abrams, 1960.
ROSENBERG, HAROLD. *Arshile Gorky.* New York: Grove Press, 1962.

RUBIN, WILLIAM. "Arshile Gorky, Surrealism and the New American Painting," *Art International,* VII, No. 2 (February 25, 1963).
———. "Notes on Masson and Pollock," *Arts,* XXXIII (November, 1959).
SCHAPIRO, MEYER. "Gorky: The Creative Influence," *Art News* (September, 1957).
SCHWABACHER, ETHEL K. *Arshile Gorky.* New York: Whitney Museum of American Art, 1957.
———. *Arshile Gorky: Memorial Exhibition.* New York: Whitney Museum of American Art, 1951.
SEITZ, WILLIAM C. "Abstract Expressionist Painting in America." Unpublished Ph.D. dissertation, Princeton University, 1955.
———. *Arshile Gorky.* New York: Museum of Modern Art, 1962.
———. *Hans Hofmann.* New York: Museum of Modern Art, 1963.
———. *Mark Tobey.* New York: Museum of Modern Art, 1962.
Tiger's Eye. Nos. 1–9 (1947–49). Ed. R. and J. Stephan.
VVV. Nos. 1–4 (1924–44). Ed. David S. Hare. Editorial advisers: A. Breton, M. Duchamp, M. Ernst.

CHAPTER SEVEN

ALLOWAY, LAWRENCE. *Barnett Newman: The Stations of the Cross.* New York: Solomon R. Guggenheim Museum, 1966.
———. "The New American Painting," *Art International,* III, Nos. 3–4 (1959).
———. "Sign and Surface: Notes on Black and White Painting in New York," *Quadrum,* No. 9 (1960).
American Paintings: 1945–1957. Minneapolis, Minn.: Minneapolis Institute of Arts, 1957.
American Vanguard. Washington, D.C.: United States Information Agency, 1961–62.
ARNASON, H. H. *Abstract Expressionists and Imagists.* New York: Solomon R. Guggenheim Museum, 1961.
Artforum (September, 1965). A special number devoted to Abstract Expressionism.
ASHTON, DORÉ. *Philip Guston.* New York: Grove Press, 1959.
———. *The Unknown Shore: A View of Contemporary Art.* Boston: Little, Brown and Co., 1962.
BRYANT, EDWARD. *Jack Tworkov.* New York: Whitney Museum of American Art, 1964.
Catalogues of the annual exhibitions: Art Institute of Chicago; Whitney Museum of American Art; Corcoran Gallery; University of Illinois Biennial; "Americans" exhibitions, Museum of Modern Art, selected by Dorothy Miller.
Clyfford Still: Paintings in the Albright-Knox Art Gallery. Buffalo, N.Y.: Buffalo Fine Arts Academy, 1966.

Contemporary American Painting. Columbus, Ohio: Columbus Gallery of Fine Arts, 1960.

DE KOONING, ELAINE. *Franz Kline.* Washington, D.C.: Washington Gallery of Fine Art, 1962. Memorial Exhibition Catalogue.

Expressionism 1900–1955. Minneapolis, Minn.: Walker Art Center, 1955.

The Face of the Fifties. Ann Arbor, Mich.: University of Michigan Art Museum, 1961.

FRIEDMAN, B. H. (ed.). *School of New York: Some Younger Artists.* New York: Grove Press, 1959.

FRIEDMAN, MARTIN. *Adolph Gottlieb.* Minneapolis, Minn.: Walker Art Center, 1963.

GOLDWATER, ROBERT. "Reflections on the New York School," *Quadrum,* No. 8 (1960), pp. 17–36.

———. "Reflections on the Rothko Exhibit," *Arts,* XXXV (March, 1961).

GOOSSEN, E. C. "The Big Canvas," *Art International,* II, No. 8 (November, 1958).

———. "Clyfford Still, Painting as Confrontation," *Art International,* IV, No. 1 (January, 1960).

———. "The Philosophic Line of Barnett Newman," *Art News* (Summer, 1958).

GOTTLIEB, ADOLPH. "Artist and Society, A Brief Case History," *College Art Journal,* XIV, No. 2 (Winter, 1955).

———. "My Paintings," *Arts and Architecture,* LXVIII (September, 1951).

GREENBERG, CLEMENT. "American-Type Painting" and "The Crisis of the Easel Picture," in *Art and Culture.* Boston: Beacon Press, 1961.

———. "The 'Crisis' of Abstract Art," *Arts Yearbook,* No. 7 (1964).

HAMILTON, GEORGE HEARD. *Josef Albers: Paintings, Prints, Projects.* New Haven, Conn.: Yale University Art Gallery, 1956.

———. "Object and Image: Aspects of the Poetic Principle in Modern Art," in *Object and Image in Modern Art and Poetry.* New Haven, Conn.: Yale University Art Gallery, 1954.

HESS, THOMAS B. *Abstract Painting: Background and American Phase.* New York: Viking Press, 1951.

———. *Willem de Kooning.* New York: George Braziller, 1959.

HUNTER, SAM. *Art Since 1950.* Catalogue, Seattle World's Fair, 1962.

———. "USA," in *Art Since 1945.* New York: Harry N. Abrams, 1958.

HUNTER, SAM, and LIPPARD, LUCY R. *Ad Reinhardt.* New York: Jewish Museum, 1966.

"Is Today's Artist With or Against the Past?," *Art News,* Part I (Summer, 1958); Part II (September, 1958).

KAVOLIS, VYANTAS. "Abstract Expressionism and Puritanism," *Journal of Aesthetics and Art Criticism* (Spring, 1963).

KOZLOFF, MAX. "The Impact of De Kooning," *Arts Yearbook,* No. 7 (1964).

———. "The Many Colorations of Black and White," *Artforum,* II, No. 8 (February, 1964).
MOTHERWELL, ROBERT. "The Painter and His Audience," *Perspectives USA,* No. 9 (Autumn, 1954).
MOTHERWELL, ROBERT, and REINHARDT, AD (eds.). *Modern Artists in America.* First Series. New York: Wittenborn, Schultz, 1952.
Museum of Modern Art Bulletin, XVIII, No. 3 (Spring, 1951). Statements by members of the New York School.
The New American Painting. New York: Museum of Modern Art, 1959.
New York School. Los Angeles, Calif.: Los Angeles County Museum of Art, 1965. Baziotes, De Kooning, Gorky, Gottlieb, Guston, Hofmann, Motherwell, Newman, Pollock, Pousette-Dart, Reinhardt, Rothko, Still, Tomlin.
O'HARA, FRANK. *Robert Motherwell.* With Selections from the Artist's Writings. New York: Museum of Modern Art, 1966.
Paintings by Clyfford Still. Buffalo, N.Y.: Albright-Knox Art Gallery, 1959.
ROSENBERG, HAROLD. *The Anxious Object.* New York: Horizon Press, 1964.
———. "Hans Hofmann's Life Class," *Art News Annual (Portfolio),* No. 6 (1962).
———. "Tenth Street: A Geography of Modern Art," *Art News Annual,* No. 28 (1959).
———. *Tradition of the New.* New York: Horizon Press, 1959.
ROSENBLUM, ROBERT. "Abstract Sublime," *Art News* (February, 1961).
RUBIN, WILLIAM. "Adolph Gottlieb," *Art International,* III, No. 3–4 (1959).
SCHAPIRO, MEYER. "The Liberating Quality of Abstract Art," *Art News* (Summer, 1957).
———. "The Younger American Painters of Today," *The Listener* (London) (January 26, 1956).
SEITZ, WILLIAM C. "Spirit, Time, and Abstract Expressionism," *Magazine of Art,* XLVI (February, 1953).
SELZ, PETER. *Mark Rothko.* New York: Museum of Modern Art, 1961.
SHARPLESS, TI-GRACE. *Clyfford Still.* Philadelphia: University of Pennsylvania Press, 1963.
60 *American Painters, 1960.* Minneapolis, Minn.: Walker Art Center, 1960.
SWEENEY, JAMES J. "Recent Trends in American Painting," *Bennington College Alumnae Quarterly,* VII, No. 1 (Fall, 1955).

CHAPTER EIGHT

ALLOWAY, LAWRENCE. *The Shaped Canvas.* New York: Solomon R. Guggenheim Museum, 1964.
———. *Six Painters and the Object.* New York: Solomon R. Guggenheim Museum, 1964.
———. *Systemic Painting.* New York: Solomon R. Guggenheim Museum, 1966.

CAGE, JOHN. *Silence.* Middletown, Conn.: Wesleyan University Press, 1961.

COPLANS, JOHN. "John McLaughlin, Hard Edge, and American Painting," *Artforum,* II, No. 7 (January, 1964).

Exhibition catalogues, Venice and São Paulo biennials.

FRIED, MICHAEL. "Frank Stella's New Paintings," *Artforum,* V, No. 3 (November, 1966).

———. *Kenneth Noland.* New York: Jewish Museum, 1965.

———. "Modernist Painting and Formal Criticism," *The American Scholar* (Autumn, 1964).

———. *Three American Painters.* Cambridge, Mass.: Fogg Art Museum, 1965. Olitski, Noland, Stella.

GOODRICH, LLOYD. *Young America 1965: Thirty American Artists Under Thirty-Five.* New York: Frederick A. Praeger, 1965.

GREENBERG, CLEMENT. "After Abstract Expressionism," *Art International,* VI, No. 8 (October 25, 1962).

———. "Louis and Noland," *Art International,* IV, No. 4 (May 25, 1960).

———. *Post-Painterly Abstraction.* Catalogue of the Los Angeles County Museum, 1964.

HOPPS, WALTER. *Catalogue of the VIII São Paulo Biennial.* Washington, D.C.: National Collection of Fine Arts, 1966. Additional bibliography: Larry Bell, Billy Al Bengston, Robert Irwin, Donald Judd, Barnett Newman, Larry Poons, Frank Stella.

HUNTER, SAM. *Larry Rivers.* New York: Jewish Museum, 1966.

KAPROW, ALLAN. "The Legacy of Jackson Pollock," *Art News* (October, 1958).

KIRBY, MICHAEL. *Happenings.* New York: E. P. Dutton, 1965.

LIPPARD, LUCY R. *Pop Art.* New York: Frederick A. Praeger, 1966.

MCSHINE, KYNASTON. *Josef Albers.* New York: Museum of Modern Art, 1964.

New Abstraction, Das Kunstwerk. XVIII, Nos. 10–12 (April–June, 1965).

OLDENBURG, CLAES. "The Artists Say," *Art Voices,* IV, No. 3 (Summer, 1965).

Richard Diebenkorn. Washington, D.C.: Gallery of Modern Art, 1964.

ROSENBLUM, ROBERT. "Morris Louis at the Guggenheim Museum," *Art International,* VII, No. 9 (December 5, 1963).

RUBIN, WILLIAM. "Ellsworth Kelly: The Big Form," *Art News* (November, 1963).

———. "Younger American Painters," *Art International,* IV, No. 1 (January, 1960).

SEITZ, WILLIAM C. *The Responsive Eye.* New York: Museum of Modern Art, 1964.

SOLOMON, ALAN. *Robert Rauschenberg.* New York: Jewish Museum, 1963.

———. *XXXII International Biennial Exhibition of Art, Venice 1964, United States of America.* New York: Jewish Museum, 1964. Chamberlain, Dine, Johns, Louis, Noland, Oldenberg, Rauschenberg, Stella.

STEINBERG, LEO. *Jasper Johns.* New York: George Wittenborn, 1963.

TILLIM, SIDNEY. "The New Avant-Garde," *Arts,* XXXVIII (February, 1964).
———. "Optical Art: Pending or Ending?," *Arts,* XXXIX (January, 1965).
———. "Realism and the Problem," *Arts,* XXXVII (September, 1963).
———. "What Happened to Geometry?," *Arts,* XXXIII (June, 1959).

CHAPTER NINE

ANDERSEN, WAYNE V. *The Sculpture of Herbert Ferber.* Minneapolis, Minn.: Walker Art Center, 1962.

ARNASON, H. H. *Theodore Roszak.* New York: Whitney Museum of American Art, 1956.

Arts Yearbook: Contemporary Sculpture. Introduction by William C. Seitz. No. 8 (1965).

Catalogues of the Whitney Museum of American Art Annual. (Sculpture and painting in alternate years.)

CONE, JANE HARRISON. *David Smith.* Cambridge, Mass.: Fogg Art Museum, 1965.

FORSYTH, ROBERT J. *John B. Flannagan.* Notre Dame, Ind.: University of Notre Dame Press, 1963.

GIEDION-WELCKER, CAROLA. *Contemporary Sculpture: An Evolution in Volume and Space.* New York: George Wittenborn, 1955. Calder, Ferber, Hare, Lassaw, Lippold, Lipton, Smith.

GOODALL, DONALD. "Gaston Lachaise, 1882–1935," *Massachusetts Review* (Summer, 1960).

GOOSSEN, E. C. "The End of the Object," *Art International,* III, No. 8 (1959).

GREENBERG, CLEMENT. "Cross-breeding of Modern Sculpture," *Art News* (Summer, 1952).

———. "David Smith" and "Modernist Sculpture, Its Pictorial Past," in *Art and Culture.* Boston: Beacon Press, 1961.

———. "David Smith's New Sculpture," *Art International,* VIII, No. 4 (May, 1964).

GREGOR, WAYLANDE. "The Present Impasse in Sculpture." First American Writers Congress, 1936.

GRIFFEN, HOWARD. "Auriga, Andromeda, Cameoleoparalis," *Art News* (December, 1957). On Joseph Cornell.

HESS, THOMAS B. "New Directions in American Sculpture," *Art News Annual (Portfolio),* No. 1 (1959).

HUNTER, SAM. "David Smith," *Museum of Modern Art Bulletin,* XXV, No. 1 (1957).

"The Ides of Art: 14 Sculptors Write," *Tiger's Eye,* No. 4 (June, 1948).

KIRSTEIN, LINCOLN. *Elie Nadelman.* New York: Museum of Modern Art, 1948.

———. *Gaston Lachaise.* New York: Museum of Modern Art, 1935.

KRAMER, HILTON. *David Smith.* Los Angeles, Calif.: Los Angeles County Museum of Art, November 3, 1965–January 30, 1966. Memorial Exhibition.

———. "The Sculpture of David Smith," *Arts,* XXXIV (February, 1960).

MCSHINE, KYNASTON. *Primary Structures.* New York: Jewish Museum, 1966.

MILLER, DOROTHY C. (ed.). *The Sculpture of John Flannagan.* New York: Museum of Modern Art, 1942.

MORRIS, GEORGE L. K. "Relations of Painting and Sculpture," *Partisan Review,* X (January–October, 1943).

———. "Le Sculpture Abstraite aux U.S.A.," *Art d'aujourd'hui* (January, 1953).

MORRIS, ROBERT. "Notes on Sculpture," *Artforum,* Part I, IV, No. 6 (February, 1966); Part II, V, No. 2 (October, 1966).

"The New Sculpture: A Symposium." New York: Museum of Modern Art, 1952. Typescript of a symposium with H. Ferber, R. Lippold, T. Roszak, and D. Smith.

NOGUCHI, ISAMU. "Meanings in Modern Sculpture," *Art News* (March, 1949).

O'HARA, FRANK. *Nakian.* New York: Museum of Modern Art, 1966.

RITCHIE, ANDREW C. *Sculpture of the Twentieth Century.* New York: Museum of Modern Art, 1952.

RUBIN, WILLIAM. "David Smith," *Art International,* VII, No. 9 (December 5, 1963).

SCHNIER, JACQUES. *Sculpture in Modern America.* Berkeley: University of California Press, 1948.

Sculpture in America Today. Los Angeles, Calif.: Los Angeles County Museum, 1967.

SEITZ, WILLIAM C. *The Art of Assemblage.* New York: Museum of Modern Art, 1961.

SMITH, DAVID. "The Language Is Image," *Arts and Architecture,* LXIX (February, 1952).

———. "The Secret Letter," in *David Smith.* New York: Marlborough-Gerson Gallery, 1964. Interview by Thomas B. Hess. Exhibition Catalogue.

SWEENEY, JAMES J. *Alexander Calder.* New York: Solomon R. Guggenheim Museum, 1964.

CHAPTER TEN

ANDREWS, WAYNE V. *Architecture, Ambition and Americans.* New York: The Free Press of Glencoe, 1964.

BURCHARD, JOHN, and BUSH-BROWN, ALBERT. *The Architecture of America.* Boston: Little, Brown and Co., 1961.

BUSH-BROWN, ALBERT. *Louis Sullivan.* New York: George Braziller, 1960.

Bibliography

CONDIT, CARL W. *The Chicago School of Architecture.* Chicago: University of Chicago Press, 1964.

HITCHCOCK, HENRY-RUSSELL. "Frank Lloyd Wright and the 'Academic Tradition' of the Eighteen-Nineties," *Journal of the Warburg and the Courtauld Institutes,* VII (January–June, 1944).

HITCHCOCK, HENRY-RUSSELL, and DREXLER, ARTHUR (eds.). *Built in USA: Post-War Architecture.* New York: Museum of Modern Art, 1952.

HITCHCOCK, HENRY-RUSSELL, and JOHNSON, PHILIP. *The International Style: Architecture Since 1922.* New York: W. W. Norton, 1932.

JACOBS, JANE. *The Death and Life of Great American Cities.* New York: Random House, 1961.

KIDDER SMITH, G. E. "The Tragedy of American Architecture," *Magazine of Art,* XXXVIII (November, 1945).

MOCK, ELIZABETH (ed.). *Built in the USA, 1932–1944.* New York: Museum of Modern Art, 1944.

MORRISON, HUGH. "Buffington and the Invention of the Skyscraper," *Art Bulletin,* XXVI (March, 1944).

MUMFORD, LEWIS. *Roots of Contemporary American Architecture.* New York: Grove Press, 1959.

———. *Sticks and Stones.* New York: Dover Publications, 1955.

SCHUYLER, MONTGOMERY. *American Architecture and Other Writings.* New York: Atheneum Publishers, 1964.

SCULLY, VINCENT J. "Archetype and Order in Recent American Architecture," *Art in America,* XLII, No. 6 (December, 1954).

———. *Frank Lloyd Wright.* New York: George Braziller, 1960.

STEIN, C. S. *Toward New Towns for America.* Cambridge, Mass.: The M.I.T. Press, 1966.

SULLIVAN, LOUIS H. *The Autobiography of an Idea.* New York: American Institute of Architects, 1924.

———. *Kindergarten Chats and Other Writings.* New York: Wittenborn, Schultz, 1947.

WRIGHT, FRANK LLOYD. *The Living City.* New York: Bramhall House, 1958.

———. *On Architecture.* New York: Duell, Sloan & Pearce, 1941.

———. *Writings and Buildings.* New York: Horizon Press, 1960.

PLATES*

* Unless otherwise noted, all paintings are oil on canvas.

1. MAURICE PRENDERGAST, *The East River,* 1901. Watercolor, 13¾" x 19¾". Collection The Museum of Modern Art, New York. Gift of Abby Aldrich Rockefeller

2. ROBERT HENRI, *Gypsy of Madrid,* 1924. 32″ x 26″. Courtesy Chapellier Galleries, New York

3. GUY PÈNE DU BOIS, *Father and Son,* 1929. 21½″ x 18″. Collection Whitney Museum of American Art, New York

4. WILLIAM GLACKENS, *Portrait of the Artist's Wife,* 1904. 75″ x 40″. Courtesy Wadsworth Atheneum, Hartford, Conn.

5. GEORGE BENJAMIN LUKS, *The Old Duchess,* 1905. 30″ x 25″. The Metropolitan Museum of Art, New York. George A. Hearn Fund, 1921

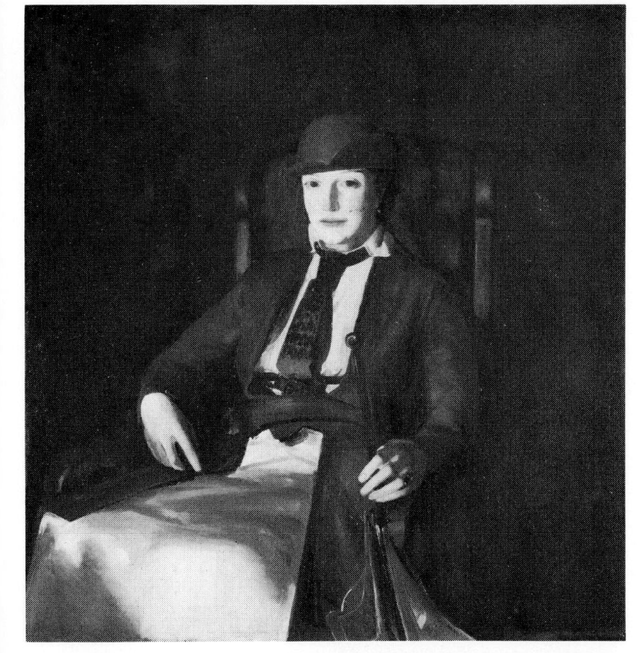

6. GEORGE BELLOWS, *Mrs. Chester Dale* (Maud Murray, 1883–1953), 1919. 42½″ x 40″. The Metropolitan Museum of Art, New York. Gift of the Chester Dale Collection, 1954

7. ALFRED MAURER, *Flowers, ca.* 1912. Oil on cardboard, 21¼″ x 18″. Collection Whitney Museum of American Art, New York

8. BEN BENN, *Mother and Child,* 1915. 36″ x 27″. Collection Whitney Museum of American Art, New York

9. JOHN SLOAN, *Sixth Avenue Elevated at Third Street,* 1928. 30″ x 40″. Collection Whitney Museum of American Art, New York

10. JOHN SLOAN, *Nude and Nine Apples,* 1937. Tempera and oil on composition board, 24″ x 30″. Collection Whitney Museum of American Art, New York

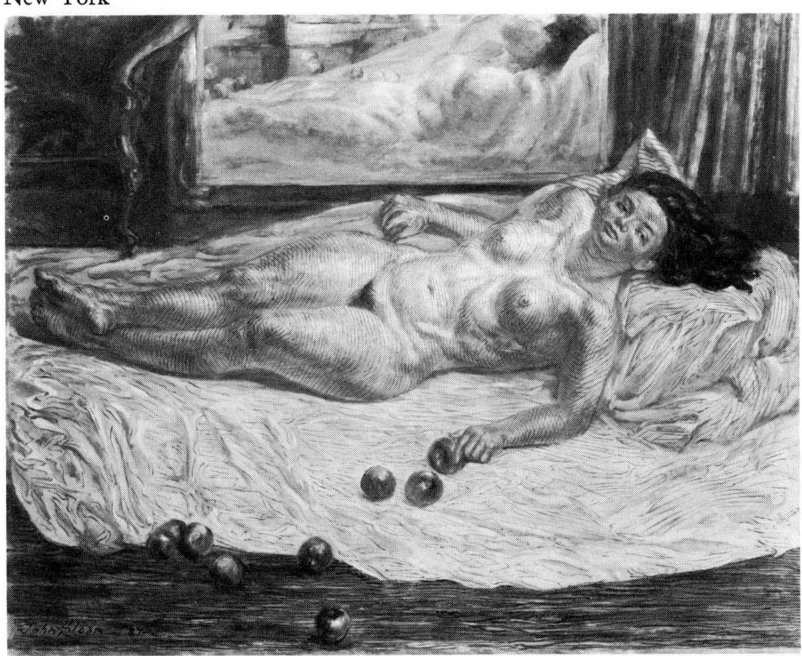

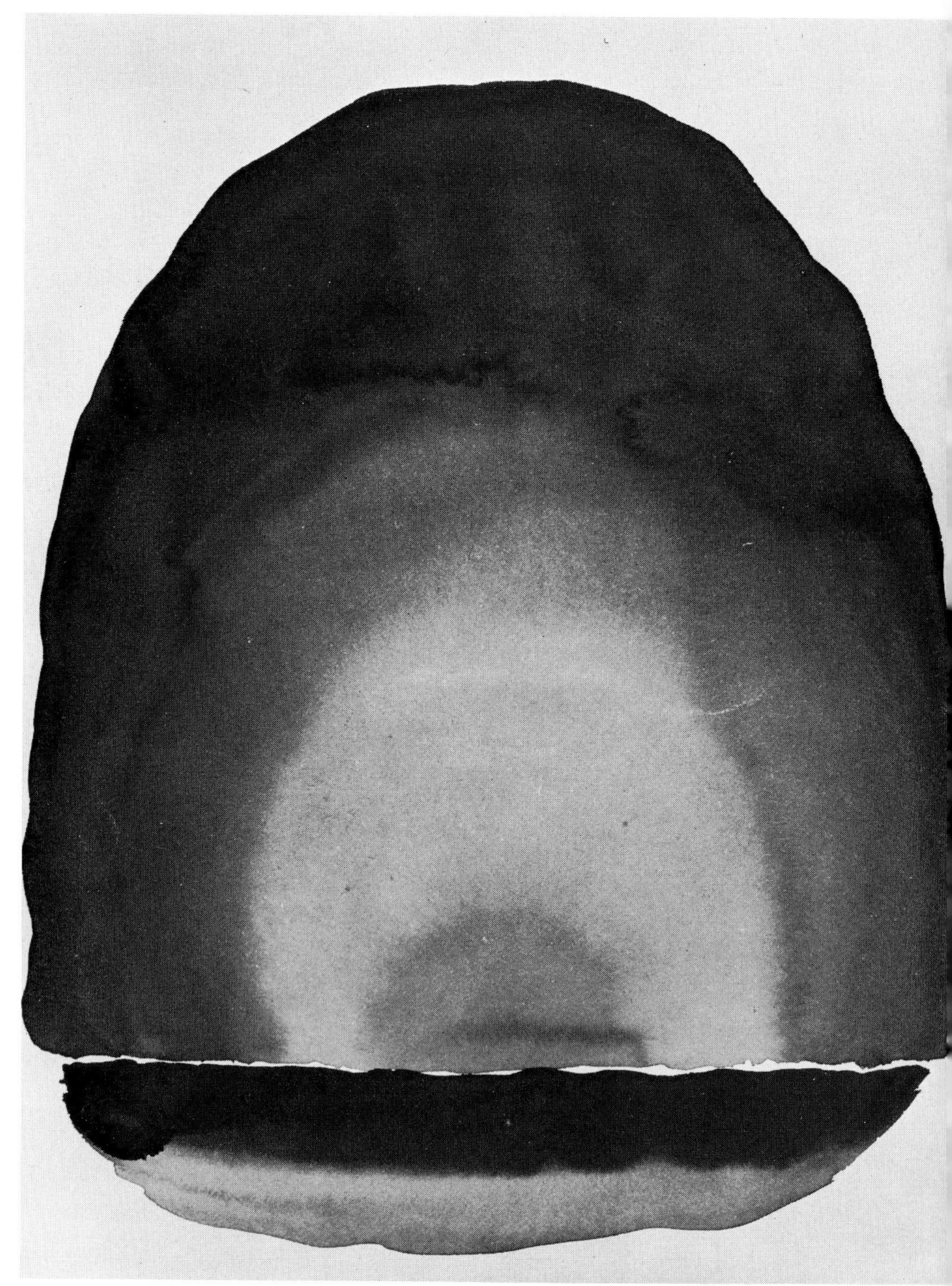

11. GEORGIA O'KEEFFE, *Light Coming on the Plains III,* 1917. Watercolor, 9″ x 12″. Courtesy The Downtown Gallery, New York

12. CHARLES DEMUTH, *August Lilies,* 1921. Watercolor, 11¾″ x 17⅞″. Collection Whitney Museum of American Art, New York

13. GEORGIA O'KEEFFE, *The White Flower,* 1931. 30″ x 36″. Collection Whitney Museum of American Art, New York

14. MARCEL DUCHAMP, *The Bride Stripped Bare by the Bachelors, Even,* 1912. Pencil drawing, 9″ x 13″. Courtesy Cordier & Ekstrom, Inc., New York

15. MARSDEN HARTLEY, *Military Symbols 2*, 1914. Charcoal on paper, 24¼" x 18¼". The Metropolitan Museum of Art, New York. Purchase, 1962, Rogers Fund

16. MORGAN RUSSELL, *Four Part Synchromy, Number 7*, 1914–15, 15⅜″ x 11½″.
Collection Whitney Museum of American Art, New York. Gift of the artist

17. STANTON MACDONALD-WRIGHT, *"Conception" Synchromy,* 1915. 30″ x 24″. Collection Whitney Museum of American Art, New York. Gift of George Of

18. CHARLES DEMUTH, *Buildings, Lancaster,* 1930. Oil on composition board, 24″ x 20″. Collection Whitney Museum of American Art, New York. Anonymous gift

19. ARTHUR B. CARLES, *Bouquet Abstraction, ca.* 1930. 31¾″ x 36″. Collection Whitney Museum of American Art, New York

20. OSCAR BLUEMNER, *Composition,* 1931. Oil on wood, 23″ x 30″. Collection Whitney Museum of American Art, New York

21. ANDREW DASBURG, *Taxco,* 1933. Watercolor, 14½″ x 21½″. Collection Whitney Museum of American Art, New York

22. JOHN MARIN, *Bryant Square,* 1932. 21½″ x 26½″. The Phillips Collection, Washington, D.C.

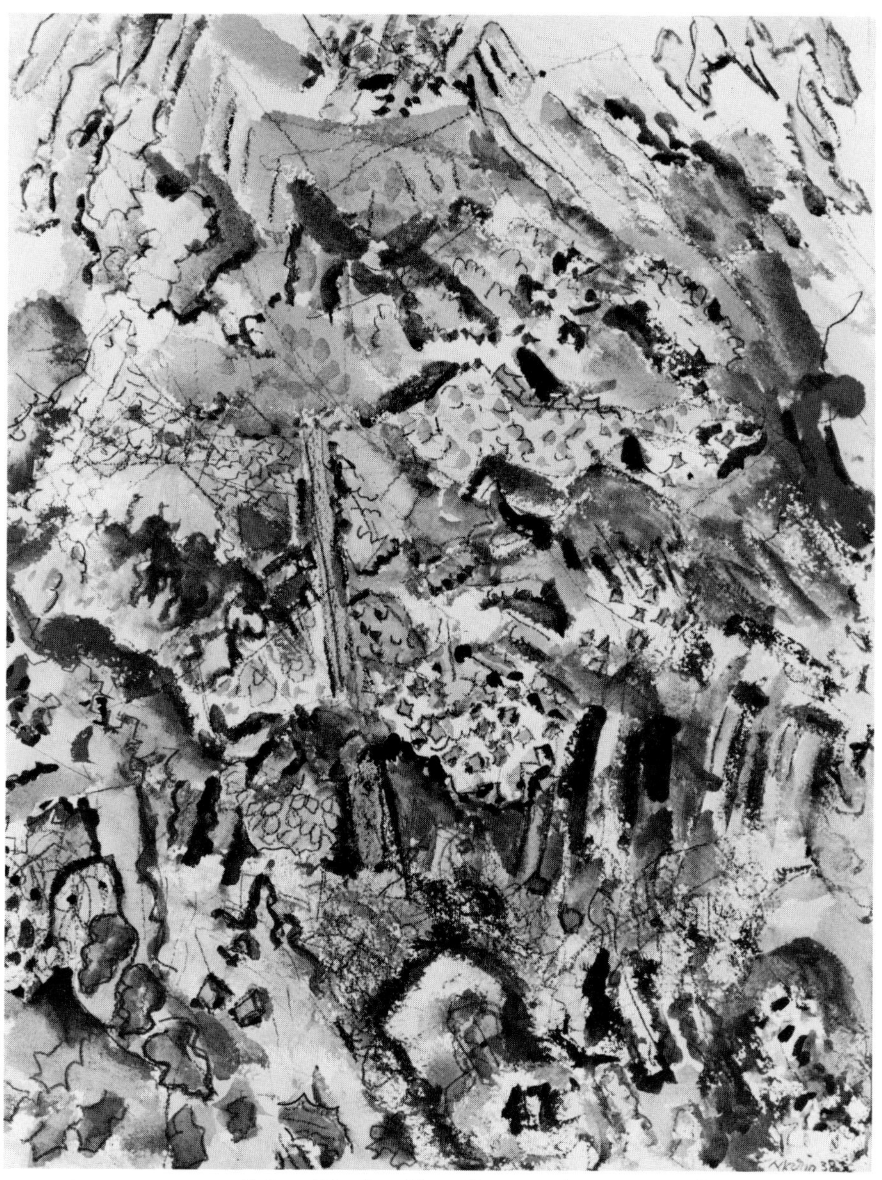

23. JOHN MARIN, *Alpine District, New Jersey—Autumn, 1938,* 1938. Watercolor, 14⅞" x 20½". Courtesy The Downtown Gallery, New York

24. JOSEPH STELLA, *La Crêche,* 1930. 60″ x 76″. Courtesy of The Newark Museum, Newark, New Jersey

25. THOMAS BENTON, *Cotton Pickers, Georgia, ca.* 1932. Oil and egg tempera on canvas, 30″ x 35¾″. The Metropolitan Museum of Art, New York. George A. Hearn Fund, 1933

26. CHARLES BURCHFIELD, *The Parade,* 1934. Watercolor, 24⅜" x 33¼". Collection Dr. and Mrs. Irving F. Burton. Courtesy Frank Rehn Gallery, New York

27. CHARLES BURCHFIELD, *Old House by Creek,* 1932–38. 34½" x 57". Collection Whitney Museum of American Art, New York

28. REGINALD MARSH, *Twenty-Cent Movie,* 1936. Egg tempera on composition board, 30″ x 40″. Collection Whitney Museum of American Art, New York

29. REGINALD MARSH, *Coney Island Beach, Number 1,* 1943. Watercolor and ink, 21½″ x 29½″. Collection Whitney Museum of American Art, New York

30. JOHN GRAHAM, *Self-Portrait,* 1944. 24″ x 20″. Courtesy André Emmerich Gallery, New York

31. EDWARD HOPPER, *Seven A.M.*, 1948. 30″ x 40″. Collection Whitney Museum of American Art, New York

32. IVAN ALBRIGHT, *Roaring Fork, Wyoming*, 1948. Gouache, 22½″ x 30¾″. Collection Whitney Museum of American Art, New York. Gift of Mr. and Mrs. Lawrence A. Fleischman

33. ARTHUR DOVE, *Flour Mill Abstraction,* 1938. Watercolor, 9″ x 5½″. The Phillips Collection, Washington, D.C.

34. ARTHUR DOVE, *Pozzuoli Red,* 1941. 22″ x 36″. The Phillips Collection, Washington, D.C.

35. GEORGE L. K. MORRIS, *Nautical Composition,* 1937–42. 51″ x 35″. Collection Whitney Museum of American Art, New York

36. CHARLES SHEELER, *Water,* 1945. 24″ x 29⅛″. The Metropolitan Museum of Art, New York. Purchase, 1949, Arthur H. Hearn Fund Income

37. MILTON AVERY, *Brook Bathers,* 1938. 30″ x 40″. Collection Mr. Brooke A. Makler, Philadelphia, Pennsylvania

38. MARSDEN HARTLEY, *Off the Banks at Night,* 1942. Masonite panel, 30″ x 40″. The Phillips Collection, Washington, D.C.

39. RICHARD POUSETTE-DART, *Untitled, ca.* 1938–39. 37″ x 49″. Collection the artist

40. BALCOMB GREENE, *The Ancient Form,* 1940. 20″ x 30″. Collection The Museum of Modern Art, New York

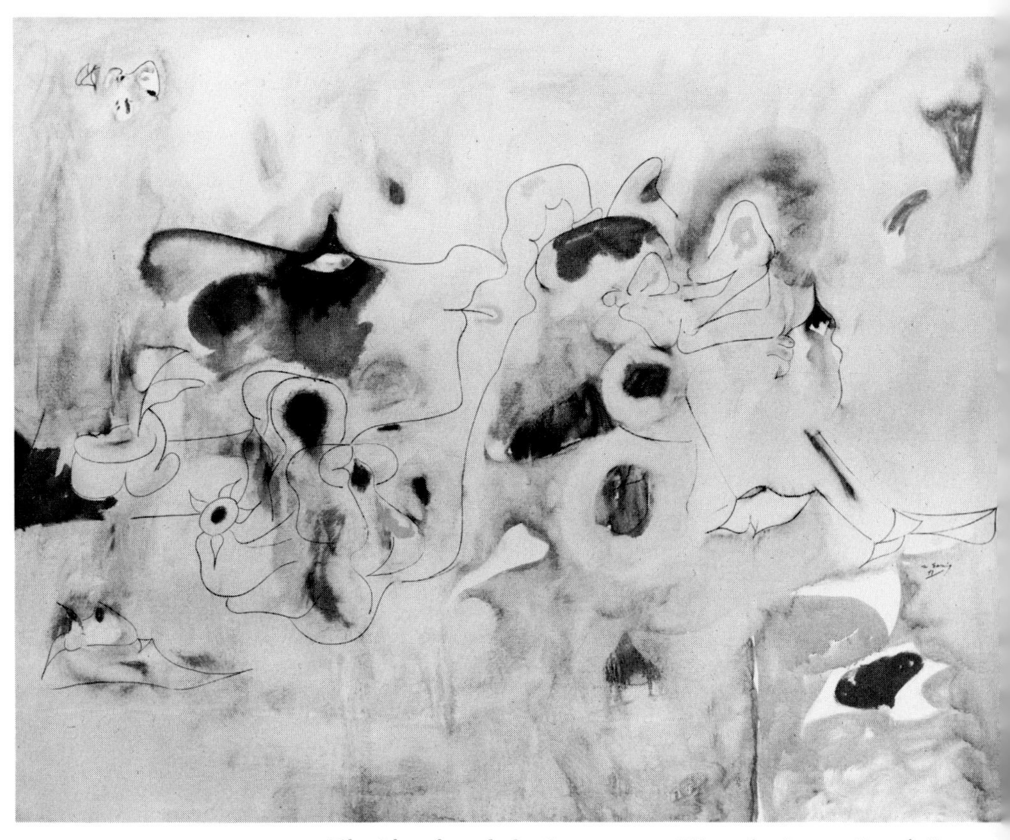

41. ARSHILE GORKY, *The Plough and the Song,* 1947. Oil on burlap, 51″ x 63″. Collection Allen Memorial Art Museum, Oberlin College. Courtesy Sidney Janis Gallery, New York

42. MARK ROTHKO, *Untitled, ca.* 1946–47. Ink drawing, 15½″ x 22½″. Collection Mrs. Betty Parsons, New York

43. WILLIAM BAZIOTES, *The Beach,* 1955. 36″ x 48″. Collection Whitney Museum of American Art, New York

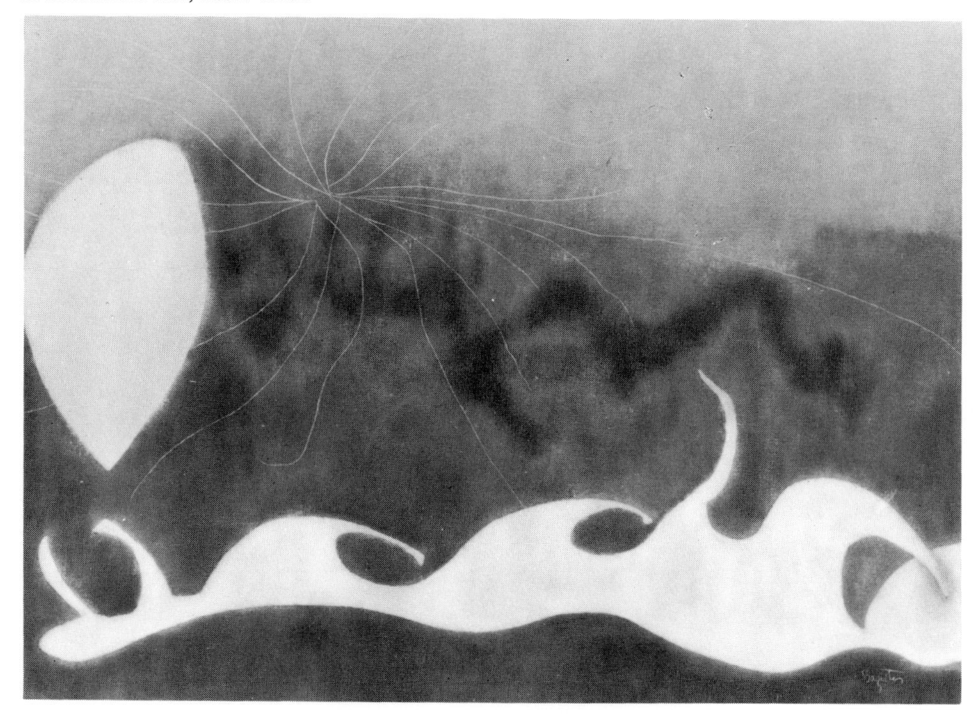

44. WILLEM DE KOONING, *Woman, ca.* 1943. 46″ x 32″. Collection Mr. and Mrs. Thomas B. Hess, New York

45. JACKSON POLLOCK, *There were Seven in Eight, ca.* 1945. 42⅞″ x 102″. Collection Lee Krasner Pollock. Courtesy Marlborough-Gerson Gallery, New York

46. AD REINHARDT, *Number 18, 1948–49,* 1948–49. 40″ x 60″. Collection Whitney Museum of American Art, New York

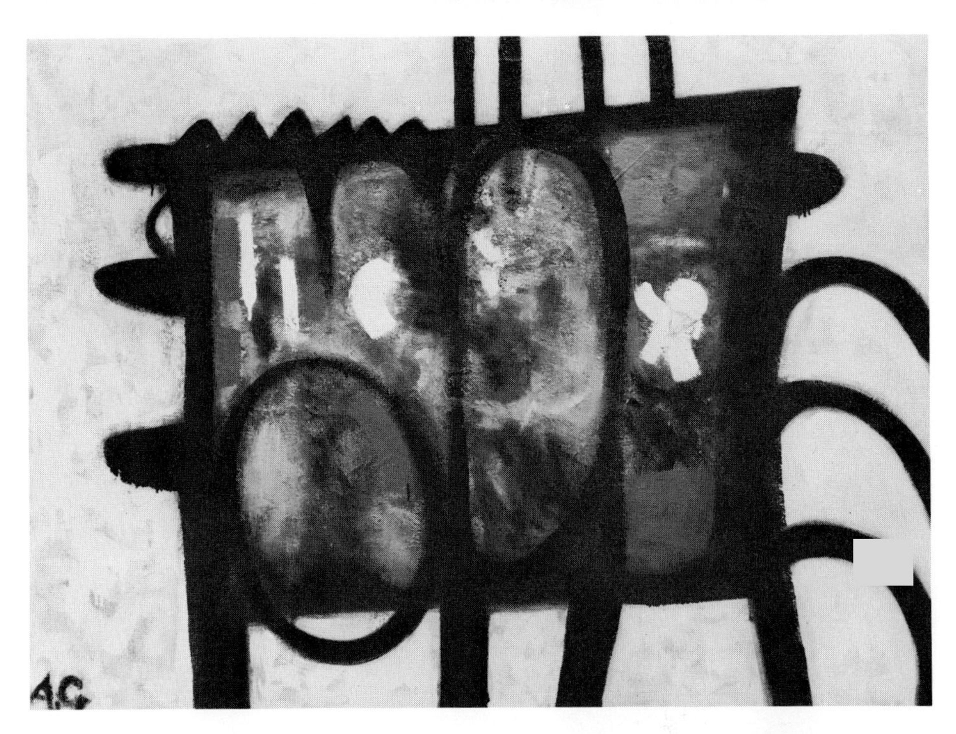

47. ADOLPH GOTTLIEB, *Unstill Life,* 1952. 36″ x 48″. Collection Whitney Museum of American Art, New York. Gift of Mr. and Mrs. Alfred Jaretzki, Jr.

48. FRANZ KLINE, *Figure Eight,* 1952. 81″ x 63½″. Collection William S. Rubin, New York

49. ROBERT MOTHERWELL, *Je T'Aime IV,* 1955–57. 70⅛″ x 100″. Collection Mr. and Mrs. Walter Bareiss

50. STUART DAVIS, *Owh! In San Pão,* 1951. 52¼″ x 41¾″. Collection Whitney Museum of American Art, New York

51. JOSEF ALBERS, *Homage to the Square: "Enfolding,"* 1965. Oil on masonite, 32″ square. Collection the artist

52. BARNETT NEWMAN, *Covenant,* 1949. 48″ x 60″. Collection Mr. and Mrs. Joseph Slifka, New York. Courtesy Betty Parsons Gallery, New York

53. ILYA BOLOTOWSKY, *Yellow Key,* 1953. 50″ x 10″. Courtesy Grace Borgenicht Gallery, New York

54. ROBERT RAUSCHENBERG, *The Bed*, 1955. Combine painting, 74″ x 31″. Collection Mr. and Mrs. Leo Castelli, New York

55. ROY LICHTENSTEIN, *Good Morning Darling,* 1964. Magna on canvas, 27″ x 36″. Collection Mr. David Lichtenstein. Courtesy Leo Castelli Gallery, New York

56. JASPER JOHNS, *According to What,* 1964. Oil on canvas with objects, 191¾″ x 88″. Collection Mr. Edwin Janss. Courtesy Leo Castelli Gallery, New York

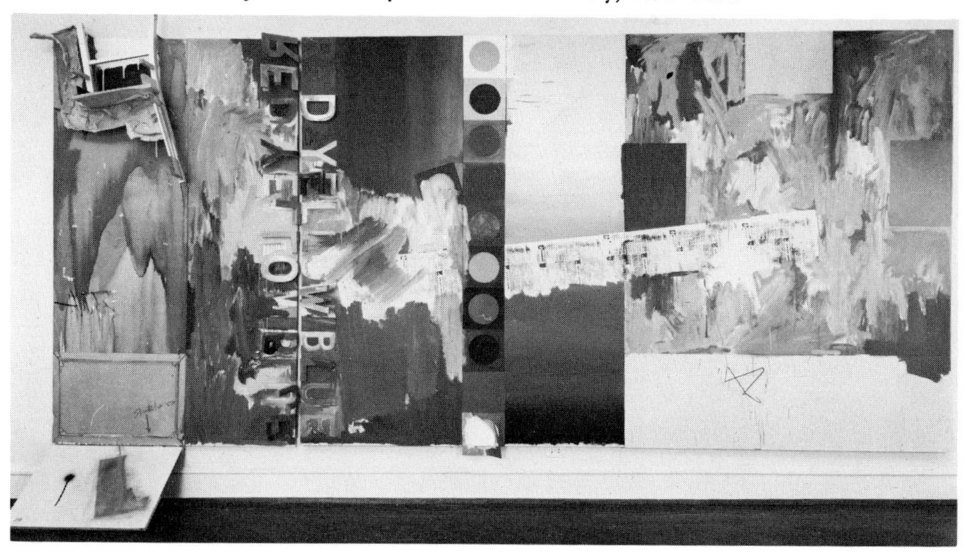

57. JOHN FERREN, *A Rose for Gertrude,* 1962. 72″ x 76″. Collection James Michener. Courtesy Rose Fried Gallery, New York

58. MORRIS LOUIS, *Iota,* 1960–61. Acrylic on canvas, 103½″ x 183″. Courtesy André Emmerich Gallery, New York

59. BURGOYNE DILLER, *First Theme: Number 10,* 1963. 72″ square. Collection Whitney Museum of American Art, New York. Gift of the Friends of the Whitney Museum of American Art

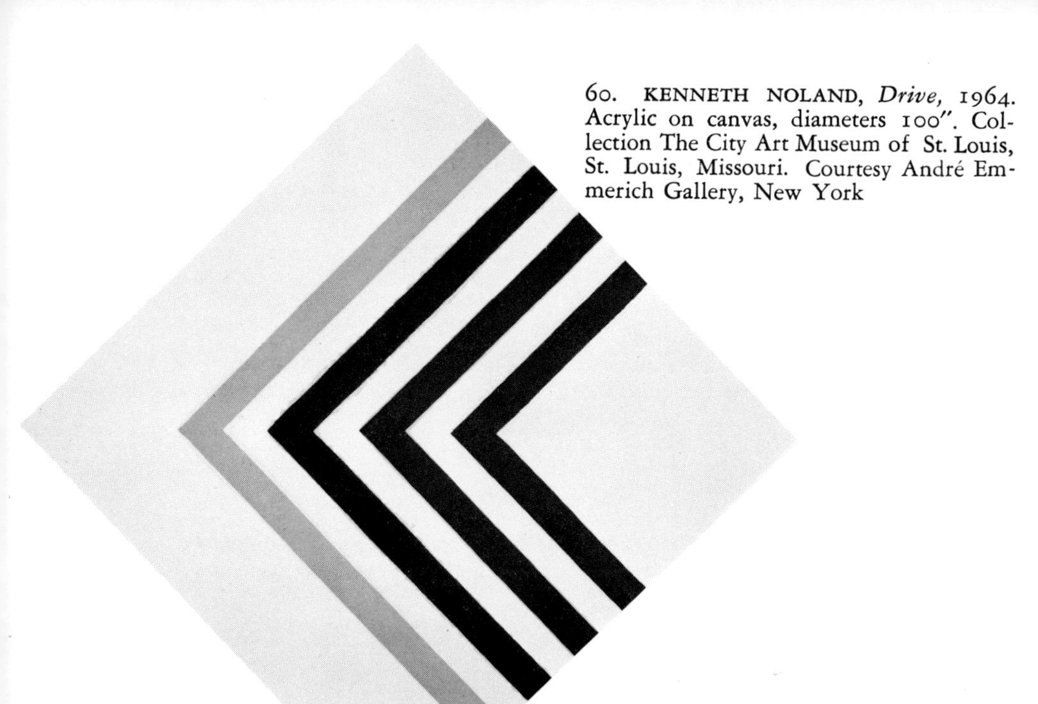

60. KENNETH NOLAND, *Drive,* 1964. Acrylic on canvas, diameters 100″. Collection The City Art Museum of St. Louis, St. Louis, Missouri. Courtesy André Emmerich Gallery, New York

61. LARRY ZOX, *Monitor I,* 1966. Acrylic on canvas, 7′ x 8′. Courtesy Kornblee Gallery, New York

62. FRIEDEL DZUBAS, *Beginning,* 1966. Acrylic on canvas, 102″ x 53″. Courtesy André Emmerich Gallery, New York

63. ELIE NADELMAN, *Man in the Open Air, ca.* 1915. Bronze, 54½″ high. Collection The Museum of Modern Art, New York. Gift of William S. Paley

64. MAX WEBER, *Equilibrium,* 1915. Polychrome bronze, 23″ high. Courtesy Galerie Chalette, New York

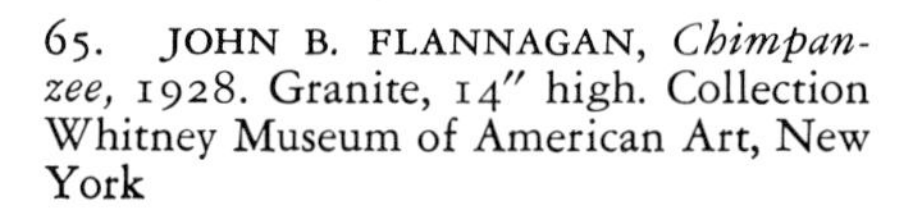

65. JOHN B. FLANNAGAN, *Chimpanzee,* 1928. Granite, 14″ high. Collection Whitney Museum of American Art, New York

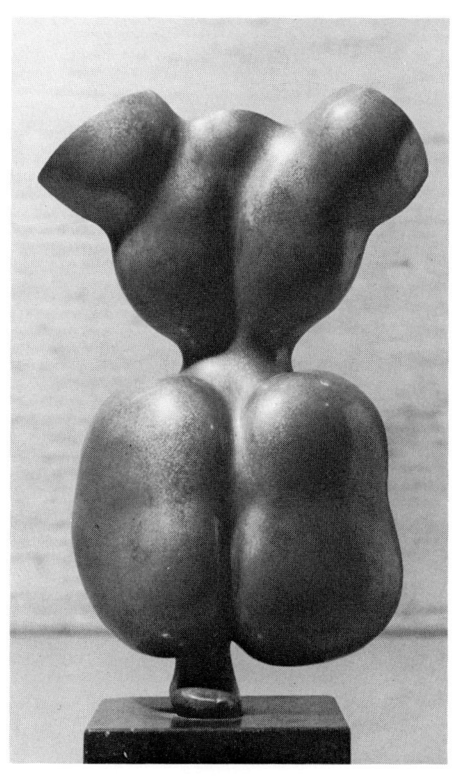

66. GASTON LACHAISE, *Torso,* 1930. Bronze, 11½″ high. Collection Whitney Museum of American Art, New York

67. JOHN STORRS, *Composition Around Two Voids,* 1955. Stainless steel, 20″ high. Collection Whitney Museum of American Art, New York

68. ALEXANDER CALDER, *The Flame,* 1967. Metal, 37″ x 60″. Courtesy Perls Galleries, New York

69. DAVID SMITH, *Cubi XI,* 1963. Stainless steel, 103⅞" high. Purchased by Morris Cafritz for Universal Building North, Washington, D.C. Courtesy Marlborough-Gerson Gallery, New York

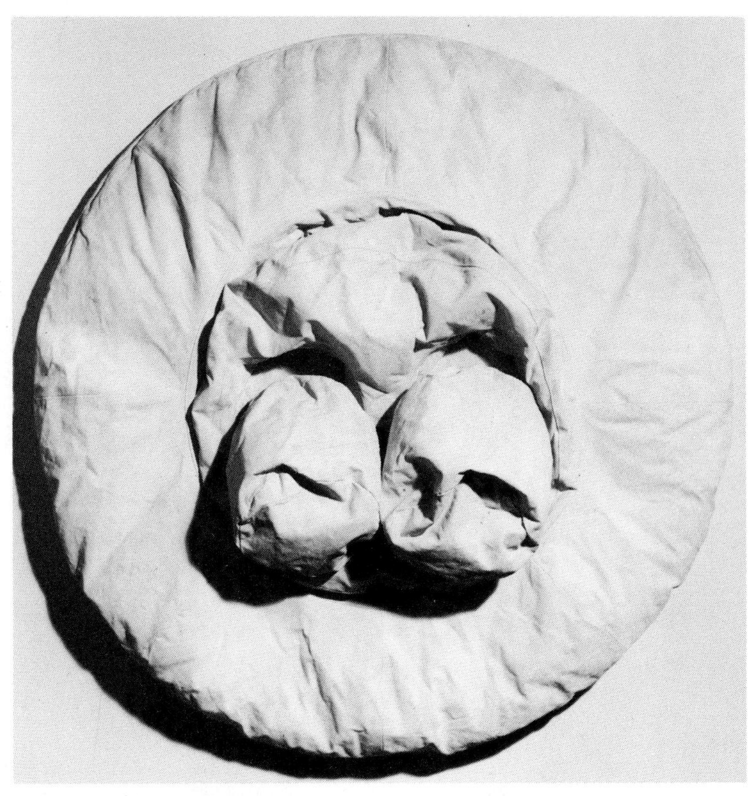

70. CLAES OLDENBURG, *Giant Soft Swedish Light Switch, Ghost Version,* 1966. Canvas, kapok, 52″ in diameter. Courtesy Sidney Janis Gallery, New York

71. DONALD JUDD, *Untitled,* 1965. Aluminum, anodized aluminum, 8¼″ x 253″. Collection Whitney Museum of American Art, New York

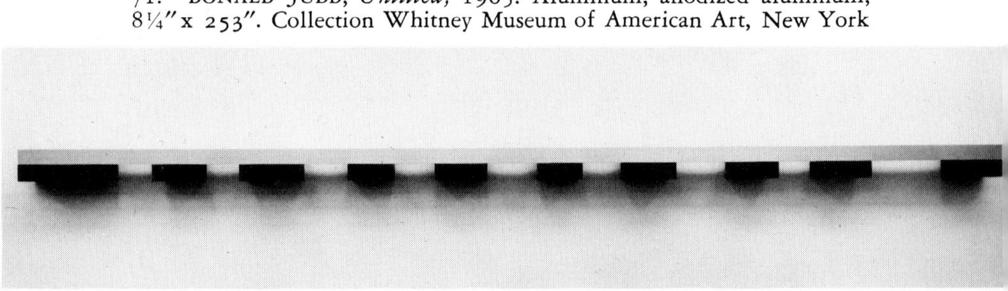